Extradition and Empire

In the first book-length study of the imperial history of extradition in Hong Kong, Ivan Lee shows how British judges, lawyers, and officials navigated the nature of extradition, debated its legalities, and distinguished it over time from other modalities of criminal jurisdiction – including deportation, rendition, and trial and punishment under territorial and extraterritorial laws. These complex debates were rooted in the contested legal status of Chinese subjects under the Opium War treaties of 1842–43. They also intersected wider shifts and tensions in British ideas of territorial sovereignty, criminal justice and procedure, and the legal rights and liabilities of British subjects and alien persons in British territory. By the 1870s, a new area of imperial law emerged as Britain incorporated a frontier colony into an increasingly territorial and legally homogenous empire. This important perspective revises our understanding of the legal origins of colonial Hong Kong and British imperialism in China.

Ivan Lee is Assistant Professor in the Faculty of Law at the National University of Singapore. His research centres on the history of ideas and practices of criminal law, jurisdiction, and procedure in the British Empire.

See the Studies in Legal History series website at http://studiesinlegalhistory.org/

Studies in Legal History

Other books in the series:

Alastair McClure, *Trials of Sovereignty: Mercy, Violence, and the Making of Criminal Law in British India, 1857–1922*
James Q. Whitman, *From Masters of Slaves to Lords of Lands: The Transformation of Ownership in the Western World*
Marie-Amélie George, *Family Matters: Queer Households and the Half-Century Struggle for Legal Recognition*
Simon Devereaux, *Execution, State and Society in England, 1660–1900*
Giuliana Perrone, *Nothing More than Freedom: The Failure of Abolition in American Law*
Christian G. Fritz, *Monitoring American Federalism: The History of State Legislative Resistance*
Ada Maria Kuskowski, *Vernacular Law: Writing and the Reinvention of Customary Law in Medieval France*
E. Claire Cage, *The Science of Proof: Forensic Medicine in Modern France*

(Continued after the Index)

Extradition and Empire

Sovereignty and Subjecthood in Hong Kong

IVAN LEE
National University of Singapore

CAMBRIDGE
UNIVERSITY PRESS

CAMBRIDGE
UNIVERSITY PRESS

Shaftesbury Road, Cambridge CB2 8EA, United Kingdom

One Liberty Plaza, 20th Floor, New York, NY 10006, USA

477 Williamstown Road, Port Melbourne, VIC 3207, Australia

314–321, 3rd Floor, Plot 3, Splendor Forum, Jasola District Centre, New Delhi – 110025, India

103 Penang Road, #05–06/07, Visioncrest Commercial, Singapore 238467

Cambridge University Press is part of Cambridge University Press & Assessment, a department of the University of Cambridge.

We share the University's mission to contribute to society through the pursuit of education, learning and research at the highest international levels of excellence.

www.cambridge.org
Information on this title: www.cambridge.org/9781009356930

DOI: 10.1017/9781009356961

When citing this work, please include a reference to the DOI 10.1017/9781009356961

First published 2025

Cover image: Henry Pottinger, Admiral Parker, and General Gough receiving the Chinese Imperial Commissioners Qiying, Yilibu, and Niujian on board HMS Cornwallis. Print on silk by James Keymer and Co., 1842. Reproduced with permission.

A catalogue record for this publication is available from the British Library

Library of Congress Cataloging-in-Publication Data
NAMES: Lee, Ivan (Lawyer), author.
TITLE: Extradition and empire : sovereignty and subjecthood in Hong Kong / Ivan Lee, National University of Singapore.
DESCRIPTION: 1. | Cambridge, United Kingdom ; New York, NY : Cambridge University Press, 2025. | Includes bibliographical references and index.
IDENTIFIERS: LCCN 2024059186 | ISBN 9781009356930 (hardback) | ISBN 9781009356961 (ebook)
SUBJECTS: LCSH: Extradition – China – Hong Kong – History. | Hong Kong (China) – Politics and government – History. | Great Britain – Colonies – China – Hong Kong. | Hong Kong (China) – History – Transfer of Sovereignty from Great Britain, 1997. | Sovereignty.
CLASSIFICATION: LCC KNQ4660 .L44 2025 | DDC 345.5125/052–dc23/eng/20241210
LC record available at https://lccn.loc.gov/2024059186

ISBN 978-1-009-35693-0 Hardback

Contents

Illustrations

Maps

Table

Acknowledgements

The PhD dissertation on which this book is based was supervised by Professor P. G. McHugh of Sidney Sussex College, University of Cambridge. Among other things, Paul taught me to hone my disparate interests in the Chinese populations of the British Empire into a feasible and impactful topic for a book-length project. In deciding to focus on the jurisdictional politics of extradition, I was also inspired by my interactions with the organisers and participants of the *Legal History and Empires: Perspectives from the Colonized Conference*, held in 2018 at the University of the West Indies at Cave Hill, Barbados. It took me years to realise how much I had learnt from those brilliant scholars in just three days, over and between delicious meals of breadfruit and mahi-mahi.

Other scholars offered generous comments on my work at various conferences and events. I am grateful to the organisers and participants of the *7th Annual Doctoral Scholarship Conference*, held in 2017 at the Yale Law School; the *48th Annual Meeting of the American Society for Legal History*, held in 2018 in Houston, Texas; the *London Legal History Seminar* of December 2018; the *3rd Conference of the International Society for Chinese Law and History*, held in 2019 at the National Taipei University; and the *3rd Asian Legal History Conference*, held in 2023 at the Chinese University of Hong Kong.

Next, I reserve special thanks for Lisa Ford, who, as the editor of this book, provided extremely detailed and helpful comments at every stage of the project, teaching me to write clearly and precisely. Michael Lobban helped to shape my thinking at pivotal junctures over several years; Christopher Munn inspired me with his deep knowledge of and passion for the history of Hong Kong, and Jenny H. Day enlightened me on Qing Chinese views of Chinese political refugees. Other scholars who provided helpful suggestions and criticism include Antony Anghie, Duncan Bell, Edward Cavanagh, Shaunnagh Dorsett, Coel Kirkby, Diane Kirkby, Jack Jin Gary Lee, Michael Ng, Gautham Rao, Christopher Roberts, Mitra Sharafi, Kevin Y. L. Tan, and the two anonymous readers who reviewed this book for Cambridge University Press.

The National University of Singapore (NUS) Faculty of Law and Centre for Asian Legal Studies provided research funding for this project – I gratefully acknowledge their generous support. More generally, I am grateful to all of my colleagues at NUS Law for their mentorship and collegiality. Andrew Halpin, Arif Jamal, James Penner, and many others offered kind words of advice whenever I needed them. I also thank the friendly staff of The National Archives in London, the Government Records Service in Hong Kong, the C J Koh Law Library in Singapore, and the University Library and Squire Law Library in Cambridge for their help in accessing historical records. Separately, Isabelle Lewis drew the maps that appear in this book, and Cecelia Cancellaro, Victoria Phillips, and others at Cambridge University Press managed its publication with patience and professionalism. Also, earlier versions of parts of Chapters 1 and 3 were originally published as two journal articles, 'From Reciprocity to Territoriality: Extradition, the Opium War, and the Idea of British Sovereignty in Hong Kong, 1842–44', *Law and History Review* 40, no. 3 (2022): 437–58, and 'British Extradition Practice in Early Colonial Hong Kong', *Law & History* 6, no. 1 (2019): 85–114. I thank Cambridge University Press and the Australian and New Zealand Law and History Society for allowing me to repurpose these works under generous licences. Finally, my family and friends know that I could not have written this book without their love and support. I am more grateful to them than words can express.

Abbreviations of Archival Sources

The National Archives, London

CO 129	Colonial Office: Hong Kong, Original Correspondence
CO 130	Colonial Office: Hong Kong, Acts and Ordinances
CO 131	Colonial Office: Hong Kong, Sessional Papers
CO 132	Colonial Office: Hong Kong, Government Gazettes
CO 133	Colonial Office: Hong Kong, Miscellanea
CO 295	Colonial Office: Trinidad, Original Correspondence
CO 323	Colonial Office: General Correspondence
CO 381	Colonial Office and Predecessors: General Entry Books, Series II
CO 403	Colonial Office: Hong Kong, Entry Books
CO 700	Colonial Office and Predecessors: Maps and Plans, Series I
CO 854	Colonial Office: Circular Despatches
FO 17	Foreign Office: General Correspondence, China
FO 83	Foreign Office: General Correspondence, Great Britain and General
FO 405	Foreign Office: China and Taiwan Confidential Print
FO 705	Private and Semi-official Correspondence of Sir Henry Pottinger
MPG 1	Maps and Plans Extracted from the Records of the Colonial Office

PCAP 9	Judicial Committee of the Privy Council: Minutes

Public Records Office, Hong Kong SAR

HKRS 100-3	Correspondence Received by the Chief Police Magistrate from the Colonial Secretary of Hong Kong

Introduction

Dimensions of Extradition and Empire

The founding of colonial Hong Kong was a turning point in modern history for various familiar reasons. It marked, for one, the end of the Opium War – the infamous war to ease Chinese restrictions on foreign trade and to punish China for trying to suppress the British-dominated opium trade.[1] The Treaty of Nanjing (1842), by which China ceded Hong Kong for British merchants to use as a trading post, also included wider concessions that enabled them to trade on favourable terms at a strategic selection of unceded ports. These commercial and jurisdictional concessions pioneered what would be known as the 'treaty port' system of Sino-foreign trade. It was an exploitative system that Britain and other imperial powers later expanded so aggressively that treaty ports and territorial leases speckled coastal China by the early twentieth century.[2] The legal infrastructure of these international enclaves embodied the Chinese experience of 'informal imperialism', the historical mode of imperial subjugation that stopped short of formal annexation.[3] This partial subjugation of China lasted a century, giving the Treaty of Nanjing its invidious reputation.

But the founding of Hong Kong was also bound up with a less familiar process of legal change: the emergence of the modern British law of extradition. Hong Kong played a pivotal role in this process because, despite being formally ceded territory, it was an ambiguous juridical space with a transient and putatively foreign population. The Treaty of Nanjing and its supplement, the Treaty of the Bogue

(1843) included provisions for the mutual exchange of fugitive criminals, which differed in important respects from two contemporaneous treaty arrangements between Britain and the United States (1842) and France (1843).[4] The legal practices and discourse generated by all these treaties laid the groundwork for the Extradition Act 1870, the Act of Parliament that defined British law until 1989, while also anchoring the laws of most British colonies until their independence.[5] The three decades between 1842 and 1870 were thus formative in crystallising this area of British imperial law. Legal actors sculpted and debated the limits of Crown authority over foreign fugitives, weighing the interests of crime control and foreign relations against the precepts of due process and the rule of law. In doing so, they developed an elaborate legal doctrine, only fragments of which existed before 1842.

This political and intellectual process of making extradition law took place across the British Empire, but it played out especially dramatically in Hong Kong. British officials were confronted in 1842, as soon as the Treaty of Nanjing was signed, with difficult questions about the rights and wrongs of conducting criminal legal proceedings in Hong Kong, either unilaterally or in collaboration with the Chinese government. These questions embroiled overlapping considerations of sovereignty, subjecthood, and criminal justice and procedure. Numerous disputes arose between the 1840s and 1870s, testing local and imperial ideas of what extradition meant and what made it lawful or unlawful.

History has forgotten the role of China in the origins of British extradition. It has also forgotten the role of extradition in the origins of British imperialism in China, as most studies have only explored British practices of extraterritorial jurisdiction at the unceded treaty ports.[6] When brought back into focus, the multifarious tendrils of extradition challenge our understanding of the legal instrumentation of the expanding British Empire. They certainly challenge the long-held view that the delegates at Nanjing instituted, instantly and in so many words, 'extradition' between Hong Kong and China in addition to British 'extraterritoriality' in mainland China, the latter being widely regarded by scholars as the legal keystone of the treaty port system.[7] The problem with this dichotomous narrative is that it presupposes ideas and practices that in fact took time to crystallise. As this book will show, it matters that the negotiators of the Treaties of Nanjing and the Bogue did not speak of 'extradition' or 'extraterritoriality' at any stage of their proceedings. Instead, they made looser promises to 'punish' or 'hand over' certain people under certain conditions.[8] Scholars rarely problematise the labelling of these promises, but 'extradition' and 'extraterritoriality' have their own intellectual histories. Put simply, these words have accumulated meanings that did not cross the minds of the people who negotiated, interpreted, and enforced the Opium War treaties.

'Extradition', for one, was a French word that only entered common usage in Britain after the publication of Charles Egan's *The Law of Extradition* (1846), a work on the Anglo-American and Anglo-French treaties of 1842–43.[9] These treaties differed from the Opium War treaties in terms of how they were understood and enforced, and the indiscriminate use of the word 'extradition' obscures these differences. Similarly, extraterritoriality captured the imagination of positivist jurists seeking to legitimise the practice in the late nineteenth and early twentieth centuries. Those jurists associated the right of territorial sovereignty with Western civilisation in order to justify preventing the likes of China, Japan, and the Ottoman Empire – allegedly semi-civilised states – from disciplining Western sojourners within their borders.[10] However, this Eurocentric positivist conception of international law was still germinating in the early 1840s, principally from the seed of Henry Wheaton's *Elements of International Law* (1836); and, although Western chauvinism undoubtedly tainted the peace negotiations at Nanjing, it is misleading to suggest that Britain approached those negotiations specifically with an eye to preserving its own territorial jurisdiction while undercutting China's.[11] '[T]he very idea of extraterritoriality seems to presuppose the authority and legitimacy of territoriality,' as Daniel Margolies and his colleagues have rightly noted.[12] If we apply the terms 'extraterritoriality' and 'extradition' ahistorically, we risk losing sight of how ideas of territorial sovereignty traded blows, at Nanjing and in Hong Kong, with non-territorial ideas of subjecthood and the relative powers and obligations of British and Chinese officials.[13]

Indeed, the analytical lens of the *emerging* law of extradition reveals wider patterns of legal inchoateness and complexity. It reveals that Britain acquired Hong Kong under a peace settlement that tried to do many haphazard things to structure bilateral control over people and territory. This was done at a time when Britain had just started developing (and naming) formal procedures for exchanging criminals with foreign countries, so Hong Kong became a site of profound contestation over the terms of such exchanges. The young colony became a testing ground for competing claims over who got to do what, where, to whom, and for what reasons. When could fugitives be tried, released, or moved around as prisoners? When did it matter if they were British subjects, Chinese subjects, both, or neither? Or if they were charged with committing crimes in British territory, Chinese territory, both, or neither? And did it matter who arrested them, how they were treated, or whether their guilt was disputed? The answers to these and other questions were not obvious at all, nor were they merely of local interest. Forged in the mid-nineteenth century, they marked the jurisdictional contours of the British Empire, in China and everywhere. Extradition as we know it was created in this complex process. The messy edges of adjacent practices such as deportation and the exercise of extraterritorial jurisdiction were also thrown into unprecedented relief.

Territory and Sovereignty

We cannot begin to rethink the early history of colonial Hong Kong without recognising that it trailed the belated rise of a British Empire of territorial sovereignty: an empire built on the idea that British judges and officials possessed the exclusive authority to discipline people within British territory. Georgian Britain exercised territorial jurisdiction in the British Isles and generally respected the territories of its European neighbours; however, it was slow to behave similarly in connection with the indigenous polities that interspersed British settler colonies. In early New South Wales, settlers and officials rarely construed Aboriginal acts of violence as crimes justiciable in court, as Lisa Ford has shown. They answered Aboriginal violence with all manner of peaceful bargains and violent reprisals but not, as a rule, with criminal prosecution. This tradition of jurisdictional exclusion was driven by 'syncretic' logics that arose from sustained interaction between settler and Aboriginal communities – logics of diplomacy, reciprocity, and retaliation. In this context, ideas of 'perfect territorial sovereignty' only took hold in the 1820s and 1830s, when the accelerating colonisation of Australia was seen to require greater legitimation.[14]

Indigenous conduct also became justiciable in Canada and New Zealand between 1820 and 1840 but not before. In Canada, Britain asserted jurisdiction over indigenous people once they had outlived their usefulness as independent allies. Indigenous tribes had weakened themselves supporting Britain against the United States in the War of 1812, and their ancestral lands, though still a vital source of widely traded animal furs, were becoming increasingly irresistible targets of appropriation for colonial agriculture. These political and economic changes stimulated jurisdictional territorialisation, as P. G. McHugh has argued.[15] Similarly, New Zealand was annexed pursuant to the Treaty of Waitangi (1840) after 'lesser, more minimalist (and less costly) forms of imperium' proved futile in managing disputes between acquisitive settlers and the indigenous Māori.[16] Having worked with and through Māori chiefs to control British subjects – but not Māori people – during the 1830s, Britain abandoned this 'personalized, jurisdictionally-oriented approach' to ordering New Zealand, in favour of 'more absolutist notions of sovereignty'.[17]

Hong Kong underwent a similar but later process of territorialisation, with a twist in the form of inchoate practices of extradition. Acquired as a safe haven and staging ground for British merchants trading at the Chinese port of Canton (Guangzhou), the small island – of only twenty-six square miles of mostly inarable land – was not originally marked for full-scale colonisation. The extent of British jurisdiction over Hong Kong's Chinese population arose as a point of contention between the delegates at Nanjing, and also between ill-prepared officials in London. Britain was torn between wanting to govern the island as it pleased and to yield to China's assertion that, with only minor exceptions, Chinese subjects fell under Chinese jurisdiction everywhere. Practical considerations compounded the issue as the 1840s rolled by: officials in Hong Kong struggled with the expense of governing Chinese people, especially amid mass migration from China.[18] Driven by these centrifugal considerations, the colony equivocated about the treaty arrangement for fugitive exchanges, as this book will show. Many Chinese criminals were tried and punished locally, but many others were sent to mainland China through legal procedures that blurred the line between the exercise and non-exercise of British jurisdiction over Chinese subjects. These procedures were reformed over time as ideas of extradition firmed up, and British sovereignty came to be seen more clearly as entailing an official duty and power to set strict criteria for exposing anyone in Hong Kong to foreign jurisdiction – anyone, regardless of nationality or subjecthood.

Geopolitics influenced the configuration of territorial sovereignty, to be sure. China was not the New World: it was populous and unified, and Britain continued to recognise its sovereignty despite taking some of its land and subjecting it to harsh terms of peace. The fact that Hong Kong was chipped off this still-sovereign Chinese Empire, and folded into a still-territorialising British Empire, was exactly why complex practices of bilateral ordering arose and evolved. The cession of Hong Kong spurred legal actors to frame claims that either emphasised or de-emphasised the new international border – claims of how people's rights and liabilities either changed or stayed the same whenever they moved between the ceded island and the unceded mainland. Things were different in North America and Australasia, where indigenous polities were largely (though never completely) absorbed into or destroyed by settler states.[19] In those contexts, Anglophone legal actors constructed, broadly speaking, normatively plural legal regimes under an unbroken canopy of British sovereignty. In New Zealand, for example, special laws applicable to Māori people replaced Māori customs in the 1840s, as Shaunnagh Dorsett has shown.[20] In Hong Kong, by contrast, official, judicial, and lawyerly constructions of the Chinese border constituted British sovereignty.

As a treaty partner, China also resisted British territorialisation. While contesting the British ordering of Hong Kong, Qing Chinese officials filled bilateral discussions with their own brand of subject-centric sovereignty. 'Qing officials primarily enforced the [Qing] legal code over people, not territories,' as Pär Cassel has argued.[21] Qing China was 'territorially organized', internally and externally, but it had a long tradition of 'ethnic legal pluralism' – partitioning domestic jurisdiction along ethnic lines.[22] In the frontier provinces of Tibet and Xinjiang, local elites were authorised to enforce Buddhist and Islamic laws against their own people. The Mongol people also had their own legal code, the Mongol Code, which they enacted in consultation with early Manchu conquerors; and, finally, the Manchu people, Qing

China's ruling class, were governed by special privileges and restrictions that did not apply to the Han Chinese or other ethnic groups. Manchu bannermen were generally exempt from capital punishment, for example, and they were only allowed to marry Manchu women.[23] So, guided by this worldview, nineteenth-century Chinese officials placed much more emphasis on the ethnicity and subjecthood of fugitives who moved between China and Hong Kong, than on the location of their misconduct or choice of refuge. In other words, Chinese officials almost always claimed jurisdiction over fugitives of Chinese descent, no matter what they did and where they went. The extent to which British officials resisted these claims explains much about how the Opium War treaties – and, later, the Treaty of Tianjin (1858) – were understood and enforced between the 1840s and 1870s. The more the British emphasised *locus* over status, or at least alongside status, the more extradition took shape as a formal mechanism for the *transborder* exchange of fugitive criminals – a mechanism that dealt not only with clashes between the laws of peoples, but also between the laws of places.

These praxes of territorial jurisdiction add a new dimension to the imperial history of extradition. Bradley Miller has recently argued that practices of extradition emerged along the Canadian–American frontier in response to 'the challenge of the border', or the perceived problem that territorial sovereignty 'undermined [states] by limiting their authority in a world in which people crossed borders with much more dexterity than law'.[24] Miller argues that the Anglo-American Treaty of 1842 alleviated this problem to a degree. But 'customary regimes of abduction' also pervaded the nineteenth century because local law enforcers were more eager to achieve 'supranational justice' than senior officials in London and Washington.[25] Practices of extradition were thus a solution to a problem in a context in which legal actors shared basic premises of state sovereignty.[26] In Hong Kong, by contrast, there was no such dynamic in 1842. There was neither a pre-existing border with China nor any shared idea of sovereignty. There were, instead, plural claims of jurisdiction, embodied in a vague bilateral agreement for fugitive exchanges, which reflected local tensions and exigencies. Extradition grew out of this embryonic agreement as legal actors enforced it, disputed its meaning, and ultimately pursued imperial uniformity in interpreting international agreements of its ilk. Extradition, then, was not an answer to any prior challenge of sovereign borders – not in Hong Kong. On the contrary, it was a product of legal manoeuvring over time and a gradual distillation of jurisdictional plurality.[27]

Subjects and Aliens of Empire

By tracking emerging ideas and practices of extradition, this book also explores the complex legal status of Chinese people under British rule. The ethnic Chinese population of Hong Kong was treated more harshly and arbitrarily than other communities, as historians know well. Early colonial officials sought legitimacy on the island, but they buckled under the combined pressures of language barriers, jurisdictional competition from China, and the absence of reliable local collaborators.[28] Fickle and coercive colonial ordinances regulated matters of housing, commerce, and public health through criminal sanctions directed at the Chinese community, bringing many thousands of people into regular contact with magistrates and policemen. These ordinances belied official promises of good governance and impartial justice; they set an ugly tone for the rest of colonial rule.[29] As the nineteenth century gave way to the twentieth, other explicitly and implicitly racist laws restricted, among other things, what the Chinese-language press could print and where people of Chinese descent could live. From 1904 to 1946, the temperate Peak District of Hong Kong – a high-altitude escape from the subtropical heat – was effectively reserved for white residents.[30]

This pattern of racialised governance exemplified wider interplays between legal coercion and unequal subjecthood in the British Empire. Systemic racism unbalanced the scales of criminal justice in India, as Elizabeth Kolsky has shown. The Indian Penal Code, enacted in 1860, applied equally to everyone in the Raj, but the Criminal Procedure Code of 1861 granted 'European British subjects' special rights, including immunities from being detained by 'native' Indian personnel. 'Native' Indians therefore bore the brunt of the general criminal law, even if they managed to avoid narrower regimes of coercion. In tea-producing Assam, indentured plantation workers – migrant 'coolies' from other parts of India – were liable to fines and even imprisonment for breaches of contract under laws reminiscent of Atlantic slavery.[31] Meanwhile, the subjecthood of trans-colonial migrants was also eroded. Natal devised a language test in 1896 to turn back Indian immigrants, while enacting other laws to disenfranchise existing residents of colour – laws that portended Apartheid.[32] Then, Australia deployed a version of the 'Natal formula' against immigrants of Chinese descent, including British subjects born in Hong Kong; and, in 1914, Canada detained and deported over 350 Punjabi British subjects who had crossed the Pacific Ocean on the S.S. *Komagata Maru*.[33] These discriminatory practices are all notorious. They dashed hopes of the inclusive subjecthood that, as Hannah Muller has argued, characterised the expanding British Empire in the late eighteenth century.[34] Subjecthood lost value in the mature empire when racial prejudices and communal interests eclipsed notions of shared identity.

But the emerging law of extradition inflected the trajectory of unequal subjecthood with the adjacent jurisprudence of alienage. Few ethnic Chinese residents of Hong Kong were regarded as British subjects before the 1860s. This was because they were mostly migrants who arrived after China ceded the island. Furthermore, British officials gradually abandoned the view that the people living in Hong Kong at the time of the cession had become British subjects, as we shall see.[35] To the extent, then, that people of Chinese descent faced formal discrimination in early Hong Kong, they did so mostly as aliens to the British Crown and not as unequal subjects. And, as aliens liable to be given up to China, these people occupied a similar legal position as other alien residents of British territory, who could also be given up to their home countries under international agreements. Crucially, those other aliens were seen to be entitled to the same procedural rights as British subjects in matters of criminal law. In 1850, the Foreign Secretary, Viscount Palmerston minuted, in relation to the procedure for surrendering fugitives to France, that 'the formal safety of a foreigner in England should be substantially as secure as that of a British subject'.[36] So, when officials extended a similar attitude to fugitives wanted by China – fitfully at first, then more consistently after 1865 – they afforded the Chinese residents of Hong Kong a sliver of formal equality in the form of legal rights that they could and did exploit. Race still mattered, to be sure, as British decisions not to hand people over to China were coloured by sensational accounts of Chinese barbarity and corruption. But, in the view of many Chinese people, these prejudices worked in their favour, shielding them from Chinese justice. In that sense, the compromised subjecthood of Chinese people was one thing; their overt alienage was another.

Chinese people were caught, then, between the mutable boons and banes of alienage and subjecthood. They were caught as the emerging logic of extradition altered what it meant for the British Empire to treat people equally. Demographic changes made it necessary, too, for officials to reassess this question after 1860. A growing number of people born in Hong Kong and the Straits Settlements could claim to be British subjects by right of birth (*jus soli*) and Chinese subjects by right of blood (*jus sanguinis*). Were these dual subjects eligible for British protection, and liable to British jurisdiction, when travelling in China? Was China treaty-bound to give them up as fugitives? Again and again, the rights of subjects and aliens of Chinese descent were compared with those of migrants and sojourners everywhere, as the empire struggled to craft rational and consistent laws of nationality and extradition.[37] This comparative jurisprudence disclosed much more than racialised colonialism. It was pragmatic and formalistic in equal parts, and local and imperial at every turn.

Executive Power and the Rule of Law

This book explores, finally, the procedural and constitutional legalities of extradition. The modern idea of extradition contemplates formality, cooperation, and restraint. It speaks of extraditable and non-extraditable crimes, standards of proof, maximum lengths of detention, and other rules that define the boundaries of the mechanism. Modern lawyers also distinguish extradition from 'alternative' procedures for moving convicts and accused persons across international borders – procedures that are either less cooperative, such as deportation, or more loosely regulated, such as 'extraordinary rendition'. Particular standards and definitions obviously differ between legal systems, but the modern use of 'extradition' generally denotes something more specific than the bare transfer of criminals between independent states.[38] The word is sometimes used in a looser sense, on the other hand, to describe historical practices of less determinate features. For example, the world's oldest known treaty, signed around 1280 BCE between Ramesses II of Egypt and Hattusili III of the Hittite Empire, is commonly said to have provided for mutual extradition.[39] As noted, many nuances in the modern legal relations between people and governments are lost in such accounts.

Rather, historicising the term 'extradition' reveals much about the legal history of empire and of international law. 'Extradition' first appeared in statutory form in a French executive order (*décret-loi*) of 1791; and, as part of international agreements, in a French treaty of 1828.[40] These instruments and their contemporaries were some of the earliest to formally regulate state practices, though scholars have traced 'prototype' French treaties to as early as 1759.[41] Other terms were used in that pre-revolutionary period, as well as in even earlier periods, when French and other European practices were discernibly more free-form. '*Restituter*' and '*remettre*' appeared in early modern French instruments, and '*remittere*' appeared in Latin ones – all meaning to restore or remit fugitive criminals to their countries of origin.[42] Anglo-American lawmakers updated their lexicon in a similar fashion, while taking equally gradual steps to regulate, reform, and reframe their practices. Processes of 'surrender' and 'delivery' were specified in English-language treaties and legislation at the turn of the nineteenth century, before 'extradition' was finally given formal recognition in an Act of the United States Congress of 1848 and in the British Extradition Act 1870.[43]

So, strictly speaking, extradition emerged late in Anglophone legal history. Medieval and early modern England exchanged traitors, murderers, and other felons with neighbouring countries, notably France and Scotland (before the union of 1603), under various treaties and ad hoc arrangements. But those practices were irregular, bound by few legal rules, and not called 'extradition'. They also died out from the 1690s, several decades after it became customary for the Court of King's Bench to supervise the detention of prisoners through the ancient writ of habeas corpus.[44] During the reign of James I (1603–25), judges of the King's Bench started issuing the writ on the King's behalf, compelling jailers in England to produce the bodies of prisoners and to explain the legal grounds of their detention. This famous process of judicial review enabled unlawfully detained people to be set free. It became even more important with the decline of royal absolutism in the same century, as Parliament legislated to make all detentions ordered by the King and his Privy Councillors, including his Secretaries of State, amenable to judicial review.[45] The legal opinion emerged, then, that the detention of fugitives for the purposes of trial or punishment in foreign countries was illegal at common law and only Parliament could authorise such proceedings.[46] The Habeas Corpus Act 1679 confirmed that, save for convicts sentenced to transportation, no 'inhabitant or resident' of the Kingdom of England could lawfully be 'sent prisoner' beyond the realm.[47]

This constitutional shift manifested itself a century later in a historic legal regime for surrendering fugitives to America. In 1794, Britain and the newly independent United States signed the Jay Treaty to stabilise their relations amid British involvement in the French Revolutionary Wars.[48] Under Article 27, the two countries agreed, 'on mutual Requisitions ... to deliver up to Justice, all Persons who being charged with Murder or Forgery committed within the Jurisdiction of [the requesting party], shall seek an Asylum within any of the Countries of [the requested party]'. A proviso added that the 'delivery' of any fugitive 'shall only be done on such Evidence of Criminality as according to the Laws of the Place, where the Fugitive or Person so charged shall be found, would justify his apprehension and commitment for Tryal, if the offence had there been committed'.[49] In this way, the proviso in Article 27 laid down what Anglophone lawyers would later call the requirement of 'prima facie' or presumptive proof of guilt for surrendering accused fugitives. The proviso also laid down an early version of the rule of 'double criminality' – the rule that each requested fugitive's conduct must constitute a crime under the laws of both the requesting and requested states.[50] In the Jay Treaty version of this rule, Britain could refuse an American request, for example, for a person charged with murder in Pennsylvania on the grounds that, under English law, the evidence disclosed not murder but manslaughter, a crime not listed in Article 27.[51]

In 1797, the Jay Treaty was implemented in Britain by an Act of Parliament, which reproduced Article 27 and established a procedure for fulfilling American requests.[52] On receiving a valid request, the King's Secretaries of State were empowered to issue warrants for the arrest of the named fugitive(s). Upon arrest, each fugitive was to be examined on oath, by a magistrate (or Justice of the Peace), along with relevant witnesses. The magistrate was then required either to discharge the fugitive if the evidence against them was lacking, or to commit them to jail if their guilt was proved to the standard required by Article 27. This, in theory, was the same standard as would cause a grand jury to endorse a bill of indictment for a crime committed in England.[53] Finally, if the fugitive was committed to jail, then it was 'lawful for one of his Majesty's Secretaries of State, by Warrant under his Hand and Seal, to order the Person so committed to be delivered to [the] United States'.[54]

The Jay Treaty regime for fugitive 'deliveries' broke new legal ground. However, it was short-lived because Article 27 expired in 1806 along with other articles that Britain and the United States had decided not to make permanent.[55] Next, the British government did not approach Parliament for more powers to remove fugitives until 1842–43, the crucial years in which treaties containing permanent extradition agreements were signed with the United States and France (see Map 0.1). In addition to reviving the regulatory framework of the Jay Treaty, the Anglo-American and Anglo-French treaties of 1842–43 provided for the surrender of fugitives charged with a longer list of crimes.[56] The Acts of Parliament that implemented these treaties also empowered judges to discharge fugitives who were still awaiting removal two months after being committed to jail, unless the Crown could justify the need for further detention.[57] The Anglo-American and Anglo-French treaties thus charted a clearer path towards legal modernity. They featured in the published works of Charles Egan (1846), Robert Phillimore (1854), and Travers Twiss (1861) – British jurists who now wrote about 'extradition' as a distinct area of law.[58] In his *The Law of Extradition* (1867), an important treatise that would see four editions over five decades, Edward Clarke argued that 'the history of the subject in England' began in 1842.[59] Later endorsed by no less prominent a jurist than James Fitzjames Stephen, Clarke's account has influenced Anglophone understandings of the origins of extradition ever since.[60]

This brings us back to Hong Kong. Unbeknown to commentators in Britain, the early colonial government sent prisoners to China without express authorisation from Westminster, and without observing most of the safeguards that were starting to gain currency elsewhere. The colonial government was able to do this because Hong Kong was regarded as a ceded territory, not 'settled' by British subjects

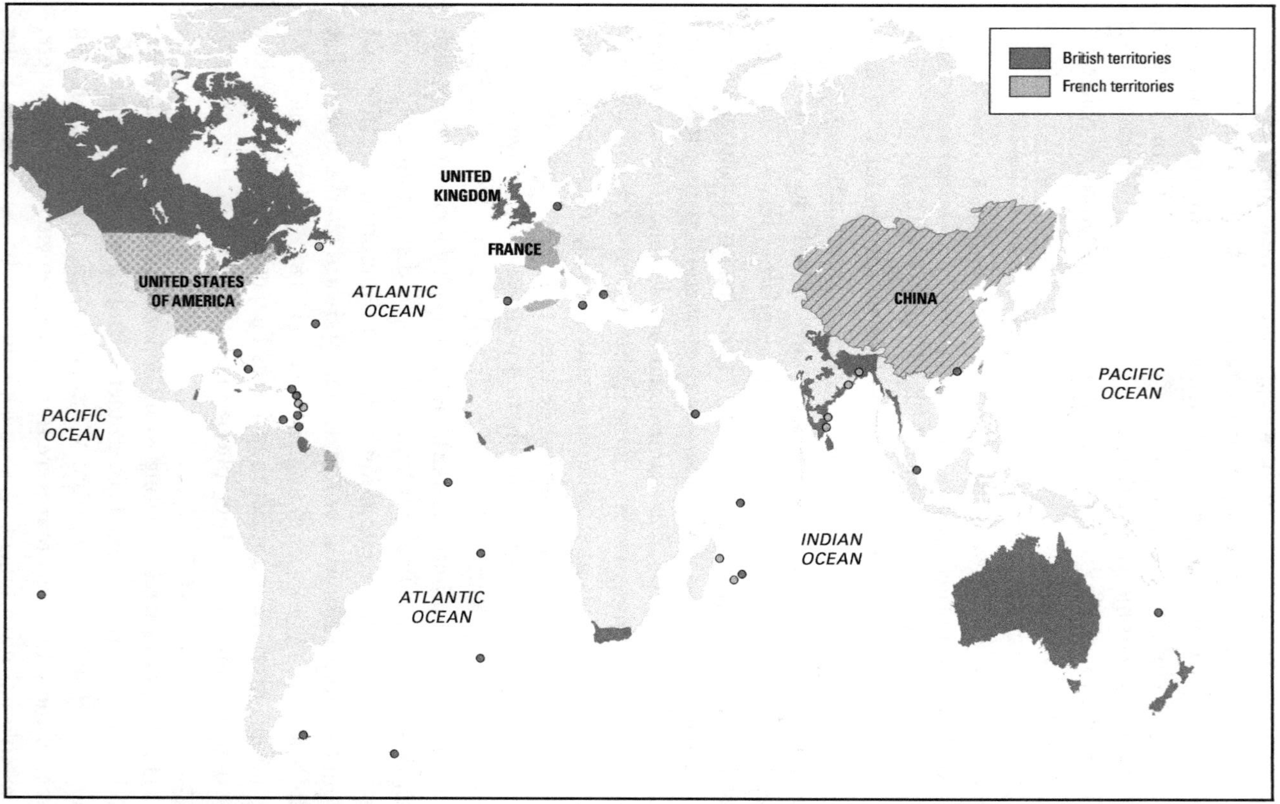

MAP 0.1 The territories of Britain, France, the United States, and China, *c.* 1843.

taking the common law with them, and the Crown was long understood to have the power to legislate for ceded territories where it had not decided to establish representative legislatures.[61] However, the Crown's divergent approach in Hong Kong was also shaped by the jurisdictional idiosyncrasies of the Chinese treaties; and, crucially, it was further enabled by the fact that imperial standards for extradition were not clarified until 1870.

Indeed, apart from enforcing narrow treaties with the United States (1842), France (1843), and Denmark (1862), Westminster was reluctant to make further legal provision for removing fugitives from British territory.[62] This was because liberal parliamentarians viewed foreign legal systems with suspicion, and they vaunted Britain's reputation as a place of political asylum.[63] So, whereas France and other European countries had made strides to bring border-crossing fugitives to justice, Britain remained, as Clarke argued in 1867, 'one of the least ready of all the nations of the world to perform her duty in this matter as a member of the family of civilised communities'.[64] Concerns that Britain was falling behind international custom finally caused the House of Commons to appoint a Select Committee on Extradition in 1868.[65] The report of this Select Committee led in turn to the enactment of the Extradition Act 1870. This historic statute empowered the Crown to implement future treaties by Orders in Council, instead of having to obtain an Act of Parliament on every occasion. To offset the risks of injustice, the Extradition Act codified a number of additional safeguards that still survive today in some form, including the famous 'political offence exception' – the blanket prohibition against the extradition of political refugees who faced official persecution in their countries of origin.[66] Armed, then, with its new powers, the British government proceeded to sign and implement extradition treaties with thirty-six nations in Europe, Asia, Africa, Latin America, and the Pacific Ocean by 1903, making up for its reticence before 1870.[67]

The law of Hong Kong was brought almost entirely in line with imperial standards between 1865 and 1873. But it was brought there from a very different starting point, one in which prisoners were sent to China with relative abandon, through procedures that officials did not clearly or consistently regard as extradition. For this reason, the early history of Hong Kong offers a unique window into official ideas and practices at a pivotal time, just before the rights of foreign fugitives were ossified in British imperial legislation and doctrine. The early experience of Hong Kong reveals what the British Empire was willing to do – what motivated it and how far it was prepared to go – when unshackled by metropolitan politics and preconceptions.

Strands of Legal Change

In short, this book argues that the origins of extradition involved crucial experiments in the colonial ordering of territory, people, and executive power. Key experiments were carried out in mid nineteenth-century Hong Kong – experiments deeply interwoven with the origins of the colony itself. What follows is therefore as much a colonial history of an area of British law as a constitutional history of a Crown colony at Britain's Chinese frontier. The wider British presence in mainland China sits in the background of this layered narrative. Although this book does not discuss the 'extraterritorial' empire directly, it suggests that developments in Hong Kong played a bigger role in shaping that project than other studies have recognised. As British rule in Hong Kong became more territorial – more similar to how other sovereign British territories were governed – so did the extraterritorial British Empire in China appear more aberrant and objectionable.

The chapters that follow are organised thematically and in semi-chronological order. Chapter 1, 'Improvising Sovereignty', covers the period between 1841 and 1844. It argues that British sovereignty in Hong Kong was built on inchoate ideas of extradition: half-formed ideas of whether and how the colony would surrender Chinese criminals to China. A bilateral agreement for such surrenders was made in 1842, but its terms were disputed primarily because British officials struggled to articulate the scope of their jurisdiction over the Chinese population of Hong Kong. Events on the ground then short-circuited efforts to resolve this problem. In *The Queen v. Lo A-tow* (1843), Governor Henry Pottinger conflated his power to refuse Chinese requests for fugitives for lack of evidence (which China did not dispute) with the power of British courts to try Chinese subjects and sentence them to punishment (which China did dispute). Pottinger's interpretation of *Lo A-tow* established a tenuous precedent for territorial sovereignty in a turn of events that would have far-reaching consequences.

The next three chapters examine different aspects of extradition law-making over the same period between the 1840s and 1860s. Chapter 2, 'Domesticating Mobility', shows how the Hong Kong government's efforts to bolster its legitimacy carved a distinction between extradition and deportation, or between the cooperative and unilateral removal of Chinese people to China. As China continued to press its jurisdictional claims after *Lo A-tow*, Hong Kong attracted thousands of Chinese migrants whose transient habits created practical and diplomatic challenges of governance. Faced with these challenges, the colonial government promised to 'protect' Chinese people from lawlessness and arbitrary punishment. These promises buttressed the government's tenuous claim to the right to keep the peace and to remove people discretionally. Governors gave themselves flexible powers of 'rendition', 'banishment', and 'deportation' (using these words), while vesting other powers of policing and population control in a mercurial office of 'Registrar General and Protector of Chinese Inhabitants'. Colonists, imperial officials, and British diplomats in China challenged these powers. Their contestations served to refine the colonial practice of extradition.

Chapter 3, 'Navigating Disorder', examines Hong Kong's practice of giving people up to foreign authorities on charges of crimes committed at sea. Between 1850 and 1865, the colony's 'rendition' procedure, its early version of extradition, was used to remove hundreds of accused pirates, mutineers, and other criminals of Chinese origin – criminals that officials believed China was better suited to punish. Other seafarers were also given up to French and American authorities, as the colony sought to take pressure off its overstretched and barely functional courts and prison system. Ideas of British sovereignty and the international law of piracy fuelled this pragmatic policy. Notably, officials believed that maritime crimes should only be tried in Hong Kong if they implicated 'British interests', specifically British victims, offenders, or territory. This rationale for jurisdictional restraint reached a controversial zenith in 1861. In the case of the French coolie ship, *Ville D'Agen*, a Peruvian sailor, Juan Pastor was nearly given up to China despite the absence of any treaty or statutory basis for his rendition.

Chapter 4, 'Rationalising Reciprocity', explores the question of Hong Kong's legal right, or lack thereof, to request the surrender of fugitives who had taken refuge in Chinese territory. To what extent did British officials expect China to reciprocate the surrender of Chinese fugitives from Hong Kong? The Anglo-American and Anglo-French treaties for extradition were fully reciprocal, as were narrower agreements between some British colonies (such as Trinidad) and their sovereign neighbours (such as Venezuela). But Britain's treaty relations with China were far more complex. This was not least because British subjects were not amenable to Chinese jurisdiction, while the jurisdictional status of Chinese subjects was disputed. As this chapter will show, the British effort to rationalise the Chinese treaties led to a key conclusion in 1865–66 that a state's right to discipline its subjects in foreign territory – its right of extraterritorial jurisdiction – did not necessarily imply a right of extradition, or a right to retrieve absconded subjects from foreign territory. The distinction between extradition and extraterritoriality was therefore a product of gradual practice and discourse: it was decidedly not written into the Opium War treaties during 1842–43.

Finally, Chapter 5, 'Founding Alsatia', tracks the modernisation of the extradition law of Hong Kong against the backdrop of empire-wide legal reform between 1865 and 1873. This process unfolded through two explosive scandals, which caused imperial officials and judges to impose belated restrictions on the colonial removal of fugitives to China. The first, the case of *How Yu-teen* (1865), involved embarrassing allegations of British complicity in China's violent execution of a political refugee; the second, *Attorney General of Hong Kong* v. *Kwok-a-Sing* (1873), was a habeas corpus dispute born of colonial infighting and the only extradition dispute to reach the Judicial Committee of the Privy Council in the nineteenth century. These scandals propelled Hong Kong away from the flexible and jurisdictional practice of rendition. The new reality – the imperially homogenous, late-Victorian law of extradition – carried drastically heightened expectations of individual rights and executive comportment.

In these ways, *Extradition and Empire* tells the story of the contested emergence of a modern mechanism or modality of criminal law, the origins of which are steeped in Victorian ideas of sovereignty and subjecthood. Needless to say, this book does not tell the whole story of international extradition, not least because it does not explore American or continental European perspectives. But neither is this story merely local, as the formative developments in Hong Kong drew from and fed back into wider shifts in British legal thought. As a focal point of these wider shifts, the emergent extradition law of the young frontier colony is more historically and juridically revealing than the sum of its parts.

1

Improvising Sovereignty

British troops occupied Hong Kong in January 1841. But British officials did not firmly assert jurisdiction over the island's Chinese population until the winter of 1843–44, more than a year after the end of the Opium War. What explains this delay, and what is its significance? By re-examining diplomatic and colonial records from this period, this chapter shows that the legal status of Hong Kong's Chinese population was an emergent issue. It was not foreseen before the war as Britain had only coveted a Chinese island for commercial reasons and to put British merchants beyond the reach of Chinese law enforcement. In that context, officials struggled to articulate the legal implications of the territorial conquest. Would the Chinese people of Hong Kong remain under Chinese jurisdiction? Or would they come under British authority, either as British subjects or alien residents of British territory? These diplomatically sensitive questions forced British officials to explore complex compromises that engaged legal ideas of sovereignty, residency, and subjecthood. The shifting strategies of officials influenced, in turn, the drafting and early interpretation of key provisions in the Opium War treaties: the Treaties of Nanjing (1842) and the Bogue (1843).

The process by which Hong Kong's Chinese population came under British jurisdiction and ordering is especially significant because it incorporated an inchoate discourse of extradition. As we shall see, the negotiators of the Opium War treaties did not distinguish the scope of British criminal jurisdiction over Chinese subjects from the scope of the

British obligation to deliver Chinese fugitives to China. These questions were conflated. A similar conflation later guided official conduct in *The Queen* v. *Lo A-tow* (1843), the murder case that became an unlikely precedent for what Governor Henry Pottinger described as 'the entire Sovereignty of England over this Colony and its Chinese population'.[1] Pottinger made this important claim to sovereignty in December 1843 amid ongoing uncertainties about the position of the British Crown in Hong Kong. He did so by construing a pre-trial hearing for the possible surrender of seven accused murderers as a full criminal trial, and its outcome – the discharge of the accused on evidential grounds – as a complete acquittal. As we shall see, this remarkable manoeuvre ended further discussion between British officials about sovereignty in Hong Kong, though not bilateral disputes between Britain and China. In short, *The Queen* v. *Lo A-tow* confirms that British sovereignty in Hong Kong was cobbled together from fluid ideas of fugitive surrenders – evolving ideas of whether, why, and how different categories of people ought to be given up to British or Chinese authorities.

Dubious Occupation: The Roots of Jurisdictional Uncertainty

British rule in Hong Kong was rooted in the Opium War and the maritime 'China trade' of the eighteenth and early nineteenth centuries. The war got its name, of course, from the drug that predominantly private British merchants exported from India to China in exchange for silver to line their pockets and to pay for tea, silks, and other Chinese goods that sold well in Europe. The East India Company, which held the British monopoly on the China trade until 1834, profited from a distance as the largest supplier of Indian-grown opium. The Chinese government had prohibited opium imports since 1729, but enforcement waxed and waned in the estuarine environs of Canton, the hub of the China trade. In the spring of 1839, Chinese efforts to suppress the opium trade led to the confiscation and destruction of nearly 20,000 chests of British opium. Britain declared war later that year, after hawkish merchants persuaded the government to demand 'satisfaction' for the opium incident, a trading post similar to Portuguese Macau, and other trade-related concessions from China.[2]

In doing so, merchants used the opium incident as a convenient casus belli to justify a commercially motivated war: a strategic war that was already years in the making. As Song-Chuan Chen has shown, merchants spent the 1830s gathering political support for the view that Britain was legally and morally entitled to demand freer access to Chinese goods and markets.[3] Standing in the way of such access was China's extant policy of restricting Western trade to the port of Canton. Merchants in Canton were required to play by the restrictive rules of the *Cohong*, a state-licensed guild of Chinese monopolists.[4]

A related grievance was the precarious status of British merchants under Chinese law. By a local custom that developed during the eighteenth century, Western merchants enjoyed considerable autonomy in Canton. They could resolve their own disputes and discipline their own people for minor offences against Chinese victims.[5] However, bitter disputes arose whenever Chinese people died at Western hands.[6] In 1784, a British gunner on a British merchant ship, *Lady Hughes*, caused the death of two Chinese boatmen while firing a gun salute. The Chinese authorities demanded the surrender of the offending gunner. The British merchants and officials of the East India Company were reluctant to cooperate, but they relented after Chinese officials threatened to cut off their access to food and water. After being handed over, the gunner was convicted of a homicide offence and executed by manual strangulation on the direct order of Emperor Qianlong. The British were scandalised, as they felt that China had wrongly executed their countryman for an 'accidental homicide' – in other words, a blameless act.[7]

Convinced of the barbarity of Chinese law, the British merchants of Canton resolved never again to submit to it. To this end, they mounted a decades-long campaign to acquire an island or coastal base in China, specifically to create a refuge from Chinese persecution. By lobbying the Crown and East India Company, the merchants put this issue on the imperial agenda. Consequently, the British quests for self-governance and free trade in China became two sides of the same strategic coin. For both reasons, the merchants demanded the abolition of the Canton system of trade. Writing in 1830, in an influential petition to Parliament, they argued that 'the acquisition of an insular possession near the coast of China [would] place British commerce in that remote quarter of the globe beyond the reach of future despotism and oppression'.[8]

None of these early discussions addressed wider questions about how Britain would govern conquered Chinese territory. Things only changed after British and Chinese diplomats signed the Convention of Chuanbi (Chuenpi) on 20 January 1841 in a bid to bring the Opium War to a speedy end, and Royal Marines took formal possession of Hong Kong six days later. The British delegation at Chuanbi was led by Charles Elliot, the Minister to China and Chief Superintendent of British Trade in China. In addition to the 'cession' of Hong Kong, Elliot had negotiated for the reopening of the port of Canton (China had suspended trade in 1839) as well as an indemnity to Britain of 6 million silver dollars.[9] So, while the Convention of Chuanbi awaited bilateral ratification, Elliot made temporary arrangements for governing Hong Kong as an occupied territory. He issued two proclamations in February 1841 in the name of Queen Victoria, both claiming to have effect 'pending Her Majesty's further pleasure'.[10] These royal proclamations amounted to a provisional constitution for Hong Kong. Their complex contents foreshadowed later disputes.

Elliot's first proclamation provided obliquely for the governance of British subjects by subsuming them under the capacious category of 'other persons than natives of the island or of China'. This proclamation purported to place all crimes committed by non-Chinese persons 'under the cognizance of the Criminal and Admiralty Jurisdiction presently existing in China'.[11] The 'Jurisdiction' described here was that of the 'Court of Justice' that Elliot was authorised to hold in his capacity as Chief Superintendent of British Trade in China. The Chief Superintendent's judicial powers stemmed from an Order in Council issued under the China Trade Act 1833, the statute that encapsulated Britain's preparations for the end of the East India Company's China monopoly in 1834.[12] The China Trade Act enabled the Crown to perform regulatory functions that the Company used to perform, particularly in relation to dispute resolution and customs control. Under the old monopoly system, the duty to regulate British trade in Canton fell on the Company's resident Council of Supercargoes.[13] The China Trade Act authorised the replacement of this body with Crown-appointed officials led by a chief superintendent. Lord William Napier was the first holder of this new office; Elliot was the fourth.

The China Trade Act 1833 and accompanying Order in Council sought to address the historical difficulty of disciplining British subjects without acceding to Chinese jurisdiction. In theory, a number of imperial statutes dating back to 1541 empowered courts in England to try British subjects for murder and manslaughter committed in non-European territories. The latest of these statutes was the Offences Against the Person Act 1828.[14] Cases like the *Lady Hughes* were thus regarded as justiciable in England, certainly by the nineteenth century. In the days of the Company's monopoly, however, Company officers rarely bothered to bring accused persons all the way to British soil.[15] They had little incentive to do so because the impunity of British criminals never proved intolerably disruptive to trade. A similar problem pervaded the jurisdictionally plural Indian subcontinent: white violence against native Indians often went unpunished because British subjects could only be tried by the King's courts in the cities of Calcutta, Bombay, and Madras, and not by the Company's courts in the *mofussil* or Indian hinterland.[16]

Even when cases from China went to trial in England, the extraterritorial jurisdiction of the metropolitan courts was demonstrably limited and contestable in cases that involved lesser crimes than murder and manslaughter – crimes not named in the imperial statutes. In 1836, for example, a British sailor, Thomas Allen, objected to being tried for larceny at the Central Criminal Court at the Old Bailey in London. Allen had stolen three chests of tea from a British ship that was 'lying off' Whampoa (Huangpu), an anchorage downstream on the Pearl River from Canton. He argued that the court had no jurisdiction because the crime took place 'twenty or thirty miles from the sea' and 'not ... on the high seas', where the court could exercise its admiralty jurisdiction. The Crown did not dispute the location of the crime. Nor did it analogise Whampoa to the high seas by adducing 'evidence as to the tide flowing or otherwise at the place where the vessel lay'. But the court decided nonetheless that the crime fell within admiralty jurisdiction, 'the place being one where great ships go'.[17] This ruling implied that crimes other than murder and manslaughter, committed in shallower parts of the Pearl River were not justiciable at the Old Bailey. By this logic, similar crimes committed on the banks of the river, perhaps in the Western 'factories' or warehouses at the port of Canton, were also not justiciable.

The Chief Superintendent's Court of Justice might have solved these problems, had it been established in Canton before the Opium

War. The Court of Justice was authorised, at least on paper, to try all 'Offences committed by His Majesty's subjects within the dominions of the Emperor of China, and the ports and havens thereof, and on the high seas within 100 miles of the coast of China.'[18] Again, however, complications arose in practice. Whitehall still had some intention in 1834 to reform the Canton system through peaceful diplomacy, so the first Chief Superintendent, Napier, was instructed to placate China by delaying the establishment of the Court of Justice.[19] War subsequently broke out before this policy was revised, and Elliot shook things up by obtaining Hong Kong in the Convention of Chuanbi but without securing a wider concession guaranteeing the autonomy of British subjects in China. Indeed, even the terms concerning Hong Kong were unclear: the Chinese-language version of the Convention provided only for British subjects to use the island as a 'temporary dwelling' and not for Britain to annex it outright.[20] After occupying Hong Kong, therefore, Elliot took it upon himself to use the limited tools at his disposal – his statutory powers and the skimpy Convention of Chuanbi – to establish a variant of the Chief Superintendent's Court of Justice.

Elliot's move to exercise his jurisdiction was illegal in imperial eyes. The Law Officers of the Crown had advised the Foreign Office in 1840 that the Chief Superintendent could only establish his Court of Justice *in Canton* and not elsewhere unless the Crown issued another Order in Council under the China Trade Act 1833.[21] Elliot might have put himself on firmer legal ground if he had proclaimed the establishment of a domestic court instead of one that was expressly designed to operate in foreign territory. Imperial officials later agreed that the Chief Superintendent was vested with a delegated prerogative power to govern any territory ceded by China as long as the treaty of cession was unratified. Only upon ratification were more formal instruments, such as letters patent, required to place the government of the ceded territory 'on a basis of greater solemnity'.[22] There was also the related issue, which went undiscussed in 1841, that the Chief Superintendent's jurisdiction extended only to British subjects and not anyone else; so, even if Elliot could lawfully establish the extraterritorial Court of Justice in the ceded territory of Hong Kong, he could not use it to discipline all non-natives of Hong Kong and China.[23]

Elliot's mistakes were no mere technicalities. They disclosed, instead, ambivalent conceptions of the status of Hong Kong. In simple terms, was Hong Kong sovereign British territory? The indications were mixed. This ambivalence was embodied, too, in Elliot's plans for people of Chinese descent. Elliot's first proclamation of February 1841 declared that Hong Kong had been 'ceded to the British Crown'. Accordingly, 'pending Her Majesty's further pleasure, the natives of the island of Hong Kong, and all natives of China thereto resorting, shall be governed according to the laws and customs of China, every description of torture excepted'. The second proclamation was then addressed to 'the Chinese Inhabitants of Hong Kong'. It repeated parts of the first proclamation before adding that since Hong Kong had 'become part of the dominions of the Queen of England', 'all native persons residing therein must understand that they are now subjects of the Queen of England, and to whom and to whose officers they must pay duty and obedience'. These new 'subjects' were to be 'governed ... by the elders of villages, subject to the control of a British magistrate'. To this office of 'British magistrate,' Elliot appointed William Caine, an infantry captain who would go on to have a long career in the permanent colonial government of Hong Kong. For now, Caine was issued with a warrant 'to exercise authority, according to the laws, customs, and usages of China, as nearly as may be'.[24]

These declarations exhibited tensions of subjecthood and territorial sovereignty. If the 'natives' of Hong Kong had become British subjects, then it is unclear why they should come under the supervisory jurisdiction of a separate 'British magistrate' instead of the Chief Superintendent's Court of Justice. Some scholars have argued that Elliot's 'dual system of law', as it came to be known, sprung from an intention to preserve Hong Kong's indigenous society: it was a calculated move to govern a community of non-European British subjects indirectly, through their own customary leaders.[25] That may be so, but Elliot also claimed the authority to govern – again, through a 'British magistrate' – 'all natives of China ... resorting' to Hong Kong. These migrants and sojourners were certainly not British subjects, and they had few if any ties to the villages in Hong Kong. Elliot's failure to address this complication suggests that he did not merely harbour a bifurcated or racialised idea of subjecthood. On the contrary, he was likely unwilling or unable to regard Hong Kong as fully sovereign territory, or as a place where the jurisdiction of British judges and officials could be framed more simply and comprehensively. This explanation also accounts for Elliot's messy arrangements for British subjects and other non-Chinese subjects in Hong Kong. It situates Elliot's measures in the wider context of the Opium War, in which territorial conquest was incidental to the war goals of the British government and merchant lobby. Although Elliot's administration was short-lived, closely similar tensions regarding the legal status of Hong Kong and its inhabitants would resurface during 1842–43.

The Terms of Peace: Faulty Provisions for Dividing Jurisdiction

Elliot's proclamations were quickly invalidated because London and Beijing rejected the Convention of Chuanbi. The British government wanted to push for more concessions, while the Chinese government believed, wrongly, that its armies could still turn the tide of the war.[26] Elliot was therefore dismissed and hostilities resumed until another peace conference was held in Nanjing in late July 1842. The Nanjing negotiations then presented the novel solution of an agreement for Britain to surrender Chinese criminals from Hong Kong. As a result, it was in the course of negotiating this surrender agreement that Elliot's successor, Henry Pottinger – an East India Company officer with thirty-eight years' experience – continued to demonstrate Britain's ambivalence towards becoming a territorial power in China.

Pottinger managed to obtain a full package of concessions to satisfy the merchants who pulled the strings of Whitehall's China policy. Like Elliot, however, he stumbled over the issue of Hong Kong. This was partly because he and his Chinese counterparts at Nanjing agreed to construct a peace settlement in two stages: they decided to send for the mutual ratification of a skeletal treaty containing the main terms of peace – the Treaty of Nanjing of 29 August 1842 – while continuing to discuss other terms, mainly by correspondence.[27] The upshot of this staggered approach was a quick peace in 1842 followed by the preparation of two additional treaty instruments during 1843. The first of the additional instruments was a set of 'General Regulations' for the conduct of British trade in China – this was finalised in July

1843 and appended to the main Treaty of Nanjing.[28] The second was the 'Supplementary Treaty' of 8 October 1843, also known as the 'Treaty of the Bogue'.[29] The Bogue, or Bocca Tigris, is a strait in the Pearl River estuary. Its opening into the sea was partly guarded by a Chinese fort on the island of Chuanbi, the location of Elliot's failed Convention.

The most important elements of Pottinger's peace package were included in the main Treaty of Nanjing: the cession of Hong Kong to Britain, reparations to Britain of $21 million, the opening of five ports to British trade – Canton, Amoy (Xiamen), Fuzhou, Ningbo, and Shanghai – and, finally, the abolition of the *Cohong* monopoly in Canton.[30] The cession of Hong Kong was provided for in Article 3, as follows:

> It being obviously necessary and desirable that British subjects should have some port whereat they may careen and refit their ships when required, and keep stores for that purpose, His Majesty the Emperor of China cedes to Her Majesty the Queen of Great Britain, etc., the Island of Hong-Kong, to be possessed in perpetuity by Her Britannick Majesty, her Heirs and Successors, and to be governed by such laws and regulations as Her Majesty the Queen of Great Britain, etc., shall see fit to direct.

This article provided for the right of the British Crown to make laws for Hong Kong. Crucially, however, the permissible scope of those laws was unclear. Could they be enforced against Chinese subjects? This was not discussed before Article 3 was drawn up. Neither did the main Treaty of Nanjing give Britain a more general right to control British subjects at the five unceded ports. The records suggest that the delegates at Nanjing decided to defer the drafting of such a provision because they regarded the general issue of British autonomy or self-governance as uncontroversial. The senior Chinese delegate, Imperial Commissioner Qiying (Keying) had already decided to concede the point, and, knowing this, Pottinger had no reason to insist on addressing it immediately.[31]

For these reasons, it only transpired in September 1842, a week after the Treaty of Nanjing was signed, that the scope of Article 3 could not be decoupled from the issue of the scope of British jurisdictional autonomy. This problem arose insidiously. First, Pottinger and Qiying agreed that the enlarged and formally autonomous British presence in China should not undermine China's authority over its own people. So, although it was common ground that British officers would discipline British subjects at the treaty ports, Qiying believed it was equally important for the treaty instruments to stipulate that Chinese subjects would 'receive punishment from their own Country'. Qiying was concerned that Chinese fugitives would systematically 'betake themselves' to British ships under the new system of trade. He argued that such fugitives should be 'delivered up' to Chinese authorities and not 'concealed' from justice.[32] Pottinger agreed; and, since Chinese fugitives were just as likely to take refuge in British Hong Kong as on British ships visiting the treaty ports, Pottinger took the initiative to propose a wider agreement for the reciprocal surrender of fugitives between Chinese and British officials. In a report to the Foreign Office, Pottinger remarked that these arrangements seemed 'so reciprocal and advantageous, that they require no comment'.[33]

This was where difficulties arose. It was one thing for Britain to surrender Chinese subjects who 'betook' themselves to Hong Kong: what about the Chinese subjects who were already in Hong Kong? How would *they* be governed? To reconcile the forthcoming agreement for fugitive surrenders with Article 3 of the Treaty of Nanjing, Pottinger tried to justify restricting the surrender agreement. First, he proposed to distinguish the permanent residents of Hong Kong from transient residents of Chinese origin. In this approach, the 'Chinese people residing at present on the Island of Hong Kong', who chose to remain there, would 'become subject to whatever Laws and Regulations [that] may be formed for the management of that Settlement'. Meanwhile, 'all temporary Sojourners and casual Traders will be considered Subjects of the Emperor of China and will come under [the surrender agreement]'.[34] When Qiying rejected this approach, Pottinger proposed an alternative approach: he suggested making all Chinese subjects in Hong Kong liable to surrender, but only for 'serious crimes … involving Capital or other severe punishment' and not for 'trifling offences' such as 'theft, assault, shoplifting, picking pockets, gambling, rioting, [and] drunkenness'.[35]

Qiying rejected the second proposal, too. He argued that Pottinger's proposals were less acceptable than the status quo in Portuguese Macau, where all Chinese subjects came under the jurisdiction of a resident Chinese magistrate. Qiying indicated, then, that he was willing to modify the Macau model as a compromise. Instead of posting a Chinese officer in Hong Kong, he would do so at Tsim Sha Tsui, on the southern tip of the Kowloon Peninsula (which China later ceded to Britain in 1860). Qiying argued that this arrangement would allow China to punish misbehaving Chinese residents of Hong Kong without interfering with British subjects on the island.[36] It would also save British officers the trouble of bringing Chinese criminals to the magistracy or *yamen* of Xin'an (Sunon), the Chinese county of which Hong Kong was part.[37] The *yamen* of Xin'an was located in a fortified city almost thirty miles north of Hong Kong (see Map 1.1), so Qiying implied that his proposal to receive Chinese criminals in Kowloon was a fair and practical compromise.[38]

Pottinger admitted at this stage to being taken aback by the escalating difficulty of the question of Chinese subjects in Hong Kong. In a letter to the Foreign Secretary, the 4th Earl of Aberdeen, he remarked that 'the [Chinese] High Officers appear to be anxious to a degree that I had not anticipated'. Pottinger added that he was 'quite prepared to meet their views in all instances of serious offences or crimes, but I cannot yet see how a large and mixed Native Population is to be kept in order unless our Officers on the spot are vested with what may be termed *Police* Authority, in contradistinction to *Judicial* Powers'.[39] Pottinger was surprised, then, not only by the anxiety of the Chinese delegation but also by the complexity of the task of framing the surrender agreement. His correspondence suggests that he was struggling to figure out even the parameters of the task. Was it more important for the agreement to define the range of people that Britain would surrender? Or should it focus on defining the authority of British officials to decide whether and how to surrender any particular person? Pottinger was unsure, and his uncertainty contributed to the emergence of a contested agreement.

When negotiations resumed in January 1843, the best that Pottinger could do was to repeat to the Chinese delegation what he had said to Aberdeen. He said that he was prepared to send all Chinese criminals to Kowloon: his only condition was that 'the British authorities at Hong Kong must be allowed to exercise Police jurisdiction to a certain extent, else it will be impossible to keep in any degree of order or restraint the large assemblage of People of all Nations, who have settled at, or who occasionally resort, to Hong Kong'.[40] In response,

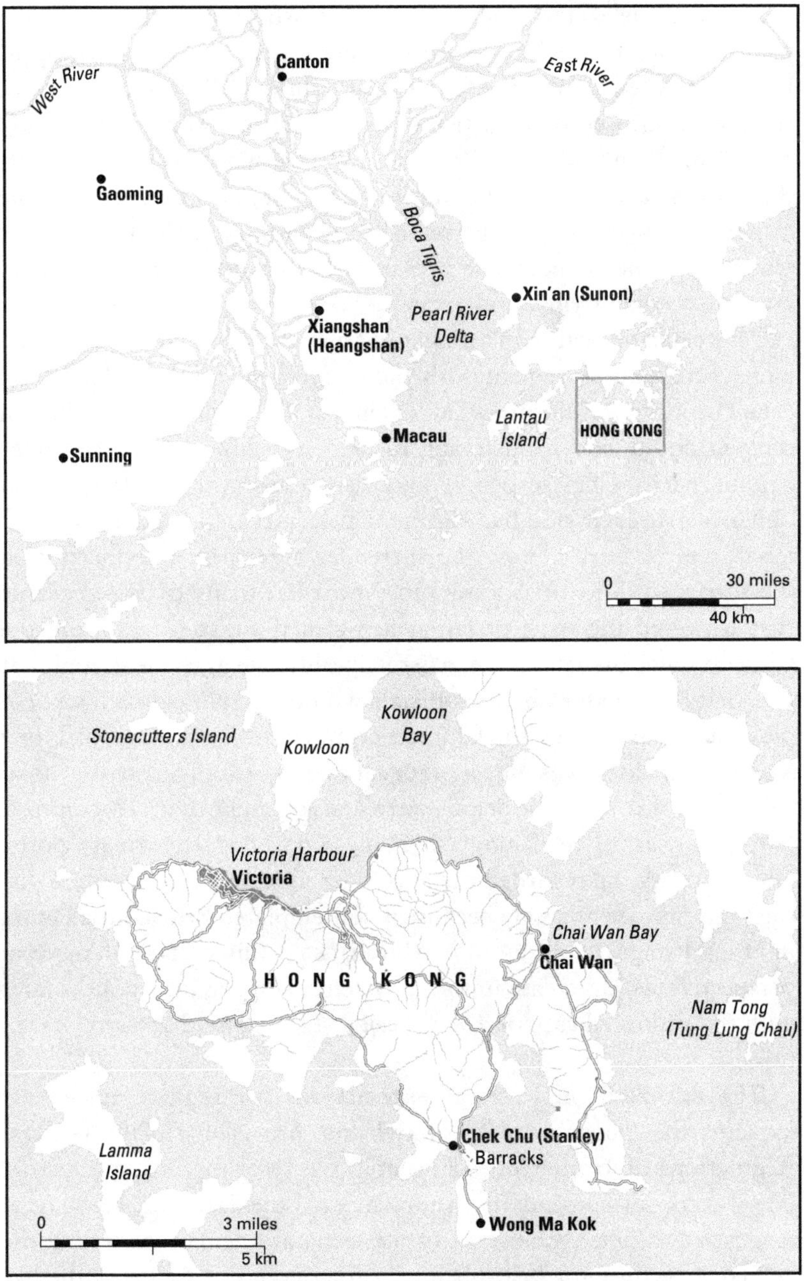

MAP 1.1 Hong Kong and the Pearl River Estuary, *c.* 1845.

the Chinese delegates proposed to let British officers administer the surrender process as long as *all* Chinese criminals were given up to Kowloon, 'even should the Crime be a light one'.[41] Pottinger agreed, though he stressed that 'British officers must in all cases investigate' crimes involving Western 'foreigners', 'and where [in these cases] the Chinese are found to be in the wrong they will be sent with the evidence to Kowloong to be punished according to the Laws of the Chinese'.[42] The Chinese delegates agreed: they declared this arrangement 'exceedingly right and proper'.[43]

This exchange caused Pottinger to believe, by March 1843, that he had reached an agreement with the Chinese government. However, even Pottinger was unsure what 'extent' of 'Police jurisdiction' British officials could exercise in Hong Kong, especially in cases of crimes committed by Chinese people against Chinese victims. It was also obvious that each side had different priorities and, as a result, different conceptions of how the surrender agreement interfaced with the agreement for British autonomy at the five treaty ports – the issue that triggered the issue of Hong Kong in the first place. From the Chinese point of view, there was really only one agreement, and that was that British and Chinese officials would discipline their own people. The arrangement for Chinese criminals to be sent from Hong Kong to Kowloon was only a practical means of applying that general rule; so, in this view, the details were not very important. By contrast, Pottinger wanted to distinguish Hong Kong from the treaty ports. Consequently, he regarded the surrender agreement as having a distinct importance precisely because it contemplated British jurisdiction in Hong Kong. Unaddressed in March 1843, this subtle difference in perspective would create untold problems, starting just months later with the contested case of *The Queen* v. *Lo A-tow* (discussed later in this chapter).

The mismatch in bilateral expectations for fugitive surrenders explains the messy wording of two key provisions in the General Regulations of Trade (July 1843) and Treaty of the Bogue (October 1843) – the instruments that supplemented the Treaty of Nanjing of August 1842. First, Clause 13 of the General Regulations set out the agreed procedure for British subjects to govern themselves at the five treaty ports.[44] But it also alluded vaguely to a British obligation to surrender Chinese criminals from Hong Kong:

XIII. Disputes between British Subjects and Chinese

Whenever a British subject has reason to complain of a Chinese, he must first proceed to the [British] Consulate and state his grievance; the Consul will thereupon inquire into the merits of the case, and do his utmost to arrange it amicably. In like manner, if a Chinese ha[s] reason to complain of a British subject, he shall no less listen to his complaint, and endeavour to settle it in a friendly manner. If an English merchant ha[s] occasion to address the Chinese authorities, he shall send such address through the Consul, who will see that the language is becoming; and, if otherwise, will direct it to be changed, or will refuse to convey the address. If, unfortunately, any disputes take place of such a nature that the Consul cannot arrange them amicably, then he shall request the assistance of a Chinese officer, that they may together examine into the merits of the case, and decide it equitably. *Regarding the punishment of English criminals, the English Government will enact the laws necessary to attain that end, and the Consul will be empowered to put them in force; and regarding the punishment of Chinese criminals, these will be tried and punished by their own laws, in the way provided for by the correspondence which took place at Nanking, after the concluding of the peace.*[45]

This composite clause was extremely ambiguous. Although it did not explicitly mention Hong Kong, its concluding sentence was almost certainly a reference to the negotiations that included Hong Kong. This is because the question of punishing Chinese criminals was not discussed in any other context, and Chinese criminals were not mentioned in the General Regulations' fourteen other clauses. Yet Hong Kong was omitted from the full title of the General Regulations: the 'General Regulations, under which the British Trade is to be conducted at the Five Ports of Canton, Amoy, Foochow, Ningpo, and Shanghai'. Also, contrary to what Clause 13 implied, the British government never planned to station consular officers in Hong Kong. China had ceded Hong Kong under the main Treaty of Nanjing, so Whitehall decided in December 1842 to establish colonial institutions of government on the island, and to appoint Pottinger Governor.[46] Since Pottinger knew about these plans, it seems very unlikely that he intended Clause 13 to provide for a British *consul* to control British subjects in Hong Kong.[47] It is more likely that the odd phrasing of Clause 13 was the result of a poorly coordinated effort, involving multiple parties, to gesture at the agreement (such as it was) for fugitive surrenders. It was thus deeply unclear whether Clause 13 applied to Hong Kong. Unsurprisingly, Chinese officials would later suggest that the Clause expressed the general rule that, without exception, all 'subjects of China should be judged by Chinese Mandarins'.[48] British officials and judges would assert, to the contrary, that Clause 13 applied only to the unceded treaty ports.[49]

Fugitive surrenders were more explicitly provided for in Article 9 of the Treaty of the Bogue:

> If lawless natives of China, having committed crimes or offences against their own Government, shall flee to Hong-Kong, or to the English ships of war, or English merchant-ships, for refuge, they shall, if discovered by the English officers, be handed over at once to the Chinese officers for trial and punishment; or if, before such discovery be made by the English officers, it should be ascertained or suspected by the officers of the Government of China whither such criminals and offenders have fled, a communication shall be made to the proper English officer, in order that the said criminals and offenders may be rigidly searched for, seized, and, on proof or admission of their guilt, delivered up. In like manner, if any soldier or sailor, or any other person, whatever his caste or country, who is a subject of the Crown of England, shall, from any cause or on any pretence, desert, fly, or escape into the Chinese territory, such soldier or sailor, or other person, shall be apprehended and confined by the Chinese Authorities, and sent to the nearest British Consular or other Government officer. In neither case shall concealment or refuge be afforded.

This article was also flawed: it mentioned Chinese subjects fleeing to Hong Kong but not Chinese subjects committing crimes in Hong Kong. There was also no mention of Kowloon or Tsim Sha Tsui and no attempt to incorporate Pottinger's demand for 'Police jurisdiction'. Indeed, Article 9 contradicted itself in specifying how closely 'English officers' could control the surrender process: it was unclear whether Chinese criminals were to be 'handed over *at once*' or only 'on proof or admission of their guilt'. Again, these ambiguities would sour relations between Britain and China; again, they demonstrate the Nanjing delegates' failure, and probably reluctance, to set clearer conditions for fugitive surrenders. Hidden throughout the Opium War treaties of 1842–43 were the scatterings of an illusory agreement and the seeds of a chronic dispute.

Imperial Intervention: Abortive Ideas for Naturalisation and Jurisdictional Plurality

From February to April 1843, officials in London made their own attempt to justify asserting partial jurisdiction in Hong Kong. In doing so, they brought important ideas to bear on the Nanjing peace settlement – ideas of subjecthood and the executive and legislative powers of the Crown, drawn from past treaties and judicial precedents. This discussion produced a tentative policy for Hong Kong, but imperial indecision and poor communication with Pottinger's delegation doomed this policy to failure.

The imperial officials started by rejecting the idea of surrendering all Chinese criminals from Hong Kong without exception. The Secretary of State for War and the Colonies, Lord Stanley (later 14th Earl of Derby) persuaded his colleagues that 'it would, according to European maxims and usages, be a great anomaly that an offence committed within the precincts, and against the Law, of an Independent Country should be tried in the Courts of another Country'. Stanley was thus minded to assert territorial sovereignty in Hong Kong, and to refrain from giving any impression that Hong Kong was only 'transferred to Great Britain in occupancy not in Sovereignty'. Stanley argued, furthermore, that injustice could arise from surrendering Chinese subjects accused of murder, rape, and other serious crimes. Differences between Chinese and British legal doctrines and judicial practices meant that if surrendered to China, Chinese subjects might be punished more leniently than British perpetrators of the same crimes – if, indeed, they were punished at all.[50]

Officials also agreed, however, that Britain could not entirely refuse to reciprocate China's concession on British jurisdiction at the unceded treaty ports. Sensing that Stanley's views would cause embarrassment if adopted as official policy, the Foreign Secretary, Aberdeen pointed out that 'the Chinese Government could hardly be expected to place greater reliance on British Courts or on British Law, than the British Government is willing to place on Chinese Courts or on Chinese Law'. Aberdeen added that '[i]f therefore Her Majesty's Government insist on the exemption of British subjects residing in the dominions of the Emperor of China from Chinese Jurisdiction in criminal matters, there appears no alternative but to grant similar exemption to Chinese subjects residing in Hong Kong'.[51] The Permanent Secretary at the Colonial Office, James Stephen agreed that Britain should, in principle, govern Hong Kong on reciprocal terms: 'As we do so we must expect and submit to be done by.'[52] Stephen shared Stanley's concerns about British sovereignty and the fair punishment of criminals, but he doubted whether those factors were determinative. For Stephen, '[p]erhaps the answer to them all is that they are not collectively of so much account as would be the difficulty of raising a new quarrel with the Chinese'.[53]

For these reasons, Whitehall pivoted quickly towards finding a compromise between jurisdictional reciprocity and territorial sovereignty. Borrowing from Pottinger's ideas, Aberdeen initially proposed to draw a distinction 'between the Chinese who have their permanent domicile on the Island [of Hong Kong], and those who only resort to it for the purposes of trade'. Aberdeen argued that the 'position' of the latter, the sojourners, 'more closely corresponds with that of British subjects in Chinese Ports'. Conversely, the permanent residents of Hong Kong were unique: Aberdeen intimated that, because those residents did not correspond to any British demographic in China, Britain was not obliged to concede jurisdiction over them.[54]

Opinions differed as to whether Aberdeen's proposal comported with British law. On the one hand, the Law Officers of the Crown advised that it did. This was because

> the persons residing on the Island, and continuing to reside there after the cession to the British Crown are no longer subjects of the Emperor of China: they are subjects of the Crown of England, and are bound to pay obedience to the Laws which the Sovereign Power in this Country may think fit to declare for the Govt. of the Island.

In the opinion of the Law Officers, it followed that Britain could lawfully refuse to surrender the 'continuing' residents of Hong Kong. Indeed, the Crown could adopt the general principle that 'the subjects of the one Sovereign committing crimes within the territories of the other may be delivered up to the authorities of the Country of the Criminal to be dealt with according to the Law of that Country'.[55] This principle of general reciprocity was basically the same principle that China asserted, except that it regarded more people as British subjects.

On the other hand, Stephen argued that the permanent residents of Hong Kong were still subjects of the Chinese Emperor: 'They are not his subjects while there [in Hong Kong], i.e., are not locally subject to him. But they are still his subjects ... and if they return to China are still Chinese.'[56] In this argument, Stephen invoked the common law distinction between the 'acquired' allegiance that naturalised British subjects owed the Crown and the 'local' allegiance that was owed by alien inhabitants of British territory.[57] As Stephen explained, alluding to Edward Coke's famous interpretation of *Calvin's Case* (1608), 'every alien owes a local and temporary allegiance to the Sovereign and to the Law of the Country, within which he happens to be'.[58] This logic certainly entailed that Britain could rightfully claim jurisdiction over all crimes committed by Chinese subjects in Hong Kong. Stephen had already questioned the wisdom of that approach, however, so his point here was not to reopen that discussion; it was rather to challenge the Law Officers' account of subjecthood.

Stephen's disagreement with the Law Officers embodied contemporary uncertainties about how people in conquered territories could 'acquire' British subjecthood. In the historic case of *Campbell* v. *Hall* (1774), the Chief Justice of the King's Bench in London, Lord Mansfield had decided that 'conquered inhabitants once received under the King's protection, become subjects, and are to be universally considered in that light, not as enemies or aliens'.[59] *Campbell* v. *Hall* concerned the status of the residents of Grenada, the Caribbean island that France had ceded to Britain, along with Quebec and other colonies, under the 1763 Treaty of Paris. By ruling that the French residents of Grenada who remained there after the cession had become British subjects, Mansfield laid down an important precedent that still endured in the nineteenth century.[60] Nevertheless, it was unclear whether this rule in *Campbell* applied to all treaties of cession, or only to those, such as the Treaty of Paris, that spelled out the rights of conquered residents.[61] This question persisted because most treaties from the Georgian period gave conquered residents an explicit choice: they could either move out of ceded territories within specified periods of time, or stay put and be deemed to have accepted British subjecthood.[62] It was, as a result, in this relatively simple way that Whitehall resolved the disputed status of two residents of Mauritius in 1838, twenty-four years after France ceded that colony to Britain under the 1814 Treaty of Paris.[63] Now, Hong Kong posed a more intractable problem because the article of cession, Article 3 of the Treaty of Nanjing, was silent on the rights and liabilities of the island's existing residents.

Judges and officials had dealt with other ambiguous acquisitions of territory, to be sure, but their efforts had yielded unhelpful results. Notably, the East India Company recaptured Calcutta from the

Nawab of Bengal in 1757 under terms that did not clarify the rights of the residents of the town. The residents who remained in Calcutta were subsequently not consistently protected as British subjects in the 1770s and 1780s, as Hannah Muller has shown.[64] The uncertainties of British sovereignty in Calcutta (and, more generally, in Bengal) were later revisited in *Mayor of Lyons* v. *East India Company* (1836), an appeal before the recently established Judicial Committee of the Privy Council.[65] A wealthy Frenchman, Claude Martin, who served the East India Company for over thirty years, had bequeathed certain estates in Calcutta in his will. Various parties contested the will, claiming that, as an alien person, Martin could not devise real property under English law, so his lands had 'escheated' or reverted to the Crown upon his death in 1801.[66] On appeal to the Privy Council, the Crown agreed, arguing that '[t]he law disabling aliens from holding real estates, was necessarily introduced *eo instanti* [i.e. immediately when] the sovereignty of these territories [in Bengal] became vested in the Crown'. 'At that instant,' the Crown acknowledged, 'the natives and inhabitants became subjects of Great Britain, and the lands therefore in their hands did not become liable to escheat.' Since Martin was a later immigrant, however, the Crown argued that *his* lands were liable to escheat.[67] Lord Brougham rejected this argument. In Brougham's view, treaties, charters, statutes, and regulations expressed 'the will of the sovereign' in relation to what laws applied in conquered territories and what rights conquered residents had. By this logic, 'without *express provision* in a treaty, the subjects conquered [from foreign powers] are aliens'.[68] Nevertheless, aliens *could* lawfully hold and devise land in Calcutta. For Brougham, this was because they had done this for decades, and the Crown had not expressed any intention to change this status quo. In fact, the Crown had facilitated the property rights of aliens in Calcutta through executive action and legislative enactments.[69]

In 1843, officials in London could not agree on whether the cession of Hong Kong had instantly caused the island's Chinese residents to become British subjects. This suggests that *Lyons* was regarded as inconclusive on the question of acquired subjecthood, or at least less conclusive on that question than on the separate question of the property rights of aliens in conquered territories. Relatedly, officials were unsure if the Crown could sidestep the problem in Hong Kong by naturalising its Chinese residents after the fact. Everyone agreed that Article 3 of the Treaty of Nanjing enabled the Crown to make laws in Hong Kong; so, Aberdeen suggested that the Crown could perhaps 'require from the Chinese settlers in Hong Kong a renunciation of their allegiance to the Emperor of China, and a recognition of the absolute supremacy of England, as the price of their being allowed to remain on the island'.[70] Again, Aberdeen implied that Britain should not assert jurisdiction over Chinese sojourners: he proposed to compel only Chinese *settlers* to swear allegiance to Queen Victoria. However, even this idea was dropped after Stephen cautioned that it 'might lead to embarrassment and could be of no practical advantage'.[71] Like other officials in future years, Stephen may have sensed, rightly, that few people of Chinese descent were willing to expressly renounce their birth allegiance.[72]

The imperial discussion culminated in a decision to pursue a rather different kind of compromise: a judicial compromise. In March 1843, officials decided that: 'Her Majesty's Government would willingly receive [in Hong Kong] one or more judicial authorities selected by The Emperor of China, who should administer in the name of The Queen the law of China in cases where the Chinese subjects of the British Crown are concerned.' Britain would pay the salaries of these officers: they 'would not be a charge upon any province of the Emperor's dominions'.[73] However, these Chinese officers would 'hold their offices at the pleasure of the Crown – that is, of the Governor [of Hong Kong] – not at the pleasure of the Emperor'. As Stephen explained, they 'should be understood to be the Queen's Judges and not the Emperor's'.[74] In other words, Whitehall was willing to host Chinese judges in Hong Kong at British expense, in lieu of sending Chinese criminals to the Chinese mainland.

Whitehall was willing to do this – to let China exercise a form of consular jurisdiction in Hong Kong – because this compromise was easier to rationalise than the allegiance-based strategies that Aberdeen had proposed. Indeed, Stephen noted with some satisfaction that 'the distinction between transient and domiciled Inhabitants might well be laid out of account'.[75] The Colonial Secretary, Lord Stanley, added that any Chinese person who wished to accept British protection as a British subject could still apply to be naturalised on an ad hoc basis.[76] Since Hong Kong was due to become a Crown colony – letters patent establishing its constitution were later issued on 5 April 1843 – its Legislative Council would have the power to enact ordinances to give individual aliens rights comparable to those of natural-born British subjects.[77] Meanwhile, it was not much of a problem for Chinese-appointed judges to serve 'at pleasure' in Hong Kong: most British colonial judges also served without security of tenure, as officers with limited authority to challenge the Crown.[78] The terms that Whitehall was prepared to offer were thus not fully reciprocal, as China did not claim any power to dismiss British consular personnel. But these terms were reasonably consistent with Article 3 of the Treaty of Nanjing, and – more importantly, from Whitehall's point of view – with British ideas of sovereignty and subjecthood.

As it happened, Hong Kong never did host Chinese-appointed judges. This was because communications between Whitehall and Pottinger's diplomatic mission broke down in early 1843. When the discussion at Whitehall was still in progress, Pottinger heard 'some verbal remarks' from an officer and courier in his mission, Lieutenant Colonel George Malcolm, to the effect that the Crown would accept nothing less than territorial sovereignty.[79] This misunderstanding caused Pottinger to propose a registration system, which resembled Aberdeen's abortive idea for naturalising Chinese settlers. Pottinger's proposal was more convoluted, however. As he explained, he would require all residents of Hong Kong, of all nationalities, to register at a 'Registry Office'. He would prohibit unregistered persons from residing in the colony even temporarily. Then, he proposed, 'all Persons registered are to be considered amenable to the Police Laws of the Island'. In other words, registrants would remain aliens, but they would be allowed to reside in Hong Kong. As for the existing Chinese residents of Hong Kong, 'the option will be given to [them] whether to quit the Island being paid for their Lands and Houses, or to remain as subjects of the British Crown and as such entitled to British Protection and subject to British Laws'.[80] What, in that case, would happen to future migrants and sojourners from China? Pottinger did not explain what registration would entail for those people: naturalisation or merely lawful residency. This ambiguity mattered because it begged the question of whether Britain would govern Chinese people only as naturalised British subjects or also as alien residents of sovereign British territory. In other words, the question of whether

Britain would govern Hong Kong as fully sovereign territory was still unanswered. As it happened, Whitehall compounded this problem by failing to send accurate and timely news about its policy discussions.

Pottinger's proposal for registration amounted to nothing. In May 1843, he presented it to Qiying for discussion, only to be told that the Chinese rejection of British law was 'a thing of the same nature' as the British rejection of Chinese law. Qiying added, pointedly, that although Article 3 of the Treaty of Nanjing 'stipulates that Hong Kong shall come under the authority and government of England, this had reference to the cession of the ground for the merchants and people of the Honourable Country to repair their vessels and store their goods there; it was not therein provided, that its Inhabitants should become English people'.[81] Again, this rejoinder brought both sides no closer to a workable agreement. It served only to further deter British officials, especially James Stephen, from trying to naturalise the Chinese residents of Hong Kong. As Stephen had predicted by taking the *Lyons* interpretation of acquired subjecthood – that naturalisation by conquest required express treaty provision – Britain could not credibly argue that it had fought the Opium War to acquire Chinese *subjects* in addition to Chinese territory for British subjects to occupy. In response to Qiying's rejection of Pottinger's proposal for registration, Stephen noted that 'the Chinese High Commissioner has the best of the argument'.[82]

Finally, Aberdeen did not firmly instruct Pottinger to carry out the imperial plan to host Chinese-appointed judges in Hong Kong. Indeed, he presented the plan to Pottinger more as a suggestion than as a policy that Pottinger was required to implement. As Aberdeen explained, 'it would unquestionably be much more agreeable' if Pottinger could convince China to drop its jurisdictional claims entirely; 'but as there is no reasonable ground for expecting that [he] could succeed in doing so, it appears ... that the course now pointed out ... affords the best chance of obviating the inconveniences which may be apprehended from the existence in as confined a space as Hong Kong of two systems of criminal jurisdiction'.[83] Pottinger was thus led to believe that he should still hold out for some prospect of territorial sovereignty. He formed this view towards the end of his treaty negotiations with China, which was why the discussion at Whitehall did not influence the wording of the jurisdictional provisions in the Treaty of the

Bogue and General Regulations of Trade. On 27 July 1843, Pottinger reported, in response to Aberdeen's equivocal instructions, that the Hong Kong question would form 'a subject of future negotiation'.[84] In fact, it never did, as further negotiations were short-circuited by *The Queen* v. *Lo A-tow*.

Practice before Principle: A Precedent for Territorial Sovereignty

A grisly murder caused events on the ground to overtake more principled discussions about British sovereignty and the surrender of fugitives between Hong Kong and China. In 1843, the part of eastern Hong Kong known as Chai Wan, or Firewood Bay, was a quiet stretch of coast that comprised little more than a fishing community in the bay and a farming village further inland.[85] One fishing family was that of Wong Yaong-fook, who lived on his boat with his wife, Wong Nei-she, and their infant child. On the night of 6 April, a fight broke out on the Wong family's houseboat. It was witnessed by another fisherman, Po A-sye, from his own boat about 200 feet away. Po A-sye later testified that Wong Yaong-fook and five other men were present. It was too dark to identify the five men, but Po A-sye believed he heard the voice of a local farmer, Lo A-tow.[86]

Two days later, Po A-sye found Wong Yaong-fook's body floating in the bay. Among other mutilations, the corpse 'bore the mark of a severe wound inflicted on the top of the head, apparently by a knife, which had cleft the skull, and cut through the bone'.[87] Shocked by this discovery, Po A-sye alerted Wong Yaong-fook's brother, Wong Yaong-po, who was also a resident of Chai Wan. But Yaong-fook and Yaong-po also had an older brother who happened to be out at sea. Everyone called this older brother 'A-yee', so his full name was probably Wong Yaong-yee by southern Chinese convention. Yaong-po decided, then, to locate Yaong-yee before reporting the homicide to any authority (since it was obviously a homicide, if not murder). Yaong-po also buried Yaong-fook in their ancestral village of Nam Tong, about three miles from Chai Wan by boat (see Map 1.1). Nam Tong was in Chinese territory: it was not part of the cession of 1842.[88]

While Yaong-po was away, the eyewitness Po A-sye decided that the death of Yaong-fook was no longer his concern. He would later claim, when questioned by the British Chief Magistrate of Hong Kong, William Caine, that this was why he did not speak to the headmen (or elders) of the village in Chai Wan. Po A-sye would also claim that he was too poor to make the journey of ten miles to report the incident at the main British settlement in Hong Kong – the settlement that the British would soon name 'Victoria'.[89] It seems just as likely, however, that Po A-sye did not even consider travelling to Victoria. It was, after all, still an open question, even among officials in London, how the British authorities in Hong Kong would deal with crimes committed between Chinese people. If Pottinger himself was still unsure despite having been appointed Governor, it is difficult to imagine that a humble fisherman like Po A-sye would have taken British jurisdiction for granted.

Meanwhile, Yaong-po and his brother Yaong-yee decided to report their case to Lau (or Laou), the Chief Magistrate of the Chinese county of Xin'an. The brothers later claimed that they did this out of simple convenience: they had apparently travelled close to Lau's *yamen* at Xin'an.[90] Again, the real reason was more likely that the brothers did what they felt was right and customary, as Chinese subjects and residents of Xin'an County. In any case, Yaong-po and Yaong-yee entreated Chief Magistrate Lau to issue a warrant for the arrest of seven people in connection with their brother's death. Lau agreed: he instructed his officers to serve the warrant on William Caine and to request Caine's assistance in arresting the seven people in Hong Kong.

As a result of these events, Caine only received news of the incident in Chai Wan during August 1843 – news in the form of an unexpected visit by *yamen* personnel from Xin'an. Although Caine decided to cooperate in the case, he protested the way it had been handled. In a letter to Chief Magistrate Lau, Caine conceded that 'the culprits of both nations, shall be mutually delivered over for punishment by the officers of their own nations'. As authority for this rule, Caine cited 'the supplementary arrangements now pending' – that is, the General Regulations of Trade and Treaty of the Bogue. However, Caine argued that the power to arrest offenders 'must rest in the hands of the officer holding the government of the place ... It can never be admitted that the officer of one country should send to search for and seize offenders within the Territory of the other.'[91] This argument alluded to Pottinger's earlier promise to deliver Chinese criminals to

Kowloon (specifically, to Tsim Sha Tsui). The details of that informal agreement were never clarified bilaterally, as we have seen. Although Pottinger had insisted that British officials in Hong Kong should have 'Police jurisdiction to a certain extent', subsequent discussions in China and London pivoted away from that particular issue. Now, in August 1843, Caine interpreted 'Police jurisdiction' to mean that, as the Chief Magistrate of Hong Kong, he had the power to investigate and determine 'the truth of the charges' against the alleged killers of Wong Yaong-fook. According to Caine, Pottinger would then have the power as Governor to decide whether to send the accused murderers to Xin'an 'for punishment', or to release them 'as being falsely accused'.[92] Chief Magistrate Lau agreed. He did not admit to violating the treaty arrangements by issuing warrants to be served in Hong Kong, but he accepted the course of action that Caine proposed.[93]

The seven people named in Lau's warrant were charged variously with murder and being accessories to murder. There were also charges of adultery, or having 'criminal connection', but Caine did not investigate those charges in and of themselves.[94] The principal accused was Lo A-tow, the man whose voice the eyewitness, Po A-sye, reported hearing on the fatal night. Also accused were Lo A-tow's five brothers, the youngest of whom, Lo A-sam, was only thirteen years old. Next, the seventh and final accused was the victim's wife, Wong Nei-she. According to Po A-sye, Wong Nei-she and Lo A-tow were having an affair. The victim, Wong Yaong-fook, discovered the affair and confronted Lo A-tow, so the latter allegedly recruited his brothers to settle the score on Wong Yaong-fook's boat. In this account of the incident, Wong Nei-she did not kill her husband, but she led the Lo brothers to him and did nothing after they killed him.[95]

In September 1843, the seven accused were brought before the Magistrates' Court that Caine presided. Their case was designated *The Queen* v. *Lo A-tow and others*. Over five days, Caine questioned the accused, the complainants, and other witnesses from Chai Wan. At the end of the hearing, Caine advised Pottinger to send Lo A-tow and Wong Nei-she to Xin'an, but to release Lo A-tow's five brothers as falsely accused. Caine explained that the complainants' case was problematic: the evidence of the victim's brothers was all hearsay and discrepancies riddled Po A-sye's eyewitness testimony. But the defendants' evidence also reeked of deception. The defendants denied all knowledge of the murder, yet they could recall the night of Wong Yaong-fook's death, the night of 6 April, well enough to present detailed alibis. For Caine, the defendants' accounts of what should have been a forgettable night were too well coordinated to be credible: 'their prevarications afford a most melancholy instance of their wickedness'.[96] On balance, Caine found sufficient evidence to recommend sending only Lo A-tow and Wong Nei-she to Xin'an for trial.

The significance of this case lies in how Pottinger decided to resolve it. Crucially, Pottinger did not surrender Lo A-tow and Wong Nei-she: he had them released and returned to Chai Wan together with the other five defendants. In a memorandum, which he forwarded to London, Pottinger explained that, considering all the work Caine had done, to send anyone to Xin'an would be 'tantamount to pronouncing them to be guilty'. This was because Pottinger did not believe that the defendants would receive a fair trial. In his opinion, the Chinese authorities were likely to 'subject those two persons to torture, in order to extort confessions of guilt from them'.[97] This concern recalled the wider Western suspicion of Chinese law, which had long animated the British unwillingness to subject themselves to it. Now, Pottinger was equally suspicious of how China would treat the Chinese residents of Hong Kong – a demographic whose subjecthood was still unclear.

The British suspicion of Chinese law would later ossify in the 1860s into a formal rule of extradition law, by which fugitives should never be extradited to face judicial torture.[98] In 1843, however, *The Queen v. Lo A-tow* was not about the conditions of extradition so much as whether an extradition-like procedure should even be carried out when Chinese people were accused of crimes in Hong Kong. Pottinger understood this. In his memorandum on the case, he implied that he had not taken it upon himself to answer the wider question of jurisdiction. He suggested, instead, that his decision not to surrender Lo A-tow and Wong Nei-she was based only on the narrow premise that the evidence against them was weak. If the evidence had been stronger, such that, by his reckoning, China would not torture them, then he would certainly have given them up. In short, Pottinger suggested that he had only denied China's jurisdictional claims 'in this instance' and not as a blanket rule. He suggested that he had only exercised the 'Police jurisdiction' that he had reserved for the British Crown in Hong Kong: he had not asserted any jurisdiction to adjudicate crimes committed by Chinese subjects. For good measure, Pottinger instructed Caine to 'inform' Chief Magistrate Lau of this logic and the evidential basis of his decision.[99]

But Pottinger framed the case differently in a separate despatch to London. In that despatch, he described the proceedings in *Lo A-tow* as a *trial*, and not merely a pre-trial hearing for the possible surrender of fugitives requested by China – a 'Trial held by the Chief Magistrate of this Colony', which 'establishes beyond all future doubt or cavil the entire Sovereignty of England over this Colony and its Chinese population'.[100] To justify this remarkable assertion, Pottinger turned his attention from the facts of the case to the nature of Chief Magistrate Lau's involvement in it. According to Pottinger, Lau's acquiescence to the judicial proceedings in Hong Kong was sufficient proof that 'the Chinese Government has tacitly waived the right they first claimed of trying all Persons (residing on the Island of Hong Kong) who might be charged with capital or other serious crimes'.[101] So, the implication was that the seven accused persons in *Lo A-tow* were not merely discharged for lack of evidence to commit them for trial in China: they were actually tried and acquitted in Hong Kong. This was not Caine's understanding of the case, to be sure. Caine had recommended surrendering Lo A-tow and Wong Nei-she, regarding Pottinger as having the executive power as Governor to accept or reject this recommendation. *That* was the extent of what Caine had told Lau – the extent of Lau's acquiescence. Nevertheless, Pottinger read a lot more into Lau's conduct. He was able to do this because Lau and other Chinese officials were not privy to his correspondence with Whitehall; also, the extended treaty negotiations of 1842–43 were vague enough that Pottinger could claim plausible deniability for this interpretive slippage.

Pottinger's inconsistent interpretations of *Lo A-tow* troubled the Foreign Secretary, the Earl of Aberdeen, but not deeply enough to change the course of events. In March 1844, Aberdeen observed that, by agreeing not to interfere with Caine's inquiries, Chief Magistrate Lau could only be said to have acquiesced to Britain's *executive* authority to arrest Chinese subjects and not to its *judicial* authority to try them in court. Aberdeen was concerned that Pottinger may have conducted further negotiations with China, which he had neglected to report.[102] In fact, Pottinger had done no such thing. Still, Whitehall was not inclined to reopen the case. Now that Hong Kong was a Crown colony, its domestic affairs fell under the purview of the Colonial Office, and that ministry was inclined to let the matter rest. 'As the Prisoners in this case underwent no punishment,' argued James Stephen, the permanent secretary, 'it is not necessary to express any opinion on the lawfulness of the proceedings against them. There would seem to be quite reason enough why such an opinion should not be expressed without necessity.' The Secretary of State, Lord Stanley, was of the same mind.[103]

Pottinger's term as minister to China and governor of Hong Kong was also ending in May 1844. He was due to be succeeded by the sinologist and former diplomat, John Francis Davis; and, although Davis had served in Canton as Chief Superintendent of British Trade during 1834–35, he had returned to England after leaving that office.[104] Whitehall was therefore reluctant to drag Davis into *Lo A-tow*. In a despatch to Davis, Aberdeen suggested that 'if no practical inconvenience arises from leaving the question in its present state, it is on every account desirable to avoid all risk of exciting the suspicion or jealousy of the Chinese government by displaying too much anxiety respecting it'.[105] Since the Chinese Imperial Commissioner, Qiying had not protested the outcome of *Lo A-tow*, Aberdeen believed there was nothing to be gained for the new governor of Hong Kong to draw further attention to the case. Indeed, the British records do not reveal whether Chief Magistrate Lau of Xin'an had even apprised Qiying – who was then based in Canton, the capital of Guangdong Province – of *Lo A-tow*. It is possible, even likely, that the higher echelons of the Chinese government placed no importance on this case at all.

All this meant that British territorial sovereignty in Hong Kong was a fait accompli. After meeting him in person, Davis took Pottinger's word that the Chinese government had dropped its jurisdictional claims.[106] Davis also observed that judicial work in Hong Kong had expanded since *Lo A-tow*, even as Whitehall discussed the implications of the case. With Pottinger's consent, Chief Magistrate Caine had disposed of other cases of serious crimes committed by people of Chinese descent – crimes including piracy and armed robbery.[107] By July 1844, therefore, ninety-four prisoners, mostly Chinese, populated the colony's new prison, Victoria Gaol, on various charges and sentences. In Davis' view, those prisoners embodied Britain's 'virtual right and possession' of criminal jurisdiction over every Chinese person in Hong Kong regardless of subjecthood. Davis argued, accordingly, that it was now a 'practical impossibility' to share this jurisdiction with China: any compromise would reduce British sovereignty in Hong Kong to 'a mere occupancy'.[108] This was the same concern that Lord Stanley had expressed from the Colonial Office in February 1843.[109] Now it ended the discussion abruptly, as no one at Whitehall responded to Davis' report of July 1844.[110] By saying nothing, Whitehall implicitly endorsed Davis' arguments despite rejecting similar arguments throughout 1843.

*

British officials fashioned a precedent for territorial sovereignty in Hong Kong by refusing a Chinese request for fugitives. In doing so, they abandoned earlier efforts to bring the Chinese residents of the island within the fold of British subjecthood. So, by applying fluid ideas of their treaty obligation to surrender Chinese fugitives – inchoate ideas of extradition – they transformed their allegiance-based conception of British and Chinese sovereignty into a more complex conception that included jurisdictional claims over people and territory in Hong Kong and China. Other accounts of the founding of colonial Hong Kong have overlooked this entanglement between the discourses of sovereignty, subjecthood, and fugitive surrenders. This is why they have reached conflicting conclusions about who decided to assert British jurisdiction over Chinese subjects in Hong Kong: Pottinger or officials in London.[111] As this chapter has shown, the truth lies somewhere in between: everyone implicitly allowed *The Queen* v. *Lo A-tow* to become a precedent for territorial sovereignty, though no one wanted to take credit for this intellectual transformation. Again, the ambiguous and mutable Opium War 'agreement' for fugitive exchanges enabled this collective denial of responsibility.

Official practices in Hong Kong shifted quickly and radically after *Lo A-tow*. An immediate consequence of the case was that the subject status of criminals ceased to matter for crimes committed in the colony. In August 1844, a colonial ordinance established the Supreme Court of Hong Kong. Formally opened on 1 October 1844, the Supreme Court was vested with jurisdictions in 'oyer and terminer and gaol delivery, assize, and *nisi prius*' – powers possessed by the King's Bench and courts of assizes in England – under legislative provisions that were silent on the nationality or subjecthood of accused persons.[112] The jurisdiction of the Magistrates' Court was simultaneously restricted, also by ordinance, to summary offences committed in the colony.[113] Heated debates would later erupt over which court was better suited to keep the peace. Magistrates would punish thousands of Chinese subjects throughout Victoria's reign, often without observing the same procedural safeguards as the Supreme Court.[114] But these practices and debates would share an unexamined premise of territorial sovereignty: British officials would only disagree about how they ought to discipline the Chinese residents of Hong Kong and not about whether they were authorised to do so. Indeed, British territorial sovereignty in Hong Kong was seen from as early as 1849 as having always been provided for in the Treaty of Nanjing, as if the profound debates of 1842–43 never took place.[115]

Territorial thinking in Hong Kong also served to gradually reify British and Western 'extraterritorial' jurisdiction in treaty-port China. In 1845, Davis put it to Qiying that there could be no reciprocity of jurisdiction between Britain and China because the conditions were different in British and Chinese territory. Chinese subjects had, at the time, 'free permission' to move around in British territories, whereas the movement of British subjects in China was restricted to five treaty ports. Even the cities adjoining these treaty ports were off limits to all Westerners. In Davis' view, this unequal restriction justified the one-sided right of British subjects to govern themselves in China.[116] Fair or not, this argument would not have made any sense before *The Queen* v. *Lo A-tow* – before Britain became a territorial power in the region. In the ensuing decades, by contrast, British and American jurists and officials would justify their extraterritorial rights in China by excluding China from their Eurocentric family of 'civilised' and territorially sovereign states.[117] This positivist discourse in international law might have unfolded differently had Britain refrained from territorialising its jurisdiction in Hong Kong during the pivotal winter of 1843–44.

2

Domesticating Mobility

Two major obstacles stood in the way of the British governance of Hong Kong from 1844: mass migration from China and jurisdictional competition from the Chinese government. Fewer than 6,000 people lived in Hong Kong in 1841, when the Opium War was still raging, and before British jurisdiction on the island became a contentious issue.[1] Colonial censuses later counted 33,000 residents in 1850 and 95,000 in 1860.[2] The new residents were highly mobile, too: many were labourers and traders who saw rich opportunities in Hong Kong, but not necessarily a permanent home. In this context, colonial officials were ambivalent about working with China to prevent Hong Kong from becoming a hotbed of crime and disorder. They wanted to send fugitives, vagrants, and other unwanted people back to China, but they were unwilling to legitimise China's blanket claim to jurisdiction over Chinese subjects; so, they devised flexible regimes to assert the British right to regulate the removal of Chinese subjects from the colony. Entrenched in colonial legislation, these removal regimes were accompanied by strategic promises to 'protect' the Chinese residents of the colony from lawlessness and arbitrary punishment – promises that sought to justify their subjection to British authority.

Discretionary powers to decide when Chinese migrants could stay and when they had to leave were vested in the colonial Governor and a strategically named office of 'Registrar General and Protector of Chinese Inhabitants'. As this chapter will show, these powers were gradually reframed as more differentiated powers of 'deportation' – the unilateral removal of people for breaching colonial law – and 'rendition', or the surrender of people as fugitives to foreign authorities under treaty. This legal bifurcation between deportation and rendition emerged over time because various stakeholders criticised the early removal regimes as unfair, unconstitutional, and even detrimental to British military interests during the Arrow War or Second Opium War (1856–60). Changes to the British diplomatic establishment in China also accelerated legal change after 1860, as Whitehall established a new legation in Beijing and restricted the ability of the Hong Kong government to collaborate with Chinese officials. These developments fettered the discretion of the Hong Kong government while widening the distinction between unilateral deportation and cooperative rendition. Stabilised in the 1860s, this legal distinction was thus mutually constitutive with the shifting constitutional position of Hong Kong within the British Empire in China.[3] The disputes and decisions that defined how the colonial government could remove alien migrants also defined the colony itself, turning it from a jurisdictionally ambiguous trading post into a more traditional British territory – a sovereign territory where the power of officials to keep the peace was more municipal than inter-imperial.

Sovereignty in Unequal Protection

In July 1844, Governor John Francis Davis reported to the Foreign Office that the Chinese Commandant of Kowloon had requested the surrender of a Chinese resident of Hong Kong on a charge of piracy. The Commandant cited the agreement for fugitive surrenders in the Opium War treaties of 1842–43, but he supplied 'no evidence whatever' to support the piracy charge; 'moreover', said Davis, the alleged pirate was 'not a refugee from the Chinese side, but an old inhabitant of Hong Kong, and constable of a village under British appointment'. For these reasons, Davis stated his 'willingness to deliver him up on any fair presumption or proof of guilt; but his abandonment otherwise would be a final blow to that confidence which the Chinese Inhabitants of this Colony ought to feel in British protection'.[4]

The immediate context of this incident was the question of jurisdiction. The request from Kowloon had come on the back of *The Queen v. Lo A-tow* (1843), the tenuous precedent for British territorial sovereignty in Hong Kong. The Chinese government did not recognise this precedent, so the idea that the Chinese population of Hong Kong came under British jurisdiction remained highly contested.[5] Eager to defend this idea, Davis stressed the importance of vindicating the 'sense of security' that he believed British rule offered the colony's Chinese community. Davis argued that if Britain failed to protect that community from arbitrary punishment at the hands of Chinese authorities, then 'the best portion of the community would abandon the place'. In this context, Davis believed that the unsubstantiated demand from Kowloon was 'trying [his] firmness on this question of jurisdiction'. Therefore, '[a] little firmness at the commencement will put this question at rest forever, whereas undue concessions will only invite encroachment'.[6] By refusing to deliver Chinese fugitives to China without sufficient proof, Davis positioned Britain as a legitimate arbiter of the procedural rights of Chinese people in Hong Kong.

Davis was not the first official to rationalise British jurisdiction in this way. Promises of protection 'served to reinforce the legitimacy of British imperial jurisdiction' in the early nineteenth century, as Lauren Benton and Lisa Ford have argued. Such promises underpinned 'the exercise of new jurisdiction over foreign polities' in territories like Ceylon, where local rulers resisted British attempts to displace or assimilate them.[7] Other scholars have shown, likewise, that 'Protectors of Aborigines' were appointed in several Australian colonies and New Zealand in the 1830s and 1840s, as Britain asserted the authority to discipline, resettle, and even educate previously independent tribes.[8] So, too, in Hong Kong. After occupying the island in 1841, Charles Elliot proclaimed that 'the Chinese Inhabitants of Hong Kong… are hereby promised protection, in Her Majesty's gracious name, against all enemies whatever'; and, accordingly, they and the elders of their villages would come under the authority of a 'British magistrate'.[9] To justify his general conduct of the Opium War, Elliot also told the Governor-General of India, the Earl of Auckland, that the people of China 'understood [the British] to be the authors of their returning prosperity, and their surest protectors against the infatuation and oppression of their own Government'.[10] Though undoubtedly a self-serving exaggeration, this assertion revealed the pertinent truth that, like many of his contemporaries, Elliot regarded the Chinese government as an obstacle to the British reordering of Hong Kong.

In 1844, Governor Davis' promise to protect the Chinese residents of Hong Kong from arbitrary punishment retraced these jurisdictional steps. Davis hastened to stress, in particular, that his promise of due process was not conditional upon subjecthood. This was because he was trying to assert the British right of *territorial* jurisdiction in Hong Kong, or the right to control British subjects and alien persons on the island in equal measure. British officials had sidelined the language of subjecthood in 1843, as Chapter 1 has shown: they had stopped trying to regard the Chinese residents of Hong Kong as naturalised British subjects. It was therefore strategic for Davis to claim that Britain offered everyone in Hong Kong equal protection in exchange for equal obedience. As Davis said to Qiying, the Manchu statesman who negotiated the Opium War treaties and now the Governor-General of the provinces of Guangdong and Guangxi:

> No Chinese are compelled to reside here. They may retire when dissatisfied but those who choose to make it their abode of their own free will, have exactly the same privileges and protection as British subjects and if they offend against the British Law, must have the same punishment ... England, having no fear of foreign intercourse, treats foreigners and subjects alike, on condition of their all obeying the same Laws. Except on this condition, such generous and liberal treatment would be impossible.[11]

Davis' ambition to give Chinese subjects due process did not mean that he was unwilling to remove them to China. It meant, rather, that he preferred to remove them on his own terms. Indeed, Davis and his predecessor, Henry Pottinger, believed that the colony needed a system to register its Chinese inhabitants and to designate some of them for possible repatriation. For Pottinger, this was because 'the Proximity of this island to the mainland' put it at risk of becoming 'the resort of the dregs of the population of this part of China, including criminals of every class, who will flock to Hong Kong to live by plunder and to escape punishment'.[12] Fugitives and criminal migrants threatened the colonial peace; so, for Pottinger, they needed to be filtered out through legally justifiable means. Pottinger never managed to implement these ideas. But Davis, citing similar reasons, oversaw the enactment of a Registration Ordinance in August 1844. 'The necessity of [registration],' Davis argued, 'arose out of the mixed and heterogenous character of the population of this Colony, bordering loosely upon an Empire from whence the far greater proportion of its

Inhabitants are derived.' In light of his ambition to protect subjects and aliens equally, Davis added, crucially, that although the peace-keeping rationale for the registration mechanism 'dictated its application to a portion of the Community, the spirit of justice and equality seemed to demand its application to the whole'.[13]

So, the Registration Ordinance of August 1844 was worded to apply equally to everyone in Hong Kong: its provisions reflected the colonial government's dual pursuits of population control and jurisdictional positioning. The Ordinance required all men (but not women) over the age of twenty-one and 'capable of earning a livelihood' to register with a 'Registrar General'. Migrants were to report within twenty-four hours of arriving in Hong Kong, giving their age, occupation, place of birth, family contacts, and any other information requested of them. Each registrant would then receive a 'registration ticket' with twelve months' validity, but only if they paid a fee of one to five dollars and if the Registrar General deemed them a 'fit and proper person'. For anyone who appeared to be 'a vagabond or bad character or without visible means of subsistence', the Registrar General had 'full power and authority to prohibit him from residing in the Colony'. Migrants who did not present themselves for registration could be fined up to fifty dollars, and employers and 'householders' could also be fined for harbouring unregistered lodgers and labourers. 'Householders' included landlords, head tenants, and the heads of families.[14]

This Registration Ordinance was doomed by its attempt at equality, however. Even before coming into effect, it was criticised by British merchants for pursuing the 'arbitrary and unconstitutional taxing of British subjects unrepresented'.[15] The sore point was not only the registration fee that Davis wanted to impose, but also the wide discretion that the Registrar General would wield. Although the powers of the Registrar General were designed to check Chinese mobility, they could just as easily erode British liberty. In October 1844, a petition signed by 107 prominent British merchants accused Davis of 'authorizing the most unheard of inquisitorial proceedings, without appeal or remedy, and [of] placing the very power of residence to British subjects, whose name may have hitherto been unsullied and unsuspected, in the hands of any one individual'.[16] These complaints underscored the absence of an elected assembly in Hong Kong. Like in a growing number of Crown colonies where non-European people outnumbered white British subjects, the legislative power in Hong Kong was vested in a nominated Legislative Council, presided over by the Governor.[17] There was no prospect of democracy because the Chinese majority was considered unsuited to it, whereas the white British minority was not trusted to legislate for the common good.[18] In 1856, the Permanent Secretary at the Colonial Office, Herman Merivale, would note that if the Crown would not enfranchise a 'general constituency' in Hong Kong, then neither would it give the vote to a 'small autonomy of white merchants'.[19] This imperial strategy had its merits, but it enabled disgruntled subjects to level powerful criticisms of executive overreach.

The petitioners persuaded Davis to turn the registration system into something more explicitly anti-Chinese. The local Chinese community may also have had an unwitting hand in this, as some labourers and business owners went on strike, while others put up a 'riotous demonstration' in opposition to registration.[20] Davis accused the British petitioners of inciting these disturbances, though the more likely source of discontent was an error in the Chinese translation of the Registration Ordinance, which suggested that the registration fee would be due every month instead of every year, making it twelve times more expensive.[21] In a report that foretold his next move, Davis complained that it was 'a much easier task to govern the twenty thousand Chinese inhabitants of this Colony, than the few hundreds of English'. For Davis, the British petitioners' claim to an absolute right of residency in Hong Kong made it 'necessary to have a separate and summary jurisdiction for the Chinese population'.[22]

A second Registration Ordinance of November 1844 made some changes to this end. First, it abolished the registration fee, thus neutralising the British petitioners' constitutional argument. Next, specified groups were exempted from the full process of registration: they were required only to submit 'blank return[s]' for occasional censuses. In a despatch to the Colonial Office, Davis called this a 'class'-based exemption since it applied to merchants, shopkeepers, servants of the Crown and East India Company, members of the 'Learned Professions', Crown tenants paying at least $250 in annual rent, and anyone earning at least $500 in annual income.[23] These categories effectively covered all white British subjects in Hong Kong.

They also covered the 'opulent natives' by the admission of the future Governor, John Bowring, or 'the right kind of Chinese' in the view of the historian Christopher Munn.[24] Wealthy migrants from China found favour with the colonial government, though the feeling was not exactly mutual.

What about the 'wrong' kind of Chinese? The preamble to the second Registration Ordinance noted, not very subtly, that the Ordinance was enacted in light of 'the migratory habit of a portion of the population'.[25] The first Ordinance, by contrast, had referred more guardedly to the need 'to secure tranquillity and good order in the Colony', and 'to prevent the resort thereto of abandoned characters and of persons without any ostensible means of subsistence'.[26] It was clear, then, that Davis' commitment to equal protection was wavering. The registration system was becoming a system for deporting Chinese subjects, even though the term 'deportation' was not yet used. The second Registration Ordinance stopped just short of admitting that it was really designed to control the poorer migrants from China, whose livelihoods depended on irregular employment in construction, victualling, portering, and other sectors of Hong Kong's entrepot economy. For Chinese migrants who did not qualify for the class-based exemption, registration remained mandatory and subject to annual renewal at the discretion of the Registrar General. Only people 'born within the Colony' were safe from removal under the revised Ordinance. They would be 'dealt with according to [the] law provided in such cases' – that is, by the established procedures of criminal prosecution.[27]

All pretences that the registration system was not designed to assert the British right to regulate Chinese immigration were later dropped. This happened after the first Registrar General, Samuel Fearon, set a precedent for gearing his office towards suppressing crimes committed specifically by Chinese subjects. Fearon took office in January 1845. Chosen by Davis for his language skills and knowledge of Southern Chinese customs, he had been an assistant magistrate in Hong Kong and an interpreter during the Opium War.[28] By June, he had registered over 12,000 Chinese people, around half of the colony's total population.[29] His work proved reasonably useful in quelling regional disorder. In one incident from early 1845, the Chinese perpetrators of a robbery on a British ship, *John Barry*, were arrested in China by Chinese officers acting on intelligence supplied by him, gathered through the registration system. This modest victory convinced Fearon of the utility of subjecting all China-born migrants to registration, surveillance, and the constant threat of removal.

In Fearon's view, these methods worked because they incentivised obedience among two groups of migrants, whose nature it was to feel 'uneasy under the restraint of law'. The first group was the historically displaced Hakka people, described by Fearon as the 'gipsies' of China. As a rootless 'race' of people, marginalised by the Cantonese natives of Guangdong Province, the Hakkas were supposedly inclined to 'wander, unrespected, whither gain may call'. If left unchecked, said Fearon, their 'unscrupulous' habits would keep Hong Kong in 'an unsettled state'.[30] The second group of disorderly migrants were the members of the Triad societies, loyalists of the old Ming dynasty, who Fearon accused of perpetrating serious crimes 'under shelter' of their anti-Qing politics. Like the Hakka people, the members of the Triads (many of whom were also Hakka) were said to be drawn to the jurisdictional vacuum that the Opium War had created in Hong Kong. British ordering was the solution to these problems, argued Fearon. Registration would discipline Chinese migrants by instilling in them a 'fear of exposure to scrutiny' – a fear of being traceable in Hong Kong when they would rather stay hidden.[31]

Fearon's account of Chinese criminality was not simply racist. Indeed, it channelled the colonial government's anxieties about controlling a migrant population in a territory that seemed to attract disorderly migrants precisely because it was a site of jurisdictional dispute. Instead of devising a complex system of registration and shoring it up with vague promises of protection, the colony could simply have reopened itself to Chinese jurisdiction. That, however, was no longer an option in 1845, so the colonial government had no other choice but to address the very problems that it was partly responsible for creating.

In December 1846, a third Registration Ordinance stabilised the registration system for a decade, while adapting the promise of protection to justify targeting Chinese people more explicitly, on even more racialised terms.[32] First, the Registrar General was appointed 'Joint Superintendent of Police, a Justice of the Peace, and Protector of Chinese Inhabitants'. In these additional capacities, it was 'his duty to prevent the commission of crime and to discover and apprehend the perpetrators thereof, and generally to protect the Chinese Inhabitants of this Colony'. Next, 'Chinese Inhabitants' were now defined as 'Natives of China or Chinese Natives of Hong Kong or elsewhere'; and, by this definition, 'any person being a Chinese' who was brought before a magistrate for any reason, such as for not having a registration ticket, could now be ordered 'to find reasonable security for his appearance anytime within twelve months, whenever he may be required to give evidence in any Judicial Proceedings, or [to] answer any charge against him'. If the Chinese person could not find the required security, and he was not a 'permanent resident in the Colony', then he could be ordered to leave and banned from returning, on pain of a fine or up to three months' imprisonment.[33] 'Permanent resident' was not defined, but the rest of the Ordinance implied that anyone who had no registration ticket, no surety to summon, and no employer or 'householder' to vouch for them (or to be vicariously liable for their conduct) was probably deportable for having no way of proving their residency, even if they were born in Hong Kong. So, the trustworthiness of people of Chinese descent was effectively to be judged by the degree of their assimilation into the colonial order and territory. Settled and connected people were trusted; strangers and itinerants were not. According to the Ordinance, its main purpose was to expel 'suspicious characters', supposedly 'for the benefit and protection of [the colony's] well-disposed and honest Chinese Inhabitants'.[34] The catch, of course, was that most Chinese people could only hope to prove their honesty and good disposition (such as by making local acquaintances) if they were allowed to remain in the colony in the first place.

Pseudo-surrenders and Strategic Removals

The registration system and other flexible legislation allowed Davis' government (1844–47) to remove Chinese subjects without invoking the treaty agreement for fugitive surrenders. Officials in Hong Kong often wanted to get rid of the same people that China wanted to retrieve, as we have seen. But invocations of the surrender agreement tended to fuel the ongoing dispute about British jurisdiction over Chinese subjects in Hong Kong; so, to get around this problem,

Davis pioneered the strategy of prosecuting fugitives under colonial law and essentially deporting them to China upon conviction. Since these 'deportees' – again, they were not yet referred to as such – were technically punished by British authorities, their removal from Hong Kong did not risk undermining British jurisdiction and sovereignty.

The registration system proved useful to this colonial strategy because it cast a wide net while offering the convenience of summary proceedings. An incident from October 1845 illustrates these advantages. Certain 'emissaries' from China – agents of law enforcement – tried to arrest a man in Hong Kong, Chan A-lok, for unspecified crimes committed in China. However, colonial policemen caught the emissaries in the act.[35] This incident followed a few other incidents, dating back to *The Queen* v. *Lo A-tow* (1843), in which Chinese personnel entered Hong Kong without British permission. Local Chinese authorities usually offered apologies, as they did in *Lo A-tow*, so the early colonial government did not fixate on the intrusions.[36] In September 1844, for example, a magistrate's clerk from Kowloon was caught 'delivering passes to the fishing boats' in Aberdeen Bay (Shek Pai Wan), in south-western Hong Kong. The Chinese authorities in Kowloon quickly disavowed the trespass and promised to punish the clerk, so Davis let him go and said nothing more.[37] In the latest incident, however, no disavowal was forthcoming, so Davis decided to prosecute the intruding 'emissaries' for assault and trespass, causing them to be imprisoned for a month in Hong Kong. Davis also sent Kowloon a 'strong remonstrance', arguing that the imprisonment was 'absolutely necessary, in order to give security to respectable natives of China who live here under British protection'.[38] This left the question of what to do with Chan A-lok, the alleged fugitive from Chinese law. Davis had him sent to Kowloon anyway, but only because he was 'not a British subject', 'possessed no Registration Ticket, had been only a few days on the Island, and could give no satisfactory account of himself'.[39] Crucially, Davis did not verify what crimes Chan A-lok was accused of committing, let alone what evidence the Chinese government was prepared to supply. All this was presumably irrelevant because Chan A-lok was not given up to China under treaty: he was removed from Hong Kong as an unregistered person, pursuant to colonial legislation.

An Ordinance 'for the suppression of the Triad and other secret Societies' played a similar if more limited role in easing the removal of Chinese fugitives.[40] First enacted in January 1845, this Triad Suppression Ordinance enabled the colonial government to send Triad members to China but, again, without being seen as doing China's bidding. It was certainly strategic for the colony to frame laws around Triad activity: British officials knew that the statute books of Qing China brimmed with laws punishing banditry, robbery, and other crimes committed by the Triads and other 'sworn brotherhoods' in some southern provinces, including Guangdong.[41] The earliest of these special laws were made in the 1780s. Their narrow scope reflected the regional nature of the problem of organised crime, but their profusion reflected its perceived urgency. This body of Chinese law was still growing in the 1840s, as organised crime in Guangdong perturbed none other than Governor-General Qiying. In 1845, Qiying persuaded Emperor Daoguang to authorise the summary execution of organised kidnappers who held victims for ransom. This extreme measure had been used for many years to punish other serious crimes such as murder and rape committed during gang robberies.[42] By taking steps to identify and repatriate Triad members, therefore, the Hong Kong government was effectively trying to tap into China's anti-Triad legal machinery.

From Hong Kong's point of view, the need for a colonial anti-Triad regime became desperate in May 1844, when a Triad-affiliated gang robbed a British boat of 12,000 rupees in military treasure, killing four soldiers and throwing a fifth overboard. This attack was doubly alarming because it took place 'within reach' of the new barracks at Chek Choo (Stanley), on the island's south coast, so the security of the whole colony was briefly compromised. The robbers fled to the mainland, but 'one of the worst of them', Chin-tae (or Chin A-tae), was later arrested in Hong Kong. Chin-tae confessed to the crime, naming nineteen accomplices.[43] To assist in arresting those accomplices, Davis' 'Chinese Secretary', the German missionary Karl Gützlaff agreed to give Chin-tae up for questioning in Kowloon on the condition that he was returned to Hong Kong to stand trial. Gützlaff's counterparts in Kowloon later honoured this arrangement: they sent Chin-tae back in July 1844. In an ironic turn of events, however, officials in Hong Kong could find 'no sufficient evidence according to the technicalities of English law to condemn him' at the Supreme Court; so, Davis sent Chin-tae back to China.[44] Only too glad for this outcome, Qiying informed Davis on 17 December that Chin-tae had been executed and that his head was on display in Canton.[45] The Legislative Council of Hong Kong passed the Triad Suppression Ordinance three weeks later, making it a 'felony' for 'persons being of Chinese origin' to be 'members of the Triad Society or other secret Societies'. Convicted Triad members faced up to three years' imprisonment – there was notably no minimum term – after which they were to be 'marked on the right cheek [like] Military Deserters' and 'expelled' from Hong Kong.[46]

The penalty of expulsion was a key feature of the Triad Suppression Ordinance. It suggests that, although Davis balked at legislating explicitly for surrendering Triad members to China, he wanted to ensure that the law of Hong Kong was capable of bringing people like Chin-tae to justice – Chinese justice, if necessary. In a letter to Qiying, Davis was perhaps deliberately vague about whether he would punish Triad members under colonial law or give them up to China under treaty. According to Davis:

> It is extremely proper and consonant to the Treaty [i.e. the Opium War treaties of 1842–43], that any Chinese Criminals taking refuge in Hong Kong should be immediately seized and handed over to the Chinese authorities for punishment. It is the custom of the civilized nations of the West to afford no protection to crimes committed against a friendly power; and on this principle I have enacted a severe ordinance against any meeting of the Triad Society in Hong Kong, knowing that it has traitorous designs against Your Excellency's government, as well as against Social Order and security in general.[47]

This passage alluded to the contested principle in European natural law thinking, by which sovereign states were obliged to decide, in the absence of treaty arrangements, whether to prosecute or extradite the fugitives of friendly powers.[48] Contrary to Davis' intimation, however, this principle was not presently in play, as there was already a treaty between Britain and China. The more relevant question, which Davis avoided, concerned the scope of the treaty: the question was whether Britain was obliged to surrender all Triad members to China, even if that was not its preferred policy. Ever astute, Qiying detected this rhetorical slippage: he argued that 'traitors and associates of the Triad Society, villains who have taken refuge at Hong Kong ... ought to be every one sent to the local Mandarins of [Kowloon], that very severe measures may be taken against them'.[49] For Qiying, this was because it was 'a provision of the Supplementary Treaty [of 1843] that the subjects of China should be judged by Chinese Mandarins, and that native malefactors having run away to Hong Kong, should be sent back to the Chinese territory to receive there their punishment'.[50]

In response, Davis asserted the British right to punish Chinese subjects for violating colonial law, even if they were also wanted by the Chinese government. Nevertheless, Davis agreed to surrender Triad members on request. 'You have only to mention their names,' he promised, 'and I will hunt them out and give them to you.'[51] Four days later, on 8 January 1845, the Executive Council of Hong Kong resolved that since 'the Law of England' applied in the colony, Triad members were not to be given up under treaty, 'with the exception of parties specifically demanded by name as refugees'.[52] Of course, Triad members who were punished in the colony could still be 'expelled' after their prison sentences, which could theoretically be very short. By configuring the law in this way, Davis positioned himself to uphold British sovereignty while maximising his options to remove Triad members to China.

The Triad Suppression Ordinance was only rendered less effective in achieving these jurisdictional goals by the scrupulous intervention of the Colonial Office. The Ordinance was supposed to facilitate, as Davis put it, the 'condign punishment' of Triad-affiliated criminals, even when evidence of their crimes was lacking.[53] However, the Secretary of State, Lord Stanley observed that the 'mere secrecy' of anyone's societal affiliations 'scarcely seems to require a punishment so severe' as imprisonment, cheek-marking, and expulsion, 'or perhaps any punishment at all'. The penalty of expulsion also struck Stanley as 'extremely indefinite': it seemed to contemplate 'banishment for life or for any other shorter time', yet the penalty for breaching such banishment was not specified.[54] There were other problems, too: marking a convicted Triad member's cheek would 'consign him to permanent infamy' and 'obstruct his return to virtue'; there was no provision for people to plead ignorance or duress in joining the Triads; and, finally, if China were to execute banished Triad members without trial, then that would make Britain 'accessory to proceedings totally abhorrent from our principles of justice'. Ultimately, Stanley approved the Ordinance to save Davis from 'serious embarrassment'. However, he instructed Davis to reinforce the legal regime with key safeguards.[55]

Stanley's instructions led to an amended Triad Suppression Ordinance, enacted in October 1845. An exception was added for Triad members who were recruited 'in ignorance' or 'under the influence of terror'; cheek-marking was replaced with marking under the left arm; and expulsion was defined as banishment for life, the breach of which was punishable by transportation for life, to a destination within the British Empire. But what really crippled the revised regime was another amendment, which made it applicable only to Triad members who were 'duly convicted of active participation in some unlawful act arising out of his or their connection with the said [Triad] Society'.[56] In other words, mere membership in the Triads was no longer penalised and no longer punishable by banishment. More than anything else, this safeguard prevented Davis from formalising the kind of jurisdictional arbitrage that he had performed to bring Chin-tae to justice in 1844. This safeguard pressured the Hong Kong government to be more transparent about developing a jurisprudence justifying the surrender of Triad members to China. The effect was palpable, at least on paper. In August and September 1846, Davis sent four notices to local magistrates, all directing that Triad members should be 'delivered over' to Chinese officials in Kowloon on 'Requisition, and sufficient presumptive evidence of their guilt … but not otherwise.'[57]

In practice, Triad members were still removed to China on flimsy evidence because the registration system stepped in for the eroded Triad suppression system. In March 1846, the colonial police detained several 'unregistered persons for assembling at a late hour for the purpose of admitting Members to the Sam-hop-ooi or Triad Society'. The Attorney General of Hong Kong, Paul Stirling advised that the detainees 'should be dealt with summarily and not brought to trial before the Supreme Court'. This was presumably because there was no evidence that the detainees had committed any substantive crime. So, Davis instructed the magistracy 'to deal with them accordingly under the Registration Ordinance'.[58] Since the Triad Suppression Ordinance was not used, there was no need for the government even to prove that the detainees were really Triad members. The routine manner in which this case was handled suggests that it was only the tip of a very large iceberg. Similar uses of the registration system against suspected Triad members likely went unrecorded, or perhaps records have not survived.

The strategic removal of unregistered Chinese subjects did not go uncontested, to be sure, but the practice survived imperial scrutiny under complex circumstances. In April 1846, a police constable, George Hall, had just arrested a Chinese man on suspicion of stealing a plank of wood from a timber yard. As the suspect was uncooperative, Hall approached some Chinese dwellings or 'huts' for help to escort the man to the police station. In response, Hall was greeted by a 'shower of stones' thrown by a 'gang of ruffians from the Chinese side': disorderly migrants from China. Hall could not identify these attackers by the time backup arrived, so the police raided every 'hut' in the area and detained fifty-four men for being unregistered. Summary proceedings under the Registration Ordinance of November 1844 led to a fine of $5 each. When the detainees could not pay up, they were given 'twenty strokes of the rattan [cane]', deprived of their queues or pigtails, and sent to Kowloon, and the Chinese authorities in Kowloon were requested to prevent them from returning to Hong Kong.[59] The caning and pigtail-cutting were carried out under another ordinance, which authorised magistrates to punish Chinese convicts 'in conformity with the usages of China', 'in lieu of ... any penalty provided by any law', including fines issued under the Registration Ordinances.[60]

Davis was made to explain all this because the future Governor of Hong Kong, John Bowring MP, had alleged at Westminster that the detainees were sentenced to 'flogging ... for not having obtained tickets of registration; and after such infliction ... delivered over to the Chinese authorities to be subjected to further penalties'.[61] A passionate reformer, Radical MP, and protégé of the late Jeremy Bentham, Dr Bowring had read about Constable Hall's case in the *Friend of China*, a Hong Kong-based newspaper that was exposing some of the colonial government's punitive excesses against Chinese people.[62] The perceived overuse of corporal punishment was a matter of public controversy in this period, so that was the angle of Bowring's inquiry in Parliament. In this context, Davis rejoined that no civilian in Hong Kong had ever been 'flogged' in military fashion – with the cat o' nine tails – and caning with a rattan cane was a rather less severe punishment.[63] Davis also added that the detainees in Hall's case were not 'merely' unregistered, as they had 'assailed the police with a view to rescue one of [their] fraternity'. Neither were the detainees sentenced to further punishment in China: they were only prevented from returning to Hong Kong.[64] These explanations begged the question: excessive or not, were the penalties lawful? Should the government of a Crown colony be able to punish the suspects of violent crimes without proving their guilt in court? After reading Davis' report, the Under-Secretary of State at the Colonial Office, Benjamin Hawes observed that 'the prisoners were taken up it appears for one offence [i.e. being unregistered] and punished for another [i.e. assault]'.[65] The issue here was one of due process: it was about the subtle arbitrariness of the registration system.

Hawes' critique was incisive, but it was obscured by the wider debate about corporal punishment. The Secretary of State, Earl Grey ignored it and also rejected Hawes' suggestion to publish a copy of Davis' report. In December 1846, Grey decided to divulge only 'the substance' of Davis' report, so Hall's case ended there.[66] Later, the registration system attracted further criticism from witnesses testifying before the parliamentary Select Committee on Commercial Relations with China (1847). The Committee was investigating a recent slump in the British trade in China, and British witnesses attributed the slump partly to the shunning of Hong Kong by the 'respectable' people of China – people who were said to be loath either to register with British officials, or to risk being 'flogged' and humiliated. It was the general cruelty of the registration system, however, that kept the Select Committee's attention. The procedural legality of the system went nearly unscrutinised, though one witness alleged that jailers in Hong Kong had negligently 'flogged' certain prisoners in a serious case of mistaken identity.[67] On the whole, Davis' jurisdictional motive for funnelling people through the registration system was not seriously questioned; so, his manoeuvres laid the groundwork for a long colonial tradition of strategic deportation.

'Regular Systems' of Rendition and Deportation

In 1850, Davis' successor, Governor George Bonham (1848–54) expanded the colonial government's discretionary powers of removal in a different way. Bonham spearheaded the Rendition Ordinance of 1850: an Ordinance 'to provide for the more effective carrying out of the Treaties between Great Britain and China ... for the Rendition for Trial to the Officers of their own Country of such Subjects of

China as have committed Crimes and Offences against their own Government, and afterwards taken refuge in Hong Kong'.[68] Instead of vagrants and fugitives crossing over from the Chinese mainland, this Ordinance was mostly used against Chinese subjects committing crimes at sea, as Chapter 3 will show. Officials in Hong Kong had started exercising an intentionally limited jurisdiction over piracy and other maritime crimes in this period, so they were becoming less wary about surrendering fugitives to China for those particular crimes. Nevertheless, the Rendition Ordinance extended the strategy of giving the colonial government a wide discretion to control the removal of Chinese fugitives. Not only could the Governor and magistrates act on Chinese requests for fugitives, but they could also initiate rendition proceedings without receiving any request if it 'appear[ed] in the Course of any Investigation' that any Chinese subject was liable to rendition.[69] This feature of the rendition system made it substantially interchangeable with the registration system. Consequently, the distinction between treaty-based and non-treaty-based mechanisms of removal was still blurred, though it was slowly starting to take shape.

Bonham's report on the enactment of the Rendition Ordinance confirms that he was mostly eager to codify his discretion to remove Chinese subjects. On the one hand, Bonham asserted that the Rendition Ordinance was 'analogous, as far as local circumstances and the differences in the Treaties will admit', with the imperial statutes that governed the surrender of fugitives to France and the United States.[70] This comment shows Bonham's awareness of the emerging imperial law of extradition: it shows his belief that imperial expectations of fugitives' rights were at least broadly relevant to the enforcement of the Chinese treaties. On the other hand, Bonham reported candidly that the Rendition Ordinance was enacted 'so that the act of rendition … might not be questionable in a legal point of view from want of form'. Hong Kong had 'no regular system' of rendition, Bonham explained, and someone, probably the local Attorney General, Paul Sterling, had 'intimated' to him that accused pirates might apply for writs of habeas corpus to avoid being sent to China.[71] The Rendition Ordinance was thus enacted to forestall such challenges and not really to do much else.

True to its roots in discretionary governance and jurisdictional politics, the Rendition Ordinance gave Chinese fugitives less protection than the imperial statutes gave French and American fugitives. First, Chinese fugitives could be surrendered on mere 'probable Cause for believing' that they had committed 'any Crime or Offence against the Laws of China'.[72] There was neither an exhaustive list of extraditable crimes nor any requirement for charges to be proved to the same standard as would justify commencing trials in Hong Kong.[73] As long as a magistrate found 'probable Cause', he was authorised to commit any fugitive to jail to await 'transmission' to 'such Chinese Authorities as to the ... Governor shall seem fit'.[74] Second, fugitives who were committed under the Rendition Ordinance could theoretically be detained indefinitely if the Governor decided to delay their rendition for any reason. By contrast, fugitives who were committed under the imperial statutes were expressly entitled to be released if not surrendered within two months, unless the Crown could show 'sufficient Cause' for further detention.[75]

Meanwhile, the colony's earliest ordinances to authorise deportation as 'deportation' were enacted in 1857. The registration system remained formally intact between 1847 and 1857, though it seems to have fallen into disuse for reasons that are not entirely clear. The records suggest, at most, that the system fell victim to the trade depression of the mid 1840s. Whitehall instructed Governor Bonham to downsize his government in 1848, so Bonham told the incumbent Registrar General and Protector of Chinese Inhabitants, Andrew Inglis, that his job was on the line. This caused Inglis to resign to join the California Gold Rush.[76] Possibly relieved, Bonham followed up by reassigning Inglis' duties to a junior clerk in the colony's treasury department.[77] The colonial Superintendent of Police, Charles May, was then made 'Officiating Registrar General' but not Protector of Chinese Inhabitants, and the full office of Registrar General and Protector was only reconstituted in November 1856, during the governorship of John Bowring (1854–59). The reconstituted office went to Daniel Caldwell, a police officer and rather cunning handler of Chinese informants and compradors, who later embroiled himself in a major corruption scandal.[78] A new Registration Ordinance of May 1857 confirmed Caldwell's power to issue registration tickets, and to cause any unregistered Chinese subject to be 'deemed a vagrant' and thus liable to be 'deported' at the discretion of the Governor-in-Council. The adjacent practice of 'Mendicancy in the public Highways or Streets' was also made punishable by deportation: Chinese mendicants could be 'deported to any place in the Chinese Empire'. Like in the Rendition Ordinance, there was no formal limit on how long vagrants and mendicants could be detained before being deported.[79]

The Registration Ordinance 1857 was enacted four months after another ordinance that also gave the Governor-in-Council sweeping powers of deportation: the Ordinance 'for better securing the Peace of the Colony'.[80] These ordinances were both enacted in 1857 for two reasons. First, a major disturbance occurred in October 1856, when several thousand Chinese residents of Hong Kong gathered in Victoria City to protest a government campaign to enforce minimum standards of sanitation on Chinese dwellings. The colonial government was responding to the growing problem of epidemics in the Chinese quarters of the city, as well as in Chinese settlements elsewhere in the colony. Certain diseases, likely including typhus or cholera, had just killed over 800 Chinese residents in early 1856, so the government was scrambling to improve public health; however, the local Chinese community resented the government's heavy-handed use of the criminal law to achieve this goal. In November 1856, the protests in Victoria prompted the government to appoint Protector Caldwell. A royal proclamation, which preceded the Registration Ordinance of 1857, also declared that 'all unregistered Chinese will be required to depart from the colony'.[81]

The other source of tension was the outbreak of the Arrow War in October 1856. The sudden resumption of hostilities between Britain and China was unsettling enough, but it was made worse by the public efforts of the new Governor-General in Canton, Ye Ming-chen, to incite Chinese people to leave Hong Kong, destroy British property, and kill British people.[82] Ye's campaign triggered a series of attacks on land and at sea – attacks that posed an existential threat to Hong Kong. On 6 January 1857, the Legislative Council of Hong Kong responded by enacting the Ordinance 'for better securing the Peace of the Colony'. The Governor-in-Council was authorised to deport 'Pirates' of Chinese origin, 'Emissar[ies] or Abettor[s] of Her Majesty's Enemies', and other 'Chinamen disaffected to Her Majesty's Government, or otherwise dangerous to the peace and good order of this Colony'. A nightly curfew was also imposed on all 'Chinamen', and sentries were allowed to shoot them on reasonable suspicion that they were outdoors 'for an improper purpose'.[83] The latter measure was later repealed in July 1857 after the Colonial Office censured it as gratuitous. Sentences of 'deportation' were also limited to five years, but the rest of this Security Ordinance was retained despite imperial intimations that even a period of martial law might be 'a less objectionable measure ... than an ordinance altering the ordinary law of the Colony to so great an extent'.[84] Remarkably, the Hong Kong government never proclaimed martial law during the Arrow War – not even after the Indian government did so during the Mutiny of 1857, confirming, as in Ceylon (1848), Canada (1837), and other parts of the nineteenth-century empire, the brutal efficacy of this executive measure in times of war and social disorder.[85] Presumably, martial law offered no practical advantage as the ordinary powers of officials in Hong Kong were already so unfettered.

The Hong Kong government used its new security powers to detain and interrogate over 500 'suspicious and dangerous characters', including 'Emissaries of the Provincial Government of Kwangtung', in January 1857.[86] Protector Caldwell leveraged his Chinese informants for this purpose. Governor Bowring then proceeded to deport 167 detainees by shipping them to a remote location on the south coast of Hainan Island, 400 miles south-west of Hong Kong. January was the time of the north-east monsoon, so Bowring chose Hainan specifically to deny the deportees an easy way back to Hong Kong. The crew of the sailing ship that carried the deportees was even told to follow the monsoon all the way to Singapore before returning to Hong Kong by steamer.[87]

The Security Ordinance also proved useful during the most notorious incident from this period. On 15 January 1857, over 300 European residents of Hong Kong fell ill after eating bread from their regular supplier, a bakery in Victoria run by Cheong A-lum. Arsenic was found in the bread, so the colonists suspected a conspiracy. Some civilians and even officials called for Cheong A-lum and his associates to be executed, with or without trial; and, although Governor Bowring refused to practice what he called 'the Law of Lynch', he was not above invoking the Security Ordinance against forty-two people.[88] It is unclear how many of these suspected conspirators were deported: perhaps they were shipped to Hainan together with other detainees. As for Cheong A-lum, he and nine others, including his father, were tried at the Supreme Court for attempted murder. They were then acquitted in February for lack of evidence, by a jury of convalescent Europeans, no less.[89] The facts of the case were so hazy that the poisoning may well have been an accident or an act of commercial sabotage unrelated to the Arrow War, as Kate Lowe and Eugene McLaughlin have argued.[90] But the wider European community still needed placating, so Bowring kept Cheong A-lum in jail under the Security Ordinance, heard petitions on his fate, and requested instructions from London. A compromise was eventually struck in July: instead of carrying out 'the extreme measure of legal deportation', the colonial government released Cheong A-lum on a bond of $2,000, to be forfeited if he returned to Hong Kong within five years.[91] Cheong A-lum kept the deal: after spending several years in Macau, he retired in Vietnam.[92]

In short, local emergencies during 1856–57 encouraged the Hong Kong government to expand its discretionary practice of removing Chinese subjects from the colony. It was precisely at this juncture, however, that the colony first felt the effects of the differential codification of deportation and rendition. In March 1857, the Colonial Office rubber-stamped Bowring's deportation of Chinese detainees to Hainan. Permanent Secretary Merivale saw nothing wrong with the order, Under-Secretary John Ball agreed, and the Secretary of State, Henry Labouchere (later Lord Taunton) did not even comment.[93] Six weeks later, however, another despatch arrived, in which Bowring reported that, amid everything else, he used the Rendition Ordinance to surrender seventy-three Chinese prisoners to Kowloon on charges of piracy.[94] Now, everyone criticised Bowring's decision. Ball called it 'a most extraordinary proceeding', since China might 'enrol these pirates and condone any number of past murders on condition of their killing an equal number of Englishmen'.[95] The more he considered it, said Ball, 'the worse the case appear[ed]'.[96] Merivale and Labouchere offered more measured criticism, but they agreed that the rendition was a mistake.[97]

What explains these opposing attitudes to the wartime rendition and deportation of Chinese subjects? The imperial view may have been influenced by the Paris Declaration on Maritime Law (1856), the landmark treaty in which Britain and other European states agreed to abolish their centuries-old practice of commissioning privateers to attack their enemies' shipping – private seafarers who operated under legally contested commissions or 'letters of marque'.[98] Later acceded to by over fifty states, the Paris Declaration shaped the British intolerance of real and alleged practices of privateering in the Arrow War and Taiping Rebellion (*c*. 1850–64), as Bruce Elleman has argued.[99] Even so, it seems unlikely that the Colonial Office simply felt more threatened by pirates than other potential hirelings of the Chinese military. If pirates could become enemy assets, then so could the enemy 'emissaries' and 'suspicious characters' that Bowring deported to Hainan under the Security Ordinance – doubly so, if the bread poisoning incident really was a deliberate attempt at mass murder. As it happened, only three people – including Bowring's wife, Lady Maria Bowring – later died in 1858 from complications traceable to the poisoned bread. The bread contained enough arsenic to induce severe vomiting, so most of the other victims did not ingest anything close to a lethal dose.[100] But the lethality of the poison was beside the point in 1857. Imperial officials almost certainly understood, given the volatility of the situation in Hong Kong, that 'pirates', 'emissaries', and so on, were arbitrary categories that merely tracked the fluid occupations of the Chinese migrants that the colony had reasons to expel. Indeed, it was clear that 'pirates' were also deportable under the Security Ordinance, just as they were liable to rendition under the Rendition Ordinance; and, although Bowring's reports were stingy on details, they strongly implied that he did deport some 'pirates' to Hainan, or at least some seafarers who were perfectly capable of becoming enemy combatants.

It seems more likely, therefore, that the Colonial Office objected only to Bowring's choice of removal mechanism. In 1857, the procedural distinction between rendition and deportation – between handing people over to Chinese authorities and dropping them off in remote parts of China – became relevant because the colony's formal collaboration with Chinese authorities seemed risky and improper when Britain and China were at war. Bowring provoked this view by presenting the Colonial Office with an obvious opportunity to compare the Security and Rendition Ordinances. By using both ordinances in quick succession during the same emergency situation, he exposed how he and earlier governors had conflated matters of colonial governance and treaty diplomacy since 1844: matters of peacekeeping, immigration control, and the inter-imperial division of jurisdiction over Chinese subjects. The imperial criticism of the latest instance of this conflation – the wartime rendition of pirates – signalled that things were about to change, as Whitehall was rethinking the wide discretion of the Hong Kong government to seek or avoid formal collaboration with Chinese authorities.

The Rise and Fall of Jurisdictional Governance

The early Governors of Hong Kong could weave colonial governance with jurisdictional politics because they were also high-ranking diplomats: Ministers Plenipotentiary to China. As diplomats and administrators, they could control how the British governance of Chinese subjects was framed, as we have seen. They could enforce or appear to enforce the Chinese treaties, while spurning Chinese claims to jurisdiction. Because the offices of Governor of Hong Kong and Minister to China were fully merged until the mid 1850s, it was unnecessary for anyone to define the boundaries of each office. This constitutional imbrication facilitated the flexible removal of Chinese people from Hong Kong. By the same token, however, the subsequent splitting of the merged office from the late 1850s would further distinguish rendition from deportation. Legal ideas would solidify through the disaggregation of British diplomatic, consular, and gubernatorial authority in Hong Kong and China.

The first British Minister to China was Charles Elliot, the Chief Superintendent of British Trade in China between 1836 and 1841. Chapter 1 has explained that, as Chief Superintendent, Elliot was already responsible for governing British sojourners in China. Elliot was then appointed Minister in 1840, during the Opium War, because the Foreign Office needed an official with authority to negotiate peace with China.[101] The offices of Minister and Chief Superintendent were thus merged in practice, not least after Henry Pottinger succeeded Elliot in both offices during 1841. Whitehall then decided, after ratifying the Treaty of Nanjing, to appoint Pottinger Governor of Hong Kong, causing him to become Governor, Minister, and Chief Superintendent. This decision reflected the complex role of Hong Kong in Britain's early China policy. As the Secretary of State for War and the Colonies, Lord Stanley noted in June 1843, Hong

Kong was 'occupied not with a view to Colonization but for diplomatic, commercial and military purposes'. These purposes called for a Governor who was 'at once, to negotiate with the Emperor of China or his officers, to superintend the trade of the Queen's subjects in the seas, rivers and coasts of the [Chinese] Empire, and to regulate all the internal economy of the Settlement [of Hong Kong]'.[102] Accordingly, the British Subjects in China Act of August 1843 directed the Chief Superintendent to govern British subjects in Chinese territory by enacting ordinances with the advice of the Legislative Council of Hong Kong. This imperial Act directed the Chief Superintendent to do this 'so long as' he was also Governor of Hong Kong; so, an assorted bundle of diplomatic, consular, and gubernatorial powers became formally vested in one official sitting in Hong Kong.[103]

The amalgamated office in Hong Kong was more unusual in the imperial constitution than other studies have noted. Among the forty-five colonial governors and other equivalent administrators who were on the Colonial Office's payroll in 1852, only George Bonham drew a separate salary (of £3,000) for his Foreign Office appointments, in addition to his salary as Governor (also £3,000).[104] A few other administrators also held quasi-diplomatic offices, but Bonham was the only accredited Minister to a foreign government. For example, the High Commissioner of the Ionian Islands was only so titled because Russia objected to the British annexation of that territory, so Britain accepted the lesser role of 'protecting sovereign', agreeing, at least in theory, to give the Ionian Islanders internal self-governance. In practice, the High Commissioner of the Ionian Islands exercised administrative powers.[105] Similarly, the Governor of the Cape Colony was the ex officio High Commissioner for Southern Africa. According to imperial officials, the latter portfolio carried an 'undefined authority in South Africa beyond the limits of British territory', including the power to conduct diplomacy with independent tribal polities.[106] This diplomatic authority resembled that of the Minister-Chief Superintendent in Hong Kong. But it was more expansionist in nature, or more indicative of an intention to exclude rival imperial powers from the specified territory.[107] Supported by the rhetoric of protection, the early and rudimentary exercise of extraterritorial jurisdiction by British officials in Africa was later formalised as a new technique of imperial expansion, as Inge van Hulle has argued – the establishment of 'colonial protectorates'.[108] Indeed, Britain would appoint other high commissioners to administer colonial protectorates in Malaya, tropical Africa, and the Western Pacific after 1870 in further efforts to stake imperial claims cheaply and quickly.[109] China, by contrast, was not carved up in this way.

The early ministers to China were supposed to represent the British Crown in China, but they could not reside in Beijing because China had not recognised the Western paradigm and customary practices of diplomacy. The Qing imperial court regarded foreign states as less than equal in its Sinocentric worldview, so it refused to host diplomats on a permanent basis: only occasional envoys were allowed to pay 'tribute' to the Emperor.[110] In the decades before the Opium War, all other Western communications had to go through the *Cohong* in Canton, the Chinese guild of merchant monopolists.[111] Western merchants and officials resented this system, but it was only at the multilateral Convention of Beijing (1860) that Britain and other Western powers obtained the right to establish permanent legations in the Chinese capital.[112] By contrast, earlier Chinese treaties with Britain (1842–43), France (1844), the United States (1844), and other Western powers provided only for Western consuls to interact with local and provincial authorities at the treaty ports. Britain's frustration with this restrictive system of diplomacy fuelled much of its antagonism towards China until 1860, as Richard Horowitz has argued.[113] Nevertheless, Whitehall tolerated the compromise of the 1840s. In 1844, an Order in Council made the British consuls at the treaty ports answerable to the Minister-Chief Superintendent in Hong Kong.[114] As a result, the latter official developed the practice of contacting the Chinese government through the treaty-port consulates. Being closest to Hong Kong, the consulate in Canton became the main point of bilateral contact.

The combined office of Governor-Minister-Chief Superintendent was seen in 1843 as a good way to advance British interests in China, given the ongoing inaccessibility of Beijing. However, the office fractured after the trade depression of the mid 1840s caused officials in London to develop different strategies for economic recovery. On the one hand, the Foreign Office believed in the merits of revising the Opium War treaties; so, when George Bonham's term in the combined office was due to end in 1854, the Foreign Office was keen to appoint a Minister-Chief Superintendent to lead that project.[115] John Bowring was chosen for his diplomatic experience: in addition to being Consul in Canton under Bonham's administration, the China enthusiast and former parliamentarian was also a veteran of an official inquiry into Anglo-French commercial relations during the 1830s (a distinction he shared with the Foreign Secretary, the 4th Earl of Clarendon).[116] On the other hand, the Colonial Office believed the trade depression was better addressed through further cutbacks of the kind that Hong Kong had undertaken since 1848. To save money, the Colonial Office decided to promote William Caine, the colony's Colonial Secretary and former Chief Magistrate, to Lieutenant Governor, with the initial intention of leaving the more costly office of Governor vacant.[117] Without being Governor of Hong Kong, however, the incoming Minister-Chief Superintendent – the Foreign Office's appointee, Bowring – could not legislate for British subjects at the treaty ports under the British Subjects in China Act 1843. Consequently, the Colonial Office 'very reluctantly' agreed, in February 1854, to give Bowring the title of Governor but not a salary or any authority to conduct the 'ordinary civil affairs' of Hong Kong: that authority was vested instead in Lieutenant Governor Caine.[118]

This imperial compromise caused Bowring to argue – understandably, given what we know about the jurisdictional practices of the early Hong Kong government – that he could not detach governance from diplomacy, and that his official partnership with Caine was not sustainable.[119] Relations between Bowring and Caine quickly deteriorated to such an extent that the Prime Minister, Palmerston, who was an occasional patron of Bowring's, criticised Bowring's titular governorship as an 'administrative solecism ... incompatible with every sound principle of organisation'.[120] Merivale of the Colonial Office then proposed to resolve the situation by lobbying Parliament to amend the British Subjects in China Act. However, Palmerston decided to reinstate Bowring's gubernatorial powers from April 1855.[121] This, of course, allowed Bowring to continue his predecessors' practice of governing Hong Kong's Chinese population with a constant eye to treaty diplomacy.

But events relating to the Arrow War later destroyed Bowring's office, its foundations having been undermined. In October 1856, war broke out after the Acting Consul in Canton, Harry Parkes, led Bowring to believe that Chinese officers had violated British treaty rights by boarding a British-flagged ship, the *Arrow*, in the port of Canton. Bowring was persuaded to request the Royal Navy to bombard Canton in a lapse of judgement that he later came to regret. His conduct was heavily criticised at Westminster, notably by some of Palmerston's own backbenchers who regarded the bombardment as unconscionably high-handed.[122] The jingoistic electorate supported Palmerston's Whig government, however. So did merchants in London, who craved the opening of more Chinese markets to British trade. Emboldened by his political position, Palmerston defended Bowring behind the scenes, while letting the parliamentary debate spiral into a vote of no confidence against his own government. Next, Palmerston called for a general election in an all-out bid for a war mandate and promptly won the 'Chinese Election' of March 1857 by a landslide, knowing all along that he was prepared to sacrifice Bowring for this victory.[123] This was because the merchant lobby had insisted that the Crown deployed a new, 'first-class' Minister to bring China to heel, and the Foreign Office had decided, even before the election, to employ James Bruce, the 8th Earl of Elgin and former Governor-General of Canada.[124]

So, Bowring was told in 1857 that Elgin would replace him temporarily, and that his diplomatic powers would be 'in abeyance' during Elgin's 'special mission' in China.[125] But Bowring's loss of office later became permanent when Elgin obtained the treaty right to establish a British legation in Beijing: this was agreed in the Treaty of Tianjin (1858) and confirmed at the Convention of Beijing (1860). To implement this arrangement, Parliament enacted new legislation to formally detach the offices of Minister and Chief Superintendent from the Governorship of Hong Kong.[126] The Colonial Office also took the opportunity to simplify the official establishment in Hong Kong: Bowring and Caine were pensioned off in early 1859 and Hercules Robinson took office in September as the colony's first purely administrative governor.[127] The combined office of 1843 was thus abolished, with important consequences for the colonial regulation of Chinese mobility.

The Changing Formalities of Mobility Control

A bitter turf war between the colonial government in Hong Kong and the new diplomatic corps in China finally sharpened the distinction between rendition and deportation – between the cooperative and unilateral removal of Chinese subjects to China. This process took place during 1865–69, as officials feuded over the procedural implications of the establishment of the British legation in Beijing. The old promise of protection and due process resurfaced in this context – the promise that served to reinforce British sovereignty in Hong Kong during the 1840s. Previously held out mostly to usurp Chinese jurisdiction, this loaded promise now shielded the colonial government from the constitutional advances of the career diplomats, sculpting, as a result, a new legal landscape in the colony.

Hong Kong suffered a constitutional blow in the summer of 1865, after the Acting Governor, William Mercer complained that Consul D. B. Robertson of Canton had interfered with his correspondence with the Chinese government.[128] In Mercer's view, the treaty-port consuls were not entitled to withhold or modify any messages they conveyed between Hong Kong and China. Mercer accused Robertson of taking it upon himself, in recent cases of rendition, to correct instances of undiplomatic language, and to terminate communications that he deemed unfruitful. Mercer argued that these 'obstructions' amounted to the 'defeat of justice and disregard of Treaty'.[129] Robertson retorted, on the other hand, that he was obliged to practice his own idea of diplomacy – not Mercer's. Being answerable to the legation in Beijing, Robertson refused to be 'the medium of transmitting closed dispatches' between Hong Kong and China. He would not be 'forced to do [Mercer's] behests', he said, 'as if I were a servant of the colonial government'.[130] The diplomats in Beijing supported Robertson. The Acting Chargé d'Affaires, Thomas Wade (who later invented the Wade-Giles system for romanising Mandarin Chinese) argued in July 1865 that Mercer 'could no more insist' on corresponding directly with the Chinese government, 'than the Governor of Jersey [could insist on a] right of correspondence with the Government of France'.[131]

Whitehall accepted Wade's logic, so Mercer backed down.[132] But the new Governor, Richard Graves MacDonnell (1866–72) was not so easily subdued. A veteran administrator with a dour reputation, MacDonnell pounced on an incident in 1867 to expose the dangers of the diplomats' procedural gatekeeping. An eighteen-year-old Chinese domestic servant, Sun-he, had run away from her employer, a judicial clerk in Canton, citing physical abuse and his intention to 'sell me as a Prostitute'.[133] Neighbours helped Sun-He escape to Hong Kong: they 'sold' her for $98 to a trafficker of migrants, Lo A-kit, who 'sold' her on to a brothel-keeper in Hong Kong, A-fai. Sun-he did not resist because A-fai was relatively kind to her and presumably did not force her into prostitution. In an interview with the Registrar General and Protector of Chinese Inhabitants, Cecil Clementi Smith, Sun-he said she would 'not willingly go back to Canton, for my master ill-treated me very grossly'.[134]

Protector Smith questioned Sun-he because a Chinese magistrate had requested her rendition through Robertson's office in Canton. When Governor MacDonnell refused this request in light of Sun-he's testimony, Robertson accused him of breaching 'the Law that prevails among nations'. For Robertson, Sun-he's employer had 'a clear right to demand the restitution of what may be termed his property in the services of this woman, and her being conveyed into a foreign jurisdiction cannot invalidate or annul it'.[135] For MacDonnell, however, a diplomat had no right to order a Governor to perform the 'forcible rendition of a woman to slavery'. MacDonnell even felt 'a pride', he said, 'in thinking that to accede to [this] demand would cause his immediate recall from an office whose duties he had evinced so little ability to comprehend'.[136] The Colonial Office supported MacDonnell on this occasion, though his 'biting language' annoyed the Permanent Secretary, Frederic Rogers.[137] The Foreign Office was also persuaded to concede that Robertson had misinterpreted the law. The Queen's Advocate, Travers Twiss, advised that the Chinese request for Sun-he did not disclose any crime, and the 'comity of nations' did not require Britain to honour employment relations that bordered on slavery.[138]

The diplomatic isolation of Hong Kong also disrupted the work of the Protector of Chinese Inhabitants, as MacDonnell hurried to point out. Appointed in 1864, Protector Smith had worked with the 'zealous and active' Commandant of Chinese Kowloon, Pang Yuk, in a manner reminiscent of the 1840s, in which the two officials held 'semi-official' meetings to share intelligence on Chinese criminals. This was a valuable practice in Smith's view, since 'robberies were traced, and stolen property recovered, which would otherwise never have occurred'.[139] In 1868, however, Pang Yuk went dark. It later transpired that this was because Consul Robertson objected so strongly to being bypassed, that he raised the issue of Smith's meetings with Pang Yuk with the provincial government in Canton; so, to avoid allegations of misconduct, Pang Yuk suspended all contact with Smith.[140] For MacDonnell, this outcome was ludicrous. It was, he argued, 'a most extraordinarily jealous and unwise proceeding to prohibit all friendly intercourse between the Protector of Aborigines here [in Hong Kong] and the Chinese authorities of the soil immediately contiguous'.[141]

By 'Protector of Aborigines', MacDonnell meant the Protector of Chinese Inhabitants: Smith, the present embodiment of the colony's longstanding efforts to control its Chinese population. Officials in Hong Kong rarely described Chinese people as 'Aborigines', but MacDonnell likely borrowed the term from South Australia, the colony he governed from 1855 to 1862. The Aboriginal protectorate in South Australia had started evolving into a cruder system for punishing Aboriginal vagrancy, as Amanda Nettelbeck has shown.[142] Hong Kong had moved even more quickly on this front, and MacDonnell had continued to use vagrancy laws to keep the peace since becoming Governor in 1866. Apart from enacting further measures to register and police the colony's Chinese population, MacDonnell would also place Protector Smith on the Executive Council in 1869, giving him a say, in his capacity as Registrar General, in all cases of deportation.[143] The Registrar General and Protector's ability to track the movement of Chinese subjects was therefore just as important to the colony in the 1860s as it was in the 1840s.

Contact between Hong Kong and Chinese Kowloon was even more crucial because China had ceded the Kowloon Peninsula to Britain in 1860, creating a land border roughly two miles long. MacDonnell compared this state of affairs to 'persons living, as it were, in adjoining fields' – adjacent domains where neighbourly collaboration was a 'geographical necessity'.[144] Chinese people crossed the border freely, so MacDonnell argued that it made no sense for the colony to require permission from Canton to address every case of frontier disorder. Indeed, MacDonnell admitted to working with the Chinese garrison in Kowloon during August 1867, when violence erupted between a Hakka village in British territory and a Cantonese village across the border. In that case, MacDonnell travelled to Kowloon to plan a joint response with the Chinese garrison. Colonial policemen proceeded to 'prevent the effusion of blood' between the two villages, and MacDonnell later sent word to the consulate in Canton, which was three days away by return post, only when he felt that the Chinese garrison was not pulling its weight.[145] In recalling these events a year later, MacDonnell pointed out that he would have 'waste[d] three days' if he had written to the consulate in Canton before travelling to Kowloon. He avowed that he would never defer to the consulate in similar cases even if the Colonial Office ordered him to do so. Citing his long career as a colonial governor – a career spanning Canada, Australia, West Africa, and the West Indies – MacDonnell remarked that 'if I could not be trusted with that amount of discretion, I should not remain a day in my present post'.[146]

Unsettled by MacDonnell's threat of resignation, the Colonial Office finally clarified in March 1869 that 'all communication [between Hong Kong and Chinese Kowloon] ought not to be forbidden'. The rule, officials affirmed, was rather that routine communication was allowed, but any difference of 'opinion' – that is, regarding the legal status of border-crossing Chinese subjects – should immediately be referred to the diplomatic corps.[147] Similarly, the Foreign Office agreed to let colonial and Chinese officials give 'mutual assistance to prevent disorder, or to track out fugitive criminals'; however, the 'extradition [of fugitives] can still only be demanded or granted through Her Majesty's Consulate at Canton'.[148] 'Extradition' was thus regarded as an intrinsically diplomatic procedure, as distinct from other procedures that officials in Hong Kong could perform without consulting diplomats – other procedures for subjecting Chinese people to British legal ordering.

The imperial decision to restrict the colony's discretion in cases of extradition and bilateral differences of legal opinion effectively legitimised its adjacent practices of unilateral deportation. This was because Whitehall understood that Hong Kong had developed various procedures for deporting Chinese subjects, in which diplomats played only a marginal role in enforcing the law. Indeed, Consul Robertson had assisted with the deportation of vagrants and mendicants from Hong Kong, specifically by conveying messages to Chinese officials in Canton, Kowloon, and elsewhere, requesting them to prevent deportees from returning to the colony.[149] This was an established practice that, like the informal sharing of intelligence between local officials, originated in the 1840s, as we have seen. Robertson did not mind playing courier in these cases, likely because the provincial government in Canton, whose goodwill was his top priority, had little reason to object to the deportation of Chinese people from Hong Kong: every deportee was one less person under British control. Cases of treaty-based rendition were more controversial, by contrast, because officials in Hong Kong felt uneasy receiving Chinese requests for fugitives and generally preferred to initiate surrender proceedings on their own terms. Again, this mindset grew out of the jurisdictional tussles of the 1840s: an early context in which ideas of rendition and deportation had not crystallised. Now, in 1869, these processes diverged in idea and practice because career diplomats and imperial officials, who no longer considered Hong Kong a legitimate centre of British diplomacy, regarded rendition or extradition as having more diplomatic significance than deportation.

*

The legal developments described in this chapter allowed Hong Kong to develop a robust practice of deportation. Discretionary removals remained a preferred 'mechanism of social cleansing', as Christopher Roberts and Hazel Leung have recently argued. Vagrants, Triad members, and other disorderly people were deported between the 1880s and 1930s, not only to China but, for migrants of other backgrounds, also to countries in Europe, the Americas, and Southeast Asia.[150] Other 'undesirable' residents were also deported: striking labourers, critics of nations friendly to Britain, and, in the 1920s, hundreds of alleged members and sympathisers of the Chinese Communist Party.[151] The fate of deportees was usually decided by the Governor-in-Council with input from the Registrar General, who kept his seat on the Executive Council until the end of colonial rule.[152]

Crucially, these official practices attracted criticisms of what modern lawyers call 'disguised extradition', or the strategic substitution of deportation for extradition proceedings.[153] In 1931, for example, the Hong Kong government famously detained Ho Chi Minh, the future President of the Democratic Republic of Vietnam, for leading a communist uprising in French Indochina. The French authorities wanted to punish Ho, but the British law of extradition prohibited the surrender of political refugees; so, Whitehall instructed the

Hong Kong government to deport him to Indochina under a colonial ordinance.[154] In response, Ho's lawyers, Frank Loseby and F. C. Jenkin, sued for habeas corpus, arguing that this proceeding was a 'sham under cloak of deportation'. The Supreme Court of Hong Kong rejected this argument. Ho Chi Minh then appealed to the Privy Council but later withdrew his appeal after the Hong Kong government agreed to banish him to a country of his choice. Choosing Soviet Russia, he was allowed to depart for Vladivostok in 1933.[155]

Parallel controversies of disguised extradition also arose in other colonies. In 1882, the colonial government of Gibraltar used an Aliens Order in Council to deport three Cuban rebels to Spain after realising that, as political refugees, they could not be surrendered under the Anglo-Spanish Extradition Treaty of 1878. This decision caused an uproar at Westminster as well as a diplomatic dispute that ultimately drove the Spanish government to release the three rebels.[156] Similarly, several dozen French convicts landed in Trinidad in 1930, having escaped imprisonment in French Guiana. French requests for extradition were either denied or put on hold for technical and evidential reasons, so the government of Trinidad prepared to deport a number of convicts. However, humanitarian activists intervened by funding an appeal to the Privy Council, and MPs at Westminster pressured the Home Secretary, J. R. Clynes, to affirm that it was 'not the practice to use the procedure of deportation as a substitute for or to supplement extradition proceedings'.[157] The problem in Trinidad was later resolved along the lines of Ho Chi Minh's case: colonial and imperial officials agreed to implement a policy of encouraging fugitives from Guiana to accept 'voluntary' relocation to neutral countries like Venezuela in lieu of formal deportation to Guiana. The outcome of the Trinidad debate thus disclosed an empire-wide 'reconfiguration of a determined plan to expunge fugitives' from British territories, as Emily Whewell has argued.[158]

The British discourse of disguised extradition emerged only after the imperial rise of the 'political offence exception' to extradition. That exception emerged as a legal rule in the 1860s and 1870s, as Chapter 5 will explain. But the idea of disguised extradition also presupposed a distinction between extradition and deportation, and this conceptually prior distinction was no less emergent. It was itself shaped by early experiments in the cooperative and unilateral removal of alien migrants from British territory, as this chapter has shown – formative experiments that involved colonial officials wresting control of Chinese subjects from the Chinese government as well as British diplomats in China. These colonial manoeuvres were made at a time when extradition was still a new and narrow area of metropolitan legal practice. So was deportation: barring a few Aliens Acts that were in force during 1793–1826 and 1848–50, metropolitan British officials were, until 1905, famously powerless to expel aliens who were not formally requested by foreign states under treaty.[159] Against this backdrop, Hong Kong was a rare and early proving ground for the procedural and constitutional boundaries of extradition and deportation. It was a place where, by trying to control the mobility of migrants, the British Crown transformed and refined its legal powers.

3

Navigating Disorder

Strategically located at the mouth of the Pearl River, the young colony of Hong Kong was mired in maritime disorder. Piracy, an ancient problem in the region, resurfaced in the wake of the Opium War as the Chinese navy lay weakened and coastal communities lacked lawful sources of income.[1] Criminal activity also accompanied the rise of the Pacific coolie trade from the late 1840s – the poorly regulated trade in the carriage of Chinese emigrants to the Americas under legally dubious contracts for indentured labour. The crews of coolie ships committed terrible atrocities in some cases, while coolies staged violent mutinies in others.[2] The result was all the same in the eyes of early colonial officials in Hong Kong: law-breaking seafarers used the colony as a refuge, marketplace, and base of operations, embroiling it in violence and scandal.

The unruly seafarers of South China tested the British resolve to regulate the oceans. Beset by an overcrowded prison, Victoria Gaol, and other faults in the local penal system, officials in Hong Kong developed a policy of initiating the surrender of fugitives to foreign states for most crimes committed at sea, including piracy. The colony surrendered fugitives primarily to China but also to France and the United States – countries whose extradition treaties with Britain, though enforceable globally, were not made with East Asia in mind. Under this policy, local prosecutions were only preferred for crimes that implicated British people or property and crimes committed in colonial territory. Enforced mainly between 1850 and

1865, this policy amounted to the selective assertion of jurisdiction over maritime crimes. By detaining maritime criminals, Hong Kong championed the British right to police China's proximate seas; but, by offloading many detainees onto foreign states for trial and punishment, the colony moderated its regulatory responsibilities. And, by approving these practices from afar, even with some hesitation, officials in London signalled their willingness to deploy rendition and extradition as a means of calibrating British power.

With maritime cases forming the bulk of its legal practices, the small colony of Hong Kong surrendered many more fugitives than metropolitan Britain. In 1876, a parliamentary inquiry revealed that, between 1843 and 1865, the British government surrendered only one fugitive to France and thirty-five fugitives to the United States under formal treaty arrangements.[3] By comparison, the government of Hong Kong reported surrendering at least 340 and possibly over 400 Chinese subjects to China between 1843 and 1866, pursuant to the Opium War treaties (1842–43) and Treaty of Tianjin (1858).[4] This estimate included fugitives accused of committing crimes on Chinese soil. Still, piracy-related charges accounted for 233 of 247 fugitives given up to China between 1849 and 1857 (see Table 3.1). Many fugitives were also given up to China, France, and the United States on other charges, such as murder, following incidents that occurred partly or fully at sea. The Hong Kong government preferred not to prosecute all these fugitives locally, as this chapter will show. It is unclear exactly how many fugitives were given up from Hong Kong to France and the United States during 1843–65, but this number likely exceeded the metropolitan equivalent. All told, the colony surrendered several hundred fugitives with few misgivings (while deporting many others as unregistered migrants), even as Britain gained a reputation in Europe for being cautious and uncooperative in matters of extradition.[5]

To justify surrendering seafarers to foreign states, officials engaged strategically with legal ideas of piracy. In some cases, they avoided treating detainees as pirates, preferring to frame such charges as murder or kidnapping under Chinese, French, or American law. At other times, they argued that, although the law of nations made piracy justiciable everywhere, Britain was not obliged to exercise this universal jurisdiction.[6] The rendition or extradition of pirates was thus framed as consistent with international law, as officials in Hong Kong sought

TABLE 3.1 *Approximate number of Chinese subjects surrendered to China, 1849–57.*

Year	Number	Charge(s)
1849	22	Piracy (20) Assault and false imprisonment (2)
1850	10	Piracy (7) Suspicion of being pirates (2) Robbery (1)
1851	1	Murder
1852	4	Child stealing
1853	36	Piracy
1854	61	Piracy (18 + 40[a]) Robbery within Chinese dominions (2) Robbery and murder (1)
1855	10	Piracy and 'frequenting the colony for felonious purposes' (7) Burglary and robbery in Chinese territory (3)
1856	30	Confederating with pirates
1857[b]	73	Piracy

[a] Surrendered by Royal Navy officers 'without being brought before the Magistrates Court'.
[b] January to July only.
Source: The Records of the Colonial Office at The National Archives, UK, series CO 129/63, fo. 480.

to reduce their criminal caseload. On one level, these techniques were nothing new. The idea of the universal jurisdiction to punish piracy was a common 'rhetoric' that rarely saw direct application in the imperial practices of the sixteenth to nineteenth centuries, as Lauren Benton has argued: the lofty idea was 'always combined with more practical approaches that defined piracy as a crime under municipal law (the law of particular polities)'.[7] Similarly, Alfred Rubin has shown that, even as a globally dominant naval power in the nineteenth century, Britain rarely punished the '[piratical] acts of foreigners against other foreigners' without considering if other states had stronger claims to jurisdiction – narrower claims framed around the nationality of ships, victims, and offenders.[8] In that sense, piracy was construed quite similarly in early colonial Hong Kong.

On another level, however, the punishment of pirates through rendition or extradition was a municipal strategy that enforced not

British law but the laws of Britain's treaty partners – its imperial rivals in the grand scheme of things. This remarkable duality shows that nineteenth-century British officials did not simply claim or disclaim the jurisdiction to punish pirates. On the contrary, they straddled both positions, balancing the strategic advantages of ordering the oceans against the practical burdens of imposing such ordering. As ideas of extradition evolved between the 1840s and 1860s, officials marshalled them to project British authority on the cheap. This approach was almost extended to non-Chinese foreigners, too. It reached its zenith in the case of Juan Pastor (1861), the Peruvian sailor who avoided rendition to China by a hair's breadth after trafficking Chinese people on the French coolie ship, *Ville D'Agen*.

The Costs of Colonial Justice

Among the early governors of Hong Kong, John Davis (1844–47) was the first to record the view that the British system of criminal justice was unsuited to the colony's social context. Davis decried the futility of many punishments known to English law. He argued that fines were unenforceable against the many destitute residents of the colony, and prison sentences also offered limited deterrence because destitute criminals perceived short sentences as a fair trade of their freedom for bed and board. As a partial solution, Davis introduced ordinances authorising punishments ostensibly 'in conformity with the usages of China'.[9] The cutting of Chinese men's queues or pigtails was one such punishment. Though not officially practised by the Chinese government, queue-cutting was something dissidents did to themselves by way of displaying their opposition to the Qing dynasty. Law-abiding Chinese men were consequently unwilling to lose their queue: they feared being mistaken for rebels. Similarly, Davis experimented with the 'cangue' or Chinese pillory. Whereas the stocks of Anglophone tradition were usually stationary, cangues enabled Chinese convicts to be paraded around for maximum humiliation. The Colonial Office tolerated most of these unusual measures, though they barely outlived Davis' governorship. Queue-cutting was abolished around 1850, and cangues also lost local favour around the same time. Despite sharing Davis' scepticism of conventional fines and prison sentences, later governors did not attempt to Sinicise the local penal system.[10]

A key problem in the 1840s and 1850s was that Hong Kong had no capacity to keep large numbers of convicts imprisoned for long periods of time. The colonial records tell a disturbing tale of chronic overcrowding and insalubrity at Victoria Gaol, Hong Kong's only prison in those days. In 1856, a report by the Surgeon General, J. Carroll Dempster ascribed the poor health of prisoners to inadequate sanitation, the lack of outdoor space for exercise, and the deplorable condition of the prison cookhouse. Dempster noted that he had 'repeatedly condemned' the cookhouse to no avail: the colonial government would only insist at every turn that this issue was 'under contemplation'.[11] In reality, Dempster had the ear of Governor John Bowring, who prided himself on his concern for the welfare of the colony's Chinese population. However, money was very short. Hong Kong was founded as a free port, so the colonial government collected little by way of regular taxes. Instead, it leased Crown lands and auctioned monopolies on various consumer goods, the most lucrative and controversial of which was opium.[12] Annual grants from Parliament also defrayed some expenses but not the cost of public works; and, in any case, this source of revenue dried up in the early 1850s. As for special grants, Hong Kong was in a similar position as other colonies in that it was free to make requests, but the politically marginal Colonial Office was itself at the mercy of the all-powerful Treasury. In the gloomy assessment of the Permanent Secretary, James Stephen, '[the Treasury's] duties are so vast, and many of them so much more urgent and momentous than their correspondence with us, that it is hardly possible that they should give to this Office the degree of attention we require'.[13] When imperial resources were stretched, colonial requests piled up in secretarial in-trays.

So, recognising the Surgeon General's complaints, Governor Bowring lobbied hard for Victoria Gaol to receive renovations 'in harmony with the intelligence and benevolence of our times' and 'adapted to the necessities of a rapidly growing population'.[14] But Bowring's expensive requests were scaled down, imperial funds took time to arrive, and the Gaol was only rebuilt in stages between 1860 and 1864.[15] In the meantime, the original Gaol burst at the seams. Officially capable of housing only 190 prisoners during 1856–59, it reached, in 1857, an average occupancy of 322 and a peak occupancy of 497.[16] The new Gaol also filled up so quickly that the government relocated over 270 prisoners to a derelict prison hulk – a repurposed sailing ship anchored near Stonecutters Island, in the north-western corner of Victoria Harbour. Used from 1863 to 1866, this makeshift prison was predictably unsafe and insecure. Some prisoners died there of disease; others drowned trying to escape.[17] These problems pressured the colony to reduce its prison population, not only through treaty-based rendition or extradition, but also through flexible mechanisms of banishment and deportation, as Chapter 2 has shown.

In theory, convicts of capital crimes need not have strained the local prison system. In practice, however, death sentences pricked the official conscience. In 1850, for example, Chun Ah-tsup and eight other Chinese sailors of 'pirate boats' captured a Chinese 'junk', a traditional sailing ship, near Hainan Island, killing 'a great many men'. The junk ship was carrying $1,000 worth of rice from Malaya to China, so Chun Ah-tsup's gang brought it to Hong Kong, hoping to turn a quick profit.[18] Arrested by the colonial police, all nine men were tried at the Supreme Court of Hong Kong for 'piracy with stabbing', convicted, and sentenced to death. Their sentences were then commuted to transportation for life by the unanimous decision of the Executive Council. In reporting this pivotal outcome, Governor George Bonham explained that the Council refused to set 'a most inconvenient precedent' for sending large groups of convicts to the gallows: 'situated as we are, it is by no means impossible that we may have, at some time or other, one hundred convicts under Sentence of Death'. The colony 'could not carry out Sentence of Death on such a number of Prisoners', Bonham argued; 'and yet, if these nine had been executed, it would be difficult to afford any substantial reason why execution, under like circumstances, should not be done on ten times as many individuals'.[19]

In *R* v. *Chun Ah-tsup*, it mattered that the pirates had only attacked Chinese subjects carrying Chinese property, at a location far away from Hong Kong. For Bonham and other like-minded officials, the death penalty was justifiable as a deterrent to piratical interferences with British ships, people, property, or territory. Conversely, it was gratuitous if used against pirates, however vicious, who had nothing to do with the British Empire. It mattered, too, that in the latter cases, the Executive Council could not properly evaluate claims of mitigating circumstances. Having no resources in China, the Council was 'very ill-adapted to dispose of questions of this sort', in Bonham's view; so, in *Chun Ah-tsup*, the Council accepted that the prisoners were young – the youngest was only eighteen years old – but it rejected their claim that they had attacked the rice junk under duress (specifically, under compulsion from other pirates).[20] Similarly, Governor John Bowring argued in 1857 that local trials of Chinese internecine piracy put the Executive Council in a difficult position since many capital sentences must either be commuted on weak evidence or 'carried into effect in a wholesale manner'. Like Bonham, Bowring balked at either option.[21] The crux of the matter was that mass executions were 'contrary to the spirit of the present age', as Bonham put it – contrary, he implied, to the decline of capital punishment in England, which had followed Parliament's 1823 repeal of the mandatory death penalty for all crimes except murder and treason.[22]

Penal transportation was also a logistically challenging practice that Hong Kong was forced to abandon in 1858. To be sure, it was originally a favoured substitute for the death penalty because it was quite cost effective. In 1850, for example, the cost of transporting each convict to another colony was comparable to only two years' imprisonment in Victoria Gaol; so, in addition to the nine pirates whose death sentences were commuted in *Chun Ah-tsup*, Hong Kong transported 114 convicts of piracy-related crimes during 1852–58, on sentences ranging from seven years to life.[23] More generally, a total of 576 convicts, mostly of Chinese descent, were transported between 1844 and 1858.[24] However, the Straits Settlements and Labuan, the two main colonies that accepted convicts from Hong Kong, closed their doors from the mid 1850s, and the Colonial Office refused to broker alternative partnerships.[25] The dwindling availability of suitable destinations for penal transportees was a problem 'common to the whole of the British Colonies', so the Colonial Office informed Bowring in 1858 that each colony 'now has to deal with its own criminals'. Neither would Parliament bear the cost of imprisoning convicts that Hong Kong failed to transport: 'the requisite outlay must be provided for out of the Revenues of the Colony'.[26] Hong Kong was thus entangled in the wider imperial abandonment of penal transportation – a phenomenon that was rooted in shifting religious attitudes to criminal punishment, as Hilary Carey has argued.[27] Moreover, there is evidence that the demand for convict labourers receded in the Straits Settlements after free and indentured Chinese and Indian migrants started arriving in droves, providing public and private employers with a more peaceable workforce.[28] With no incentive to import more convicts, the Straits Settlements left Hong Kong in the lurch.[29]

Separately, criminal proceedings against Chinese seafarers were prone to collapsing in the first place. Governor Bowring and his successor, Hercules Robinson, were most outspoken on this issue. For his part, Bowring wrote bluntly that 'the whole administration of Criminal Justice in cases connected with Piracy is defective' since the Crown often struggled to keep Chinese witnesses in attendance, and to hire reliable interpreters for them.[30] In addition to Cantonese, the people of Guangdong Province spoke (and still speak) Teochew, Hokkien, Hakka, and other languages of limited mutual intelligibility – languages unfamiliar to many natives of Hong Kong, let alone European judges and jurors. Robinson argued, in a similar vein, that English legal procedures impeded piracy trials. By the 1860s, accused pirates '[knew] by experience that the administration of justice upon principles of British law offer[ed] many chances of escape'. With the help of British lawyers, more and more pirates were 'corrupting witnesses' and exploiting 'every legal technicality' to obtain acquittals. In fact, problems arose even at pre-trial proceedings, as Robinson estimated that only half of all pirates arrested in the colony were ever committed for trial.[31] Local records also showed that only 441 convictions for piracy-related crimes resulted from a total of 665 persons tried during 1849–66.[32] This conviction rate of 66 per cent was too low for Robinson: it was a poor return on the 'very considerable' costs of criminal trials.[33]

Finally, the early courts in Hong Kong had to deal with all regional cases of piracy: no other British tribunal in China was given admiralty jurisdiction until 1865. And, in Hong Kong, admiralty jurisdiction was vested variously in the Court of Justice (1843–44), Court of Vice-Admiralty (1846–49), and Supreme Court (1844–45 and after 1849), all colonial courts staffed and funded locally.[34] This lack of alternative tribunals coincided with Royal Navy campaigns to suppress regional piracy, unilaterally as well as in cooperation with the Chinese government. As a result, naval crews often brought prisoners to Hong Kong after battling pirate fleets, forcing the colony to decide their fate. The largest of these battles was fought in 1849 against the fleet of the Chinese pirate chief, Shap-ng-tsai – a massive fleet of sixty-four vessels, 3,000 men, and 1,200 guns. Supported by imperial Chinese forces, three British warships killed 1,700 pirates near Hainan, captured an unknown number, and routed the rest, including Shap-ng-tsai himself.[35] So, burdened by the numerous prisoners captured by their naval comrades, officials in Hong Kong felt as if the colony was subsidising the ventures of the whole British Empire in China. In 1856, Bowring invoked these sentiments to bolster his ultimately successful argument that London should at least sponsor the expansion of Victoria Gaol.[36]

To be sure, the establishment of the British Supreme Court for China and Japan later reduced the workload of judges in Hong Kong. Established in Shanghai in 1865, the new court was mainly tasked with hearing appeals against the decisions of British consular tribunals in China and Japan.[37] This appellate jurisdiction was transferred from the Supreme Court of Hong Kong, relieving the latter court of constant criticism by litigants that its judges were out of touch with the realities of treaty-port life.[38] Significantly, the Shanghai Supreme Court was also authorised to try British subjects for committing piracy and other crimes at sea and on Chinese rivers, where a small number of British seafarers had taken to preying on local shipping.[39] From Hong Kong's point of view, however, these reforms furthered British regional interests without helping the colony directly. Certainly, pirates who were not British subjects – so, the vast majority of pirates plying the China seas – could still only be tried in Hong Kong even after 1865, if they were to be tried by any British tribunal at all.[40] Moreover, the pre-1865 jurisdiction of the Hong Kong Supreme Court to hear consular appeals, though tedious for judges, did not face the same difficulties as its piracy jurisdiction: British litigants from the treaty ports usually spoke English, and their appeals (being primarily civil appeals) rarely involved sentences of death. For these reasons, the Shanghai Supreme Court would likely not have alleviated Hong Kong's piracy problem even if Britain had established it earlier.

Boundaries in Maritime Ordering

Because the punishment of pirates and other maritime criminals was fraught with difficulty, the early government of Hong Kong preferred to perform rendition or extradition 'in cases where neither British nor Colonial interests are directly concerned', as Governor Robinson put it.[41] To define these 'interests', officials drew various distinctions of territory, residency, and subjecthood in cases of maritime crimes – hasty distinctions that partitioned the oceans in a pragmatic spirit of jurisdictional clarification and containment.

The colonial reasoning was broadly consistent between 1850 and 1865. Writing in response to *Chun Ah-tsup* (1850), the troubling case of the Chinese rice junk, Bonham was the first governor to propose rendition for all cases of piracy in which the 'complainants and defendants are all Chinese and unconnected with this or any other British colony'.[42] Fourteen years later, Robinson argued likewise that the colony should continue to 'hand over, for trial and punishment, to their own authorities all persons apprehended by us for piracy in cases in which the offence has not been committed within British waters or upon the property of British subjects, or upon that of persons residing in this Colony'.[43] Like Bonham and other officials, Robinson believed that this approach was justifiable because, on the one hand, 'the obligation to suppress piracy upon the Coast of the Chinese Empire belong[ed] primarily to the Chinese Government'; but, on the other hand, the Chinese government was too 'weak and helpless' to do its duty, and Hong Kong paid the price of its ineptitude. It followed from these considerations that Hong Kong was entitled to detain pirates 'in self-defence', while doing no more than the bare minimum to protect its interests. According to Robinson:

> We cannot remain inactive and allow pirates to blockade our harbour, and prey upon the native craft frequenting it, even if the offences are committed in Chinese waters, and the vessels captured do not belong to the Colony. But because we are thus obliged to take upon ourselves a task which by right belongs to the Chinese Government it does not seem to me by any means to follow as a matter of course that we are bound to burden ourselves in addition with the punishment and custody of the offenders captured, especially if it can be shown that by our doing so we but encourage the evil which we seek to abate.[44]

How did the colony decide what cases were suitable for rendition? In practice, this task was complicated by the fact that many victims of piracy were connected in some way to the British Empire – more so than some governors were willing to admit. For example, in arguing that the offenders in *Chun Ah-tsup* could rightfully have been handed over to China, Bonham glossed over the fact that one victim in the case had testified to being employed in Malacca. Noting that this witness might thus have been 'a subject of the East India Company' (though this was never proved), the Secretary of State for the Colonies, Earl Grey was 'not satisfied that the British Government was wholly unconcerned in the matter'. So, although Grey supported the general idea of the selective rendition of pirates, he told Bonham to give 'fuller consideration' to how individual cases would be assessed for connections to British interests.[45] Tellingly, Bonham ignored this instruction and Grey did not pursue the matter.[46]

Another incident further illustrates the colony's superficial consideration of the residency and subjecthood of Chinese victims of piracy. In 1864, three pirates from Deep Bay (Hau Hoi Wan, near modern-day Shenzhen) attacked a boat in Victoria Harbour. The location of this attack might have been reason enough to bring a case in Hong Kong – the attack occurred in the colony's territorial waters – but Governor Robinson speculated further that the boat was carrying 'a Chinese family belonging to this Colony'. This was because the pirates sent the father of the family 'to obtain a ransom' in Hong Kong, while holding his children captive in Deep Bay. For Robinson, this 'impudent' act damaged British interests, making it 'necessary for the vindication of British Authority that the offenders should be tried before our own Tribunals ... [We] are therefore I think fairly burdened with the three men who are now undergoing 10 years penal servitude in our Gaol for this outrage.'[47] Here, it is unclear what was most important to Robinson: that the crime was committed in colonial waters, that the victims of the crime appeared to be residents of the colony, or that someone in the colony (not necessarily a British subject) was roped in to paying their ransom.

The legal status of the perpetrators of piracy was also swept mostly under the carpet. In 1853, the Hong Kong-based *China Mail* alleged that 'most if not all of these piratical fleets [destroyed by the Royal Navy] are fitted out in this Colony ... for scarcely a boat falls into the hands of our authorities that a portion of the crew are not identified as Hong Kong men' – that is, residents of the colony.[48] Though hyperbolic, this critical editorial exposed the reality that, as a free port with porous borders, Hong Kong was at least indirectly responsible for enabling some acts of piracy. The colony was certainly frequented by seasoned seafarers of transient habits – people whose skills and resources were equally suited to lawful commerce and unlawful associations with pirates. In this context, it is significant that the government did not feel obliged to prosecute all suspected pirates and abettors of pirates who were local residents, temporary or permanent. Indeed, there is no evidence that officials verified the residency of suspects in any systematic way. As long as they were not British subjects, all suspects of piracy-related crimes were regarded as presumptively liable to be handed over to Britain's treaty partners between 1850 and 1865. Beyond that, it was not until the 1861 case of the *Ville D'Agen* (discussed below) that non-Chinese subjects were held to be immune to rendition to China.

Officials paid more attention to the legal status of ships, by comparison. As Governor Bowring noted in 1855, 'the difficulty of deciding who is, and who ought either by right or expediency to be deemed, a British subject in a colony, so large part of whose population is constantly shifting and in which we have established only a few years, is ... embarrassing as regards the right to claim the British flag'.[49] To stop foreign ships from misusing the British flag, Bowring caused the Legislative Council to enact an 'Ordinance to Establish a Proper System of Registration for Colonial Vessels'.[50] This Ordinance required all ships owned by British subjects to be registered if they were 'employed solely in trading with the mainland of China', as opposed to other places. Registration was not mandatory for similar ships owned by Chinese subjects, but Chinese residents of Hong Kong who were 'lessees of Crown lands' could choose to register their ships if they wished to fly the British flag. In any case, ships were to be registered annually. To qualify for registration, they had to have certain fittings, including a metal-clad hull, and their master or captain had to be 'a British subject or a person conversant with the English language'. Shipowners were also required to have registered ships inspected by the colony's harbour master at least once every six months, failing which the ships were liable to forfeiture.[51]

In addition to regulating the use of the British flag, the Ship Registration Ordinance of 1855 widened the net of colonial surveillance, facilitating the discovery and investigation of maritime crimes. Unregistered ships flying the British flag raised immediate suspicion;

so did registered ships that evaded regular inspections. These practical benefits came with serious complications, however, as the crews of registered ships were incentivised to claim British protection against Chinese jurisdiction. Trouble was caused not least by the *Arrow*, the ship whose seizure by Chinese officers at the port of Canton ignited the Arrow War in October 1856. Crewed by an Irish master and sailors from mainland China, the *Arrow* was a *lorcha*, a cargo ship with a European hull and Chinese-style sails. A common sight in the Pearl River estuary, *lorchas* crowded the shipping and smuggling lanes of treaty-port China, embodying the region's ragged cosmopolitanism during the nineteenth century. In this context, it was not surprising that the Cantonese government, suspecting the *Arrow* of piracy, claimed the right to seize it. Evidence later emerged that, if nothing else, the ship's crew had received stolen property from pirates.[52] But the jurisdictional problem in Canton was twofold: not only was the *Arrow* registered in Hong Kong by her owner, a Chinese resident of the colony, her registration papers were overdue for renewal, having expired eleven days before the boarding incident. The ship's contested nationality consequently precipitated war, as British officials and politicians construed the conduct of the Cantonese government as an insult to the British flag and a breach of the Opium War treaties.[53] The *Arrow* incident is famous, of course, for illustrating the intensity of British aggression in China – the Victorian readiness 'to unleash definitive violence to extract revenge for insult, and to punish opposition, disobedience, and obduracy', as Robert Bickers puts it.[54] But, viewed through the lens of Hong Kong's internal struggles with its overloaded penal system, the *Arrow* incident also illustrates the political complications of drawing jurisdictional lines in the China seas.

Above all, officials took pains to stabilise the colony's territorial boundaries. In 1859, the Colonial Secretary of Hong Kong, William Mercer noted that the British annexation of the Kowloon Peninsula and Stonecutters Island would clarify the municipal jurisdiction of the colonial courts by defining Victoria Harbour as a '*mare clausum*' or closed sea (see Map 3.1).[55] At the time, Mercer was contributing to imperial discussions about negotiating peace with China. Beijing had recently withheld its ratification of the Treaty of Tianjin (1858), the treaty that would have brought peace without any cession of territory; so, as bilateral hostilities resumed, Whitehall solicited views on

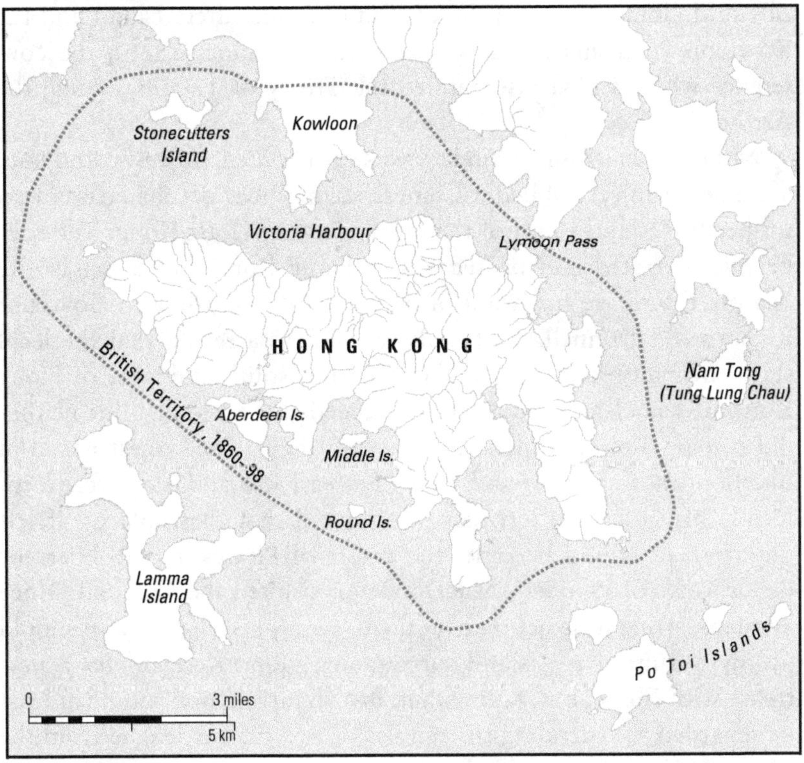

MAP 3.1 The territory and territorial waters of colonial Hong Kong, 1860–98.

the possible expansion of the territory of Hong Kong. Mercer supported this idea for practical reasons. As he explained, local judges had decided out of 'convenience' that crimes committed in Victoria Harbour were justiciable under the common law. This ruling allowed criminals to be convicted and punished more easily. However, it seemed to contradict the imperial orthodoxy that the 'authority of the Common Law' ended and 'Admiralty jurisdiction commence[d]' at the shores of British territories adjoining open waters – specifically, at the 'low-water mark' of such coasts. So, if defendants were to challenge the local ruling, then 'indictments must in future run for piracy', entailing all the difficulties of piracy prosecutions. For Mercer, enclosing Victoria Harbour would forestall this problem.[56] Whitehall agreed. Accepting this argument, and also arguments by military officers that an enclosed Harbour would be more defensible,

British diplomats secured the cession of Stonecutters Island and the Kowloon Peninsula at the Convention of Beijing (1860), the conference where China also ratified the Treaty of Tianjin, ending the Arrow War.[57]

Not every maritime boundary was easily tidied, however. In 1866, a Chinese subject robbed a Chinese fishing boat off the coast of an unspecified island south of the main island of Hong Kong. The robber was arrested and prosecuted in Hong Kong, but a magistrate dismissed the case for 'want of jurisdiction', according to Governor Richard MacDonnell.[58] Officials realised, as a result, that the legal status of many sparsely populated islands south and west of Hong Kong was unclear. China had not ceded those islands, but neither did it maintain any official presence on them. The largest island in question was Lamma Island, though other rocks and islets were technically also unceded territory. Concerned that these places, if left ungoverned, would become 'the resort of Pirates and Robbers or depositories of Plunder', MacDonnell consulted the Colonial Office about asserting jurisdiction over them. He argued that Britain should ideally acquire every island surrounding Hong Kong under a new treaty with China; but, failing that, British jurisdiction should at least be regarded as extending three miles or one marine league from the shores of Hong Kong Island, up to and around the shores of nearby islands belonging to China. Waters within three miles of both Hong Kong and any Chinese island should therefore attract the 'concurrent jurisdiction' of Britain and China, argued MacDonnell, giving his interpretation of the three-mile definition of territorial waters under international law.[59]

MacDonnell's proposals were rejected because the imperial Law Officers endorsed the competing rule that, where 'narrow straits' separated British and Chinese islands or the Chinese mainland, 'the *medium filum* [i.e. centre line] of such waters should be claimed as the boundary of territorial jurisdiction'.[60] Also supported by the Attorney General of Hong Kong, Julian Pauncefote, and grounded in the writings of Emer de Vattel, this was the same general rule that governed rivers separating the territories of continental European states.[61] The Law Officers asserted that treaties could override this rule, but the Sino-British treaties did not have this effect. That said, the Law Officers advised that the Crown could rightfully claim, as its sovereign territory, every island lying between the many headlands of Hong Kong Island; so, Middle Island, Round Island, Aberdeen Island (Ap Lei Chau), and other partially enveloped islands were regarded as rightfully British by this logic (see Map 3.1). In the opinion of the Law Officers, the British claim to Aberdeen Island was also strengthened by the fact that the Hong Kong government had issued leases and licences on that island without receiving complaints from China.[62]

Conversely, there was no existing legal basis for claiming other more isolated islands, not least Lamma Island. MacDonnell requested a new treaty of cession, but the Minister to China, Rutherford Alcock countered that it would 'neither be politic nor expedient to broach the subject' in Beijing.[63] The Colonial Office agreed, concluding in 1868 that MacDonnell's concerns about piracy and lawlessness were, in the circumstances, best mitigated through the Crown's existing right to discipline British sojourners in China. The Permanent Secretary, Frederic Rogers stressed that this was 'not an exercise of sovereignty but only of a right over British subjects'.[64] Ultimately, therefore, Lamma Island, the Po Toi Islands, and other islands around Hong Kong remained in Chinese hands, delimiting the colony through the *medium filum* rule until China leased them to Britain in 1898 as part of what would be called the New Territories of Hong Kong.[65] In 1866–68, the official effort to debate, enforce, and temper the *medium filum* rule disclosed a distinct anxiety to straighten, in one way or another, the edges of British territorial sovereignty.

Rendition and Piracy Jurisdiction

As officials in Hong Kong manoeuvred to perform and rationalise the selective rendition of maritime criminals, they navigated the jurisprudence of piracy. Was the colony obliged to prosecute pirates locally, or otherwise precluded from surrendering them to foreign states? Also, what was piracy under the law of nations? What distinguished it from crimes against the municipal laws of particular states? Whenever these questions arose before the mid 1860s, they were answered patchily, strategically, and in ways that generally downplayed the universal jurisdiction over piracy.

The Hong Kong government seemed to take a limited view of piracy jurisdiction even before developing (in 1850) its policy of surrendering

Chinese pirates selectively. In March 1845, 'certain Pirates' of Chinese origin were arrested in Aberdeen Bay, along the coast of Hong Kong Island, on suspicion of crimes committed at an unspecified location. After some discussion, the Executive Council noted that since 'no proofs [*sic*] existed of their having infringed the Laws of the Colony, the Governor [Davis] intimated his intention to hand [the detainees] over ... to the Chinese Government on demand'.[66] Here, the Council implied that the local courts had no jurisdiction to try the detainees at all. It is unclear, however, whether the Council understood 'the Laws of the Colony' as encompassing only the provisions of the common law and colonial ordinances, or also the *imperial* law of piracy as enforceable by local judges exercising their admiralty jurisdiction. In other words, the Council agreed to surrender Chinese pirates to China without clearly articulating whether foreign acts of piracy were justiciable in Hong Kong.

Meanwhile, pirates who attacked British ships were more likely to be tried in Hong Kong in the 1840s, but, again, without clear reasoning. In February 1847, a gang of eighty Chinese pirates attacked two schooners, *Omega* and *Caroline*, in Chimmo Bay, off the coast of Fujian Province, around 300 miles north-east of Hong Kong. The schooners belonged to Dent & Co. and Jardine, Matheson & Co., respectively – two of the biggest trading firms in early colonial Hong Kong. Killing thirty sailors, the pirates looted chests of opium and silver valued at a total of $160,000 or over £32,000.[67] Several suspects were later tried at the Hong Kong Court of Vice-Admiralty, resulting in few convictions because, as always, procedural and evidential problems abounded.[68] Among those convicted, Lam A-pat and Leang A-shin (who were sentenced to transportation for life) and Cheang Cho-eu (who was sentenced, as an accessory, to three years' imprisonment) petitioned the Executive Council for clemency. Supported by the jurors who convicted them, the petitioners pointed out that their convictions were based solely on the testimony of Too A-po, a fellow defendant who had turned Queen's evidence. Allegedly 'a man of unprincipled character', Too A-po had since been convicted at the Supreme Court for extorting money from people under threats of accusing them of piracy, so his testimony at the Chimmo Bay trials was now discredited. Accordingly, the Executive Council granted Lam A-pat, Leang A-shin, and Cheang Cho-eu a free pardon in July

1848.[69] Significantly, jurisdictional issues were not examined at any stage in these proceedings. None of the perpetrators of the Chimmo Bay attack were considered for rendition to China.

Further opportunities to articulate the piracy jurisdiction of the courts in Hong Kong arose from two mutinies on coolie ships during 1850–52. These incidents caused officials to discuss the legalities of prosecuting and surrendering pirates more explicitly, but still without converging on clear principles. First, 180 Chinese coolies mutinied on the French-flagged *Albert* on 7 September 1850. They killed four French sailors and a Peruvian passenger: the son and agent of the ship's charterer. The *Albert* was two weeks out of Cumsingmoon (Jin Xing Men), a Chinese anchorage twenty miles from Macau. She was bound for the city of Callao, in the Republic of Peru, a major destination of Chinese indentured emigration.[70] In Peru and other plantation economies in and around South America, the West Indies, and the Indian Ocean, hundreds of thousands of indentured migrants replaced slaves during the nineteenth century.[71] Lax regulations allowed private brokers to recruit these 'coolies' from India, China, and other parts of Asia and the Western Pacific, often without their informed consent. After being enticed, deceived, or coerced into signing contracts of indenture, many coolies were shipped across long distances under oppressive and unsanitary conditions. Mutinies were therefore a common occurrence, especially on Pacific routes, as Arnold Meagher has shown. The mutiny on the *Albert* was one of the earliest of its kind; a total of sixty-eight mutinies would take place on 736 voyages on Western-flagged ships carrying Chinese coolies to the Americas during 1847–74.[72]

Abusive brokers and sailors faced legal repercussions, to be sure, if they crossed the fuzzy line between enabling indentured servitude and perpetrating slavery. But coolies who mutinied were also regarded as criminals if they were not deemed to have been enslaved in the blinkered eyes of British, French, and other Western law – the laws of colonial powers whose subjects profited, as employers and middlemen, from global indentured emigration. So, the coolies on the *Albert* were 'frequently beaten by the Captain and Chief Mate', noted the Chief Magistrate of Hong Kong, Charles Hillier; 'and, on one occasion, for a trifling offence, two men were lashed to a boom for six hours, kept without food, and flogged thrice during the interval'. Nevertheless,

Hillier judged the ensuing mutiny to be a presumptive case of 'piracy on the high sea accompanied by murder'. Unsurprisingly, the captain and chief mate were among the four sailors killed by the mutineers.[73]

The charge of piracy with murder was framed against forty-nine mutineers who had been arrested in Hong Kong. But these mutineers were not tried because the local Attorney General, Paul Stirling advised that 'the offences having been as alleged committed by aliens on aliens in a Foreign Vessel, the Courts here have no jurisdiction in the case'.[74] Instead, the French Vice Consul in Hong Kong invoked the Anglo-French extradition treaty of 1843, and Governor Bonham agreed to surrender the mutineers to any suitable French warship.[75] The Colonial Office later approved this decision, though the Permanent Secretary, Herman Merivale questioned whether the *Albert* mutiny fell within the scope of the Anglo-French treaty.[76] According to Merivale:

> The [Anglo-French] Extradition Treaty and Act [of Parliament implementing the Treaty] do not relate to piracies, and only to murders, and when committed 'within the territories and jurisdiction of the French King.' I suppose it is assumed that upon this Act a murder committed anywhere on board a French ship is 'within' such 'jurisdiction', but the point seems rather a delicate one.[77]

In other words, the extraditability of mutineers committing murder on the high seas was a 'delicate' point that Merivale decided not to over-analyse on this occasion. As a result, Stirling's opinion that the *Albert* mutineers could not be tried in Hong Kong was allowed to stand.

Similar questions arose after another mutiny took place on the *Robert Bowne*, a United States ship, on 30 March 1852. Having taken 410 coolies on board at the Chinese port of Amoy (Xiamen), the *Robert Bowne* was sailing towards San Francisco, though her final destination may have been South America. This information was possibly hidden from the United States consul at Amoy, as Robert Irick has argued.[78] Either way, an unknown number of mutineers killed Captain Lesley Bryson and six other American sailors before compelling the surviving crew to drop anchor in the southern Ryukyu Islands, a Chinese tributary state with parallel ties to Japan. The United States Navy later rounded up sixty-nine suspects and brought them to Hong Kong in June 1852. The American chargé d'affaires to China, Peter Parker, wanted the suspects to be tried before British or Chinese courts, likely because American officials in China had no authority to hold criminal trials.[79] American consuls could not even discipline American citizens before 1860, as Eileen Scully has shown. In cases of serious crimes, they were only authorised to send people back to the United States for trial and punishment.[80]

In Hong Kong, Governor Bonham and Attorney General Stirling happened to be away on leave. In their absence, the Acting Attorney General, William Bridges doubted Stirling's opinion on the *Albert* case, arguing that mutinies perpetrated by aliens on the high seas *were* justiciable in Hong Kong as a species of 'piracy according to the Law of Nations'. Bridges acknowledged the opinion of unspecified 'text writers' that crimes committed on any ship on the high seas were only justiciable by the courts of the ship's flag state. For Bridges, however, this rule was limited to cases of ordinary crimes, where 'the governing body of the Ship carrying that Flag remains unchanged, and where the crime has no effect on the character of the vessel *quoad* its nationality its government or its destination'. By this logic, mutinies were different. In Bridges' view, 'the nationality of a ship unlawfully taken from the charge of its officers by persons assuming no national character at the time of or for the purposes of such seizure *ceases*'; so, 'in cases of this description, the Comity of Nations demands that every Nation should if possible assist another in punishing offenders'. Bridges therefore advised the colonial government to prosecute the *Robert Bowne* mutineers as pirates. He argued, in conclusion, that this was probably the only way to bring them to justice since Chinese judges were 'careless in investigation and barbarous in punishment', whereas American judges were too far away and 'ignorant of the habits of the Criminals'.[81]

Bridges clearly espoused the universal jurisdiction over piracy. However, his advice was disregarded. This was partly because his opinion was not properly considered in London, where officials reverted to framing mutinies as municipal crimes. Confessing to being unsure about the law, Merivale relayed Bridges' opinion to the Law Officers of the Crown. In doing so, he described the *Robert Bowne* mutiny as 'a murder ... effected by subjects of a foreign crown and under a foreign flag'. Crucially, Merivale did not use the word 'piracy'; and, instead of emphasising the 'ceasing' of the *Robert Bowne*'s American nationality, as Bridges had done, he noted only that the mutineers 'did not themselves hoist any flag or assume any national character'.[82] In response, the Law Officers advised, without any elaboration, that 'no British authority could, consistently with the Law of England, or, with the Law of Nations, take cognizance of such a case as that described'.[83] It was thus unclear whether the Law Officers rejected Bridges' legal opinion on piracy, or whether they simply believed, as a point of fact, that the *Robert Bowne* had continued to sail under the American flag. None the wiser, the Secretary of State for the Colonies, John Pakington forwarded the Law Officers' opinion to Hong Kong without comment, possibly creating the false impression that he had taken a stand on the international law of piracy – a general position preventing Hong Kong from prosecuting aliens committing piracy on foreign ships.[84] In reality, the Colonial Office's position on piracy was far more ambiguous.

Bridges' appeal to international law also fizzled out because the American chargé d'affaires, Parker refused to wait months for Hong Kong to receive instructions from London. With the consent of the Acting Governor, William Jervois, Parker caused seventeen of the sixty-nine suspected mutineers – the ones that the United States Navy had brought to Hong Kong – to be handed over to the Chinese authorities in Canton. Having convinced himself that these seventeen coolies were guilty of 'aggravated piracy and murder on the high seas', Parker demanded quite paradoxically that they be tried 'fairly and justly' but also executed for murdering American citizens. To Parker's frustration, Chinese judges later acquitted these men along with more than a hundred others that the government of the Ryukyu Islands had also decided to hand over.[85] Hong Kong played no part in these proceedings.

The upshot of the *Albert* and *Robert Bowne* cases was that Hong Kong continued to surrender alien seafarers under treaty as pirates as well as ordinary criminals. This routine was only disrupted in 1857 when the Arrow War soured the Colonial Office's attitude to surrendering pirates to China. Imperial officials were concerned that the Chinese government would commission surrendered pirates as privateers, as Chapter 2 has shown. Eager to recast this military concern in legal terms, officials contended that the colony was not authorised to surrender pirates because piracy *jure gentium* was 'legally cognisable by the Supreme Court of Hong Kong'; indeed, argued Merivale, 'one great object of establishing a Supreme Court at Hong Kong was that cases of this class should be heard by it'.[86] In an equally revisionist manoeuvre, the Secretary of State, Henry Labouchere also proffered a narrow interpretation of the Rendition Ordinance 1850, the colonial instrument that authorised the surrender of Chinese subjects to China for 'any Crime or Offence against the Laws of China'.[87] According to Labouchere, 'the intention of the Ordinance was limited to ordinary offenders against Chinese Law, who should take refuge in Hong Kong ... I feel sure, that the Ordinance never was designed to include persons, guilty of serious crimes against British law, and properly amenable to British tribunals.'[88]

These rhetorical salvos were fired at Governor Bowring, the unfortunate practitioner of wartime rendition. They stifled the colony's rendition practice at a time of emergency, but, crucially, without unravelling it completely. In the first place, Bowring successfully pressured Labouchere to concede that the selective rendition of Chinese pirates was 'informed by former precedents'.[89] In a follow-up despatch of October 1857, Labouchere made no further reference to legal rules, clarifying instead that it was only 'the present condition of China, and of our relations with that Empire', that 'render[ed] it very inadvisable to send back pirates' for trial.[90] This clarification then enabled Governor Robinson to argue, in 1864, for the express adoption of a permissive interpretation of the universal jurisdiction over piracy – an interpretation giving officials the discretion to decide whether to exercise that jurisdiction. For Robinson, the Hong Kong government had 'no doubt legally the power' to prosecute all cases of piracy, 'a pirate being subject to the jurisdiction of any Sovereign within whose power he is brought'. But since practical difficulties made it 'unwise to exercise this right' in every case, and Britain and China were once again at peace, Robinson argued that the colony's preference for selective rendition was just as lawful as it was expedient.[91]

Robinson's melding of international law and colonial policy was the culmination of twenty years of official experimentation and manoeuvring. It caused the Secretary of State, Edward Cardwell to encourage Hong Kong to enact a new ordinance, supplementing the Rendition Ordinance 1850, for 'the Rendition in certain Cases of Chinese Subjects charged with Piracy'.[92] Enacted in July 1865, this ordinance codified the governor's power to perform rendition whenever 'the alleged Piracy has not been committed within Colonial Waters, or against British subjects, or Residents of Hong Kong'.[93] In January 1866, however, Cardwell hastily disallowed this ordinance amid public allegations that Hong Kong had surrendered a seafaring political refugee, How Yu-teen (or 'Mo Wong'), to suffer a cruel execution in China.[94] As Chapter 5 will show, official discourse pivoted sharply towards the moral and political dimensions of rendition from 1865–66, radically reframing the legalities of piracy in the process.

Coolie Trafficking and the Legal Limits of Rendition

Supported by malleable ideas of British interests and international law, Hong Kong's early rendition practice ensnared not only robbers and mutineers, as we have seen, but also coolie traffickers – seafarers whose methods of procuring indentured emigrants were so violent or dishonest that even Western officials likened them to slavery. So, like other criminal seafarers, coolie traffickers figured in the Hong Kong government's efforts to curate its jurisdiction during 1850–65. But, more than that, traffickers prompted the government to push the limits of its authority, even to the extent of claiming, albeit unsuccessfully, a general right to surrender any fugitive to any country in the absence of treaty and statutory provision.

First, a Chinese junk ship carrying 124 men from Chiu Chao (Chaozhou), a city in eastern Guangdong, called at Hong Kong in December 1859. The passengers had agreed to travel as free migrants to work on a betel nut plantation in Sumatra, in the Dutch East Indies. But the ship's crew secretly planned to sell them to coolie brokers in Macau – co-conspirators waiting to tranship the migrants to Cuba under forced contracts of indenture. The crew made the mistake of locking the migrants under 'closed hatches' while the ship was docked in Hong Kong. This caused one migrant to panic, escape, and summon the police. Policemen then boarded the ship, questioned everyone, and arrested seven sailors, all Chinese subjects, on suspicion of kidnapping. A magistrate discharged two suspects for lack of evidence. The other five were detained under the Rendition Ordinance, and Governor Robinson promptly handed them over to the Chinese authorities in Canton.[95]

The defrauded migrants were set free. Lacking a way back to Chiu Chao, some of them were persuaded by the ship's master (who was apparently not arrested) to lodge with Shum A-hing, a Chinese resident of Hong Kong. Unfortunately for the migrants, Shum A-hing was also an associate of coolie brokers. On the pretext of giving them passage home, he escorted forty-five men to Macau and delivered them to the keepers of a coolie barracoon – an enclosure for confining and processing coolies, modelled after similar facilities used in the Atlantic slave trade. Now frightened and doubly confused, the men of Chiu Chao were forced by the barracoon keepers, on pain of being 'severely beaten', to indenture themselves in the presence of oblivious Portuguese officials.[96] Then, in January 1860, nineteen-year-old Ing A-soong escaped the barracoon and, owing to the kindness of a stranger, obtained free passage back to Hong Kong. After confronting Shum A-hing to no avail, and being threatened in turn with further abduction, Ing A-soong sought the protection of Daniel Caldwell, the Registrar General and Protector of Chinese Inhabitants. His testimony enabled Caldwell to negotiate with the authorities in Macau for the release of five other men. The Portuguese authorities insisted that the men had signed valid contracts of indenture, so the Hong Kong government agreed to reimburse the barracoon keepers the sum of $192.50. But no amount of money could save the remaining thirty-nine natives of Chiu Chao, as they had reportedly departed Macau on a French coolie ship, *Emilie Pierre*. Defeated, Governor Robinson made do by prosecuting Shum A-hing at the Supreme Court of Hong Kong for 'kidnapping and slave dealing'. Ing A-soong testified for the Crown. In February 1860, Shum A-hing was convicted and sentenced to four years' penal servitude.[97]

Robinson's decisions stretched the logic of selective rendition. Shum A-hing was tried in Hong Kong presumably because his crimes were committed locally, thus threatening the colony's interests in distancing itself from slavery. But what about the five sailors who had originally trafficked the natives of Chiu Chao into the port of Hong Kong? Robinson did not explain his decision to give them up to China, and neither did Whitehall demand any explanation. So, rendition was implicitly regarded as permissible even when coolie traffickers called at Hong Kong with victims in tow, in direct defiance of British abolition laws. Taken together, this series of events suggests that when victims were transhipped between different ports, officials preferred to frame charges around the initial location of each act of abduction: Hong Kong in the case of Shum A-hing and mainland China in the case of the five original traffickers. This approach entailed compromising the sanctity of British territory in a way that was not done even for the most serious of other maritime crimes.

Pragmatism finally shaded into illegality in the extraordinary case of the *Ville D'Agen*. In June 1861, the harbour master of Hong Kong, Henry Thomsett cleared the French-flagged *Ville D'Agen* for departure to the treaty ports of Amoy, Fuzhou, and Swatow (Shantou) for the purpose of recruiting Chinese emigrants. Thomsett did not know that the ship's master, Foursan, had no intention to call at those ports: Foursan's charterer wanted him to visit Kwangchow-wan, a coastal area in western Guangdong.[98] The French government would later lease Kwangchow-wan from China in 1898, but Foursan was instructed to obtain a false clearance because the area was still closed to Westerners in 1861. So, after arriving covertly in Kwangchow-wan, Foursan allowed two of his charterer's agents to go ashore: a Peruvian citizen named Juan Pastor and a 'Spanish or Portuguese' subject known only as Manuel. Pastor and Manuel proceeded to trick local men into boarding two Chinese-crewed *lorchas* through false offers of work and trade. Several hundred men were thus confined on the *lorchas*, some for several weeks, before being transferred to the *Ville D'Agen*. Many of these men were also beaten for refusing to sign indentures.[99] These abuses culminated on 18 August in a mutiny on one of the *lorchas*. Pastor and Manuel's crewmen scuttled the *lorcha* in reprisal, causing forty-five men to drown below decks. The *Ville D'Agen* set sail for Peru a few days later, loaded with 243 Chinese passengers – captives disguised as willing emigrants. But, as it happened, an accidental collision with a sand bank forced Captain Foursan to seek emergency repairs in Hong Kong.[100]

The mutinies on the *Albert*, *Robert Bowne*, and other coolie ships had led the British Parliament to enact the Chinese Passengers Act 1855, requiring certain ships calling at Hong Kong with over twenty passengers, 'being natives of Asia', to undergo thorough inspections. Formally deemed 'Chinese passenger ships', these ships were not allowed to depart Hong Kong on voyages longer than seven days without being certified as having enough space and supplies for all passengers. Everyone on board these ships was also liable to be interviewed, and any mistreatment of passengers or attempt to obstruct inspections could attract criminal penalties.[101] Presently, the Chinese passengers on the *Ville D'Agen* were locked up for some time in 'cages' meant for 'wild beasts', lacking in 'light, ventilation, and cleanliness'.[102] Clearly familiar with the Chinese Passengers Act, Pastor and Manuel unlocked those cages shortly after the ship entered Victoria Harbour on 30 August 1861. Thomsett, the harbour master, was initially led to believe as a result that nothing was amiss. The passengers did not appear distressed when interviewed, so Thomsett assumed that they had voluntarily embarked at the treaty ports specified on the ship's clearance papers. It was then only after the French Consul in Canton, Baron Trenqualye raised suspicions about the passengers' origins that Thomsett made further inquiries, finally uncovering the atrocities in Kwangchow-wan.[103]

The evasive conduct of the sailors on the *Ville D'Agen* complicated official efforts to frame criminal charges. Consul Trenqualye argued at first that, having 'no power over' Pastor and Manuel, Captain Foursan was not responsible for their crimes. Separately, Governor Robinson believed that Foursan was guilty, but he was unsure whether any crime committed during Foursan's expedition was justiciable in Hong Kong. As an interim solution, Robinson ordered Foursan, Pastor, and Manuel to be arrested for the relatively minor crime of false imprisonment in British territory. An arrest warrant was also issued for Pedro Helguero, a local agent of Camino & Co., the Peruvian charterer of the *Ville D'Agen*. However, Manuel escaped, allegedly to Macau, where 'all trace of him [was] lost'. Then, the commander of the French Navy in South China, Aimé Coupvent des Bois requested the surrender of Foursan. Disagreeing with Consul Trenqualye, Coupvent des Bois took the view that 'the Captain had knowingly participated in criminal and illegal operations conducted on a part of the Coast of China not open[ed] by the Treaties of Commerce'; 'accordingly, on behalf of the French government', Coupvent des Bois asserted 'the sole jurisdiction of the French tribunals' to try Foursan for 'the graver offences of Piracy and Murder'. Robinson agreed: he surrendered Foursan on 19 September 1861.[104] Significantly, the imperial Law Officers would later criticise this decision, arguing that piracy fell beyond the scope of the Anglo-French extradition treaty. But the Law Officers accepted that this was a moot point since, having obtained custody of Foursan, the French government had no cause for complaint.[105] Since no one actually complained about Foursan's extradition, Whitehall also decided not to pursue this issue.[106]

The two Peruvians, Pastor and Helguero, presented more difficulties. First, a grand jury committed them for trial at the Supreme Court of Hong Kong despite Robinson's doubts about jurisdiction. For jurisdictional reasons, the indictment ignored the events in Kwangchowwan. It stated, instead, that Pastor and Helguero had conspired to kidnap Chun A-yeong, a passenger on the *Ville D'Agen*, and 'forcibly detained' him in Hong Kong 'with intent to send him to Peru as a slave contrary to [the Slave Trade Act 1824]'.[107] Next, Robinson received two requests for the surrender of the two Peruvians. One request was made by Cantuarias, a resident of Macau claiming to be a consul of Peru. Robinson doubted Cantuarias' credentials and the Peruvian government's ability to conduct a successful trial, so he denied this request out of hand. He therefore did not seem to consider whether it mattered that Britain had not signed any extradition treaty with Peru. In the circumstances, this question was apparently ignored.[108] By contrast, Robinson took the other request more seriously because it came from the Chinese Governor-General in Canton, Lao Chong-guang, who argued that the 'subjects of powers who have no Treaty with China ought to be proceeded against ... under Chinese law'.[109] Robinson agreed to give this 'novel application' his 'careful consideration', but only if Pastor and Helguero were acquitted in Hong Kong. As he told the Colonial Office, this was because he feared that, with their 'command of money', Pastor and Helguero would exploit 'the known corruptibility of Chinese officials' to escape punishment. Barring this concern, Robinson saw the merits of the Chinese request. In his view, the rendition of Peruvian coolie traffickers and their ilk would serve to deter 'the Subjects of non-Treaty Powers who have hitherto ... taken advantage of the weaknesses of the Chinese Government to commit every species of atrocity with impunity'.[110]

Predictably, a jury acquitted Pastor and Helguero for lack of evidence. The Chinese captives on the *Ville D'Agen* could not testify to being forcibly detained in the territory of Hong Kong, let alone to any prior conspiracy to enslave them.[111] Accordingly, Robinson invoked the Rendition Ordinance in November 1861, detaining Pastor on charges of murder and kidnapping 'within the Empire of China'.[112]

Helguero, on the other hand, was released since similar charges could not be framed against him: he never joined the fateful expedition to Kwangchow-wan.[113] In response, Pastor sued for habeas corpus at the Supreme Court of Hong Kong. His lawyer, Edward Pollard argued that China had no treaty right to request the surrender of non-Chinese subjects. Treaties aside, Pollard also argued that 'the international comity of rendition between two States did not extend to the subjects of a third State'; indeed, 'comity required [Pastor's] rendition to Peru in preference to China'.[114] Pollard's arguments thus exposed a major inconsistency in Britain's existing regimes for rendition and extradition. The Opium War treaties and Treaty of Tianjin only required Britain to surrender 'natives' or 'subjects of China' hiding in Hong Kong and on British ships. By contrast, the Anglo-French and Anglo-American treaties required each signatory to surrender 'all persons' who, having committed certain crimes 'within the jurisdiction of the requiring Party, shall seek an asylum, or shall be found within the territories of the other [Party]'.[115] This disparity in scope was also embedded in legislation: Hong Kong's Rendition Ordinance was expressly restricted to 'Subjects of China', whereas the imperial statutes that implemented the Anglo-French and Anglo-American treaties were silent on the nationality of fugitives.[116]

In this way, the case of the *Ville D'Agen* boiled down to a dispute about the legal limits of discretionary rendition. On 9 December 1861, Chief Justice W. H. Adams formally declined to discharge Pastor from his detention under the Rendition Ordinance. Informally, however, Adams advised Governor Robinson to delay Pastor's rendition to China and to remit the case to London. After Robinson agreed, Adams released Pastor on bail for $10,000 on the condition that he returned to prison on 15 April 1862.[117] Adams then recorded his legal opinion for submission to the imperial Law Officers. Citing Hugo Grotius, Emer de Vattel, and other jurists, he argued that international law permitted 'independent Nations, between whom no extradition treaty existed', to request and grant the 'rendition of [any] person who having committed a capital felony in the one State, was then to be found in the other'. In Adams' opinion, '[to] deny the existence of such a right would be to proclaim immunity to murderers, man-stealers and every other class of villains *except Pirates*, all of whom might rob and slay in one Kingdom provided they could make their escape into the adjoining State'. In short, Adams propounded a general right of rendition under international law – a right that transcended the limitations of international treaties and domestic legislation – though, by his own admission, he 'entertained great doubt' on this point.[118]

Interestingly, Adams seemed to endorse the universal jurisdiction over piracy *jure gentium*, as he implied that pirates could not evade justice by crossing international borders. But he also implied that Pastor was not a pirate in this sense: his worry was precisely that, if not given up to China, Pastor would never be punished. By taking this position, Adams implicitly accepted the juristic opinion that, as Robert Phillimore had written in 1854, 'English Law does not yet hold Slave trading to be *jure gentium* Piracy.' For Phillimore, this was because, unlike robberies at sea, the maritime slave trade had not attracted the universal condemnation of sovereign states.[119] The same conclusion was previously reached in 1817 by William Scott (later Lord Stowell), the Judge of the High Court of Admiralty, in the case of *Le Louis*, a French slave ship that a British naval crew had claimed as prize.[120] Scott's famous decision to deny this claim prompted the British government to cajole various European and Latin American states into signing treaties for the cooperative suppression of the maritime slave trade – treaties that expressly framed slave trading at sea as piracy by way of justifying the reciprocal seizure of slave ships and joint adjudication of prize claims.[121] However, even those treaties were not widely understood as conferring an international jurisdiction to try or punish captured slavers. British attempts to try Brazilian slavers under a bilateral treaty of 1826 were contested in the 1840s, as Jenny Martinez has shown.[122] Meanwhile, slave trading within admiralty jurisdiction was 'deemed Piracy' and made punishable as such under the British Slave Trade Act 1824, but this was a purely domestic law that was not universally enforceable. Jurisdictional restrictions applied.[123] This was precisely why the case against Pastor collapsed at the Supreme Court of Hong Kong: most of the evidence pointed to his conduct on foreign ships, against foreign victims, beyond British waters. Now, judges and officials in Hong Kong proposed to close this jurisdictional gap, not by advocating the troubled analogy between slave trading and piracy *jure gentium* but by claiming a sweeping power of rendition.

Whitehall finally pushed back in February 1862, taking the Law Officers' advice that 'the power of mutual surrender of malefactors, as between the British Government and any other State, entirely depends upon Treaty'. The Law Officers advised that no 'general right' of rendition existed in British law, whether in relation to 'fixed residents' of British territory or 'Birds of Passage' (i.e. transient visitors) like Pastor.[124] Consequently, the Colonial Office gave instructions, with 'regret', for Pastor and his sureties to be released from their bail obligations. The Foreign Office agreed and Governor Robinson complied; so, despite being factually guilty of slave trading and probably murder, Juan Pastor walked free in the spring of 1862.[125]

*

The fact that the Hong Kong government came so close to surrendering a Western fugitive to China encapsulates the scale and audacity of its early rendition practice. Peruvian diplomats were certainly affronted by the committal of Pastor for rendition. In a formal complaint to the British government, lodged through the Peruvian legation in London, the Peruvian consul in Canton described the committal as a 'scandalous and unparaleled occurrence [and] an open breach of all International Law – of all the usages among civilized and Christian Nations'. The initial arrest of Pastor and Helguero was also denounced as a 'horrible and unjust persecution ... for they were taken and shut up in the Criminal Gaol of Hong Kong among Chinese thieves and murderers'. These criticisms were coloured by a very different view of the whole affair, to be sure – a belief that Pastor and Helguero were not slavers at all. Even so, some of the Peruvian consul's comments rang uncomfortably true, as he alleged that Robinson's decision to remit Pastor's case to London disclosed a desire to 'repent of having gone so far', while 'not wishing to assume such a heavy responsibility to do wrong'.[126] In response, the Foreign Secretary, Earl Russell did not defend Robinson's attempt to surrender Pastor to China, though he urged the Peruvian government to acknowledge Pastor and Helguero's crimes and to take steps to punish them under Peruvian law.[127] This exchange shows how Pastor's case exposed Hong Kong's overreliance on rendition and extradition treaties as tools of maritime ordering. The colony had possibly overstepped the boundaries of the French and American treaties on several occasions without repercussions, as we have seen. The Chinese treaties had also undergirded such an extensive programme of rendition that the extra-treaty rendition of a Westerner to China, supposedly a country with weak and cruel laws, was not considered completely outrageous. The Peruvian diplomatic complaint was a direct result of this systemic normalisation of rendition.

Pastor's case also confirms the close intellectual connection between rendition and jurisdictional parochialism. The idea that expensive trials in Hong Kong should mainly if not exclusively benefit British interests was only part of the story: British officials also wanted to disclaim legal responsibility for the general lawlessness that pervaded the China seas. In the latter mentality, mechanisms of rendition were attractive because they served to support arguments about which countries should 'rightfully' punish criminal seafarers and therefore which countries – other than Britain – should be blamed for particular failures of justice. So, in the case of the *Ville D'Agen*, Peru failed to control its citizens and China failed to police its territory. And, although France took responsibility for the conduct of Captain Foursan, its wider oversight of French nationals left much to be desired. For Governor Robinson, this was because the French vice consul in Hong Kong, Vaucher had known all along about the secret itinerary of the *Ville D'Agen*. In fact, Robinson reported that Vaucher was a partner of Messrs Vaucher Frères, the consignees of the ship's illicit cargo of abducted coolies. By revealing this information, Robinson hoped to exonerate Thomsett, the harbour master, from official allegations of negligence. Whitehall had accused Thomsett of failing in his duty to detect abuses in the coolie trade, so Robinson argued that Thomsett could not realistically have guarded against international schemes 'calculated to disarm suspicion'. British officials could only be expected to enforce the Chinese Passengers Act and other British laws within British jurisdiction, argued Robinson. Beyond that, 'the inhuman traffic [in Chinese coolies] can only be suppressed by other Foreign maritime nations agreeing to place their vessels under similar regulations, and by appointing independent non-commercial officials to give effect to them'.[128]

In other words, Robinson attributed the atrocities in Kwangchowwan and on board the *Ville D'Agen* to the failings of foreign states. Officials in London agreed: they expelled Vaucher from Hong Kong, absolved Thomsett of 'actual neglect', and directed only that the colony improved its procedures for inspecting foreign coolie ships.[129] Tellingly, no official in London needed any convincing that Britain could not shoulder all the problems of the China seas, even if those problems often implicated Hong Kong as a regional entrepot. To sustain the convenient view that Britain was entitled to keep to its own affairs while running a free port at modest cost, all of British officialdom exploited the idea that the legal responsibility for ordering the China seas was bounded strictly by territory and the nationalities of ships and people.

4

Rationalising Reciprocity

Early British officials in Hong Kong pored over the question of when they could or should surrender criminals to China, as previous chapters have shown. But a closely related question concerned the colonial government's right to request reciprocal surrenders from China in cases where people in China were identified as fugitives from colonial law. These cases were also significant because they triggered complex bilateral disputes, which the British imperial government gradually reframed in terms that defined British and Chinese treaty rights more systematically. This iterative discourse explored the role of reciprocity in extradition between 1844 and 1865. It also caused British officials to distinguish a sovereign state's requests for extradition from its exercise of extraterritorial jurisdiction.

Disputes arose because the Hong Kong government took to requesting the surrender of fugitives of Chinese descent, and China denied these requests on the blanket grounds that Britain had no jurisdiction over Chinese subjects. British sovereignty in Hong Kong was thus challenged in these exchanges, even as Britain tightened its grip on the colony from 1844. To address this problem, which ran into the 1860s, Whitehall adopted a conceptually formative compromise: imperial officials decided that, although Hong Kong *was* sovereign British territory, China was not required by treaty to surrender its own subjects to British authorities. In this view of the law, the government in Hong Kong had no legal recourse if Chinese criminals absconded back to China. This was not because Chinese subjects could not be tried or punished in Hong Kong – they certainly could. It was rather because Britain had no right to demand the extradition of Chinese subjects.[1]

What about British subjects? In 1865–66, Whitehall took the view that their extradition from China was also a matter of treaty arrangement. Reviewing the Chinese treaties through this lens, Frederic Rogers of the Colonial Office asserted that, unlike the Opium War treaties of 1842–43, the Treaty of Tianjin of 1858 did not provide for the *reciprocal* surrender of fugitives. The new treaty reaffirmed British jurisdiction over 'British subjects who may commit any crime *in China*,' but it said nothing about British subjects committing crimes *in Hong Kong*.[2] Meanwhile, China was still entitled to the surrender of all Chinese subjects taking refuge 'in Hong Kong, or on ... British ships'.[3] In 1866, Rogers concluded from all this that the Treaty of Tianjin formalised 'a kind of balanced one-sidedness' by giving only China a right of 'extradition' and only British Hong Kong a right of 'exclusive jurisdiction' over crimes committed within its territory.[4] So, by placing importance on *locus delicti* – the place where any crime was committed – Rogers articulated a distinction between two rights that treaties could give signatory states: first, extradition, or a state's right to retrieve its subjects from foreign territory for crimes committed in its own territory; and, second, extraterritorial jurisdiction, or a state's right to punish its subjects for crimes committed in foreign territory. In this account of the law, neither right necessarily entailed the other: the existence of either was entirely a matter of treaty construction and interpretation.

Rogers' review of the Treaty of Tianjin was an exercise in intellectual housekeeping, done belatedly to correct perceived misconceptions on the ground. As this chapter will show, the distinction that Rogers drew – between extradition and extraterritoriality – was inchoate in earlier British practice and discourse. The Chinese treaties were originally drafted and enforced upon unstable premises of jurisdiction, and this fluid practice did not encompass a British right of extradition in the sense that Rogers understood it. Rogers' distinction was originally inchoate because officials framed the treaties in conceptually divergent ways, to pursue politically divergent goals. For the British Foreign Office, what mattered more than anything else was the immunity of British subjects from Chinese jurisdiction;

for the Chinese government, it was to deny British authority over people of Chinese descent; and, for the colonial government in Hong Kong, it was to fend off Chinese interference in colonial affairs. These competing motives propelled legal practices for twenty years. Distinct modalities of dividing criminal jurisdiction only crystallised later, at the intersections of fuzzier claims and arguments.

When Rogers' distinction did crystallise, it quickly influenced imperial thinking. Whitehall's reinterpretation of the Treaty of Tianjin enabled the treaty to be cited before the House of Commons Select Committee on Extradition (1868) as a precedent for unilateral extradition, or the extradition of fugitives to foreign states without expectation of reciprocity. As we shall see, this idea was new to British jurisprudence because the Crown had made only reciprocal agreements in Europe, North America, and the West Indies. Partly inspired by the Treaty of Tianjin, witnesses from Whitehall testified to the prudence and legitimacy of non-reciprocal extradition.[5] Parliament agreed: drafted in response to the Select Committee's recommendations, the Extradition Act 1870 did not set any condition of reciprocity. So, the Crown was implicitly authorised to perform one-sided obligations. This feature of the mature British law of extradition set it apart from the laws of certain European states, notably Belgium (from 1874) and Switzerland (from 1892), which prevented officials from extraditing fugitives without reciprocity.[6]

The British review of their legal position in China also shaped the status of British subjects of Chinese descent in a remarkable way. Since the British immunity from Chinese jurisdiction was considered sacrosanct, yet Hong Kong was understood from 1866 to have no right to retrieve fugitives from China, British-born Chinese fugitives escaping Hong Kong were regarded as falling beyond the reach of the law – any law – if they were protected as British subjects in China. This gap in British justice was a logical conclusion of the positivist and analytical reinterpretation of the Treaty of Tianjin, or the reframing of British treaty rights around fixed rules of subjecthood and *locus delicti*. The fact that Whitehall accepted this conclusion – which no one had anticipated before 1865 – demonstrates the spontaneous development of the legal framework of British imperialism in China in the shadow of the jurisdictional politics of Hong Kong. This process of legal change suggests that the nineteenth-century practice of British extraterritoriality cannot be explained without a historical account of extradition, and vice versa. The origins of these areas of law were deeply intertwined.

Reciprocity and Territoriality in Early British Extradition Regimes

Two kinds of extradition regimes populated the early Victorian Empire beyond Hong Kong. The first stemmed from three treaties between Britain and the United States (1842), France (1843), and Denmark (1862), which provided for fugitive surrenders on expressly reciprocal terms. Acts of Parliament empowered the Crown to perform these treaties across the empire under rules that later provided a foundation for the more exacting Extradition Act 1870.[7] These treaty-based, empire-wide statutory regimes of extradition were also the only regimes that were recorded in the first British treatises on the subject – works by Charles Egan (1846), Edward Clarke (1867), and Frederick Gibbs (1868), all barristers at the London Inns of Court.[8] This, then, was the most prominent branch of the early British law of extradition: it was enforceable in the metropole and constitutive of metropolitan legal thought.

The imperial regimes for reciprocal extradition were rooted in a rapprochement in Anglo-American and Anglo-French relations during the early 1840s. That diplomatic climate was cultivated by the 4th Earl of Aberdeen, whose foreign secretaryship under Robert Peel's Conservative ministry of 1841–46 emphasised conciliation in Europe and North America. Aberdeen's irenic policy contrasted with the aggressive patriotism of his predecessor (and successor), Viscount Palmerston. Whereas Palmerston had antagonised France in the 1830s, and also failed to defuse old tensions with the United States, Aberdeen oversaw the conclusion of several treaties with both powers – treaties for the avoidance of war. These treaties addressed extradition and other matters of varying urgency, as Aberdeen was quick to seize diverse opportunities for cooperation and compromise.[9] On the American front, the Webster–Ashburton Treaty of August 1842, which contained the extradition agreement, also resolved a major border dispute between Maine and New Brunswick, in addition to providing for American and British cruisers to operate jointly to interdict slave ships in West African waters.[10] As for France, the Treaty of February 1843 'for the Mutual Surrender, in certain Cases, of Persons Fugitive from Justice' was signed alongside a postal convention and a fisheries convention.[11]

Other treaties for extradition were consciously avoided, however. In Europe, talks with Belgium, the Netherlands, and Naples fell through in the 1840s. A revised treaty with France also became defunct in 1852 after Parliament pressured the government into withdrawing the bill that would have brought it into force.[12] A key concern at Westminster was that the European powers wanted Britain to compromise on British legal and procedural standards. These demands, if agreed to, were thought to leave any treaty open to abuse since requests might be made on trumped-up charges, especially for political refugees. The 1852 treaty with France was a 'test case' for the potency of these feelings, as Nicholas Adams has argued.[13] The treaty of 1852 was supposed to address how British magistrates were routinely discharging fugitives requested by France under the treaty of 1843. However, Parliament had no appetite even for fixing a defective treaty. This was despite the fact that the treaty of 1852 boasted the first 'political offence exception' negotiated by British officials: a mutual promise not to extradite dissidents and other opponents of each signatory state.[14] Parliament distrusted the continent, and the Crown was loath to make international promises that it could not keep; so, the Crown chose to forgo reciprocal promises for the return of British fugitives from most European states. This official attitude of non-cooperation was aggravated by the continent-wide conservative suppression of the Revolutions of 1848. Britain was becoming a haven for political refugees, so the dictates of transnational justice foundered on the rocks of British liberalism. Indeed, Britain was so reluctant to expand its engagements in extradition, that only two other European states were given treaties before 1870: Denmark (1862) and Prussia (1864). Even then, the bill to enforce the Prussian treaty was withdrawn under heavy opposition in Parliament.[15]

Treaties across the Atlantic were similarly precluded by the awkward question of whether Britain would surrender fugitive slaves. The issue of slaves escaping to British territory had already arisen in the West Indies during the 1830s, shortly after the British abolition of slavery.[16] It later featured prominently in the Webster–Ashburton negotiations because the *Creole* incident occurred in October 1841. Around 130 African slaves from the United States brig, the *Creole*, were liberated by British officials in Nassau, the capital of the Bahamas, on the grounds that they were free persons under British law and the Bahamas government had no powers of extradition. The *Creole* was sailing from Richmond, Virginia, to New Orleans, Louisiana, as part of the still lawful domestic slave trade in the Southern United States. Nineteen slaves mutinied and steered the ship to Nassau, thus kicking up a diplomatic storm and pressuring the British delegate in Washington, Lord Alexander Ashburton, to raise this issue with the United States Secretary of State, Daniel Webster.[17]

Wrapped up in the issue of fugitive slaves was a dispute about of much wider political significance – a dispute about sovereignty. Webster was happy to accept the British position that slaves entering British territory were free persons and therefore not extraditable as slaves. But British officers had boarded the *Creole* without notice to disembark her passengers, so the British conduct in the *Creole* affair reeked of the 'right of search' system that Britain had previously failed to convince the United States to join – the system by which Spain, France, and other maritime powers had agreed to let British cruisers stop and search ships flying their flags on suspicion of slave trafficking. The separate 'joint cruising' clause in the forthcoming Anglo-American treaty was supposed to be a mutually acceptable alternative to the right of search on the high seas, so this compromise was likely to break down if British officials claimed the right to remove slaves from American ships with impunity.[18] To prevent their negotiations from unravelling on this account, Ashburton assured Webster that Britain would refrain from 'officious interference with American vessels driven by accident or by violence into [British] ports'. In return, Webster agreed to drop the *Creole* dispute and not to push for a more pro-slavery extradition agreement.[19]

Ashburton's brushing off of the *Creole* case was why the extraditability of fugitive slaves, particularly on charges of murder, would resurface as a contentious question in the Canadian case of *John Anderson* (1860). A similar question would arise in Hong Kong in the pivotal case of *Kwok-a-Sing* (1871–73), as Chapter 5 will show. Presently, in 1842, the *Creole* case simply led the Foreign Secretary, Aberdeen, to decide not to bind the West Indian colonies to any more extradition treaties. The goodwill of the United States was worth a cumbersome treaty – one that potentially undermined British abolitionism – but the same could not be said of the lesser slaveholding powers of South America.

Aberdeen articulated this policy in response to developments in Trinidad. In 1845, the Governor of Trinidad, Henry MacLeod complained to the government of Venezuela about the complicity of Venezuelan shipmasters in helping criminals escape the island colony.[20] Venezuela was a major supplier of food to Trinidad, so Venezuelan ships were exempted by a Trinidadian ordinance from calling at the customs house at Port of Spain on every visit. This arrangement created opportunities for Trinidadian fugitives to escape on Venezuelan ships. When alerted to this problem, the Venezuelan government agreed to take steps to prevent similar 'abuses' in future; however, it insisted that it would only surrender fugitives from its territory under an arrangement 'conceding reciprocally the extradition of Parties guilty, or charged with the commission of certain specified crimes'.[21] In response to this proposal, Aberdeen declared that he 'doubt[ed] the expediency of entering into a formal Treaty [with] Venezuela, for the sake of an object so purely local'. Indeed, Aberdeen believed that it was 'not desirable to augment the number of Treaties of this description, unless on the ground of great and pressing inconvenience, from the want of them'.[22]

Governor MacLeod later proposed another solution, which Whitehall accepted in 1846: MacLeod proposed to have Trinidad and Venezuela enact parallel legislation for the surrender of each other's fugitives.[23] The Venezuelan government was prepared to proceed on this basis, as it informed the British legation in Caracas that it would 'promulgate a law, allowing in general ... the surrender of Criminals from such foreign West Indies colonies as shall undertake to issue a like regulation in respect to Criminals from Venezuela'.[24] Headed once again by Palmerston, the Foreign Office approved this arrangement on the condition that the law of Trinidad did not authorise its Governor to surrender fugitive slaves.[25] A colonial ordinance that included only a short list of extraditable crimes (adapted from the lists in the Anglo-American and Anglo-French treaties) was therefore enacted in 1847. Crucially, an unusual commencement clause stipulated that:

this Ordinance shall commence and take effect when and so soon as the Governor or other officer administering the Government of this Colony shall by Proclamation under his hand and the public Seal of the Colony, declare and proclaim that the legislature of the said Republic of Venezuela hath made sufficient provision by law for the apprehension of offenders escaping to any place within the territories or dominions of the said republic, who may be charged with having committed within this colony any of the crimes or offences hereinbefore mentioned.[26]

The rest of the Trinidad ordinance borrowed heavily from the imperial statutes for the surrender of fugitives to the United States and France. As a colonial law, however, the Trinidad Ordinance applied only in Trinidad, and it was enacted by the usual process for Crown colonies: by the local legislature (in this case, a Legislative Council) and with the assent of the Governor and approval of the Secretary of State for the Colonies (at the time, the 3rd Earl Grey). The imperial Parliament was not consulted.

The Trinidad Ordinance of 1847 thus spawned the second kind of extradition regimes in early Victorian practice: colonial regimes grounded in informally reciprocal arrangements. These arrangements were informal in the sense that no country or colony was bound by treaty to enforce them. So, in this vein, other legislation covering fugitives from Venezuela were enacted during 1848–49 in Barbados, St Lucia, and Grenada – all constituent parts of the colony of the Windward Islands – as well as in the colony of Antigua.[27] These laws largely reproduced the Trinidad Ordinance, which the Colonial Office circulated in 1848 as a 'Model Law' for legislatures in the West Indies to adopt if they wished.[28] A further adaptation of the Trinidad Ordinance was also enacted in British Honduras in 1852 to enable fugitives to be given up to Guatemala for crimes committed in Guatemala.[29] Finally, the Legislative Council of Malta enacted an ordinance in 1863 for surrendering fugitives requested by the recently unified Kingdom of Italy. The Malta ordinance was also cast in the colonial mould of local and informal reciprocity: it was not based on a formal treaty, its coverage was purely local, and it was designed to commence when the government of Malta was satisfied that Italy had made reciprocal laws to extradite fugitives to Malta for crimes committed in Malta.[30]

For all their differences, therefore, the colonial and imperial models of extradition invariably presumed reciprocity and mutual territorial sovereignty.[31] As Francis Piggott, the Chief Justice of Hong Kong would write in his treatise on *Extradition* in 1910, extradition arrangements were 'entirely at variance [with] the territoriality of all law':

> A person who has not committed an offence against the laws of the country in which he is actually present is a free man, and is entitled to apply to the Courts to protect him from any violation of his personal liberty. From this bed-rock principle all subordinate principles are, or at least should be, deducible. But it is precisely this bed-rock principle which the law of extradition is designed to undermine in certain cases, as to which there is more or less agreement among all States.[32]

Whenever deviations from reciprocal territoriality arose in the early British negotiations for extradition, they were always diagnosed and either addressed or regarded as fatal to agreement. The *Creole* affair was a case in point: it complicated the Anglo-American talks of 1841–42 not only because British and American law differed on the issue of slavery, but also because both sides recognised that some limit had to be placed on the ability of British officials to board American ships, even in British waters.[33] Similarly, a key reason why the British Parliament rejected the revised French extradition treaty of 1852 was that President Bonaparte, soon to be Emperor Napoleon III, had proposed amending the French Penal Code to make all crimes against French citizens and the French state justiciable in France regardless of *locus delicti*. Because Bonaparte's proposal threatened to give rise to French extradition requests for fugitives accused of committing crimes in British territory, British legislators rejected the revised treaty wholesale, leaving the ineffectual treaty of 1843 intact.[34]

These imperial and colonial developments demonstrate the centrality of reciprocal territoriality in the early Victorian British understanding of extradition. They expose the exceptional nature of the Chinese treaties, while also providing important context for understanding why the messy enforcement of the Chinese treaties ended up motivating Whitehall to review and re-articulate the premises of extradition.

Inchoate Reciprocity in the Opium War Treaties of 1842–43

The Opium War treaties of 1842–43 did not contain an extradition agreement in the sense that British officials understood extradition agreements elsewhere – that is, as agreements between territorial sovereigns for the reciprocal surrender of fugitives to the country of the *locus delicti*. Far from endorsing territoriality, the Opium War treaties were originally meant to depart from it, as Chapter 1 has shown. They were meant to entrench a bilateral agreement to premise criminal jurisdiction not on *locus delicti* but on the nationality of criminals; or, more precisely, on each criminal's subjecthood or sovereign allegiance. Far from being designed to meet 'the challenge of the border', as Bradley Miller describes the objective of Anglo-American extradition, the Opium War treaties were designed to facilitate trade in a place where, historically, no border had separated Chinese and British people.[35] At the end of the Opium War, it was only during the extended peace process that ideas of territoriality emerged, as British officials experimented with claiming the authority to govern the Chinese residents of Hong Kong. This process led to the unilateral assertion of British territorial sovereignty over Hong Kong during the winter of 1843–44, several months after the last treaty provisions were finalised under the Treaty of the Bogue (October 1843).[36]

The belated and contested assumption of British sovereignty in Hong Kong produced a complex discourse on fugitives escaping to China. The colonial government's response to a series of incidents between 1844 and 1851 shows its tendency to request that China surrender fugitives for crimes committed in Hong Kong. These requests appealed either to reciprocity, British sovereignty, or to a vague combination of both principles. These requests were not consistent or well crafted, however. Since they involved Chinese subjects, or at least people of undisputed Chinese descent, they also tended to encourage China to assert its own position of 'personal' or allegiance-based jurisdiction – a position that contradicted British sovereignty in Hong Kong. Discussions about the Chinese treaty obligation to surrender fugitives tended to collapse as a result into less focused discussions about British jurisdiction and sovereignty. Clear references to treaty provisions were not typically made, either. This discourse shows, therefore, that the Opium War treaties of 1842–43 were not originally understood as containing discrete provisions for British territorial sovereignty in Hong Kong (Article 3 of the 1842 Treaty of Nanjing), British extraterritorial jurisdiction in China (Clause 13 of the 1843 General Regulations of British Trade in China), and reciprocal extradition between Hong Kong and China on the basis of *locus delicti*

(Article 9 of the 1843 Treaty of the Bogue). This degree of interpretive precision – grounding specific rights and obligations in specific treaty articles – was a later, imperial development. It was a retrospective refinement of earlier, looser, and more local articulations of the law.

Three Early Runaways (1844–47)

The first illustrative dispute involved the violent robbery of a British military boat near the barracks at Chek Chu (Stanley), in southern Hong Kong, by Chin-tae and his Triad gang in early 1844. This incident, described in Chapter 2, is worth revisiting in light of a revealing exchange between Governor John Davis and Qiying, the Chinese Governor-General of Guangdong and Guangxi. Chin-tae was arrested in Hong Kong in May 1844 and temporarily given up to Chinese officers in Kowloon to testify against nineteen of his accomplices, who had been arrested in China. This arrangement was made by a secretary of Davis', Karl Gützlaff, on the written understanding that Chin-tae would be given back to stand trial in Hong Kong. Chin-tae's return was delayed until July, however, because Qiying tried to nullify the Kowloon officers' arrangement with Gützlaff. According to Qiying, 'in the Supplementary Treaty [of 1843] it is said, that if British merchants have any affairs that concern [Chinese] natives, the [British] Traders will be judged by a British Officer, and native Chinese be proceeded against by the Central Empire [of China]'. Qiying cited a case from 1843, in which a Chinese man had robbed and killed a British doctor, McKinlay, in Chinese territorial waters at the mouth of the Pearl River. The perpetrator was arrested and punished in Canton to the satisfaction of Davis' predecessor, Governor Henry Pottinger.[37] Qiying argued, therefore, that Chin-tae should also be punished in China for committing 'the same crime' against British people.[38] But Davis countered that the two cases were 'not the same' because Dr McKinlay's killer was 'taken by Chinese officers, and not at Hong Kong', whereas 'Chin-tae's crime was committed at Hong Kong against the English Government, [and] he was taken by English Officers.'[39]

Davis and Qiying conflated two questions in this exchange: whether Chinese subjects could be tried in Hong Kong, and whether China was bound to surrender Chinese subjects to Hong Kong.

The contemporary British (and generally Western) view of extradition presumed a distinction between these questions because sovereign states often asserted jurisdiction over crimes committed in their own territory without asserting the right to retrieve fugitives from foreign territory. In Hong Kong, by contrast, this distinction was blurred because the very nature of British jurisdiction was contested by China and not carefully defined and defended by Britain. In Chin-tae's case, Davis notably made no demand for Chin-tae's accomplices, the ones in Chinese custody. He simply urged Qiying 'to use all the means and resources of your Government to bring these miscreants to condign punishment, as the common enemies of both Chinese and Europeans'.[40] Here, Davis seemed to recognise a concurrent British (territorial) and Chinese (personal) jurisdiction over Chinese subjects for crimes committed in Hong Kong. In this interpretation, Chinese criminals were simply punishable wherever they were arrested. If this was indeed Davis' interpretation, however, he did not articulate it well. His claim to have Chin-tae returned to Hong Kong was originally meant to give effect to an ad hoc arrangement between local law enforcement officers, but it turned into a bigger and more abstract claim because Qiying compared Chin-tae's case – improperly, in Davis' view – to the murder of Dr McKinlay. The question of whether Chin-tae was *extraditable* to Hong Kong, as distinct from whether he could be tried in Hong Kong if arrested there, was thus lost in this confusing exchange.

Subsequent events deepened this confusion. Qiying sent Chin-tae back to Hong Kong in July 1844, likely because he decided to honour the Kowloon officers' promise after all. But Davis sent Chin-tae back to China shortly afterwards because he realised that a trial in Hong Kong might result in an acquittal for lack of evidence.[41] Davis subsequently spent much of his remaining time in office formulating colonial legislation to enable the expulsion of Chinese people to China for summary crimes against colonial law, in lieu of giving them up under treaty for crimes against Chinese law. Though arguably sensible as a pragmatic means of keeping the colonial peace, this strategic use of 'disguised extradition' (as such practices would come to be known) did little to counter the Chinese position of allegiance-based jurisdiction and reciprocity.[42] Davis' decisions suggest that he was not fundamentally minded to counter that position. In fact, he sought to exploit it on occasion because he wanted Chinese wrongdoers to be punished and did not really care how this was achieved.

Another incident illustrates the colonial government's inattentive framing of the legal problem of Chinese fugitives escaping to China. In March 1845, a domestic servant, Hin-jin, 'absconded to Macau after stealing property from the house of Jacood Serang, her Master'.[43] Davis directed that 'as the offender is a Chinese woman and not a British subject, the proper course will be to forward the depositions in the case to Mr Pickett the [British] Consular Agent at Macau, with a list of the stolen property directing him to apply to the Chinese Mandarin [in Macau] for the punishment of the offender, and the restitution of the stolen property'.[44] Crucially, Davis did not request the surrender of Hin-jin for trial in Hong Kong. Did he believe now that he was constrained by *law*, that is, by his own interpretation of the Treaties of Nanjing and the Bogue? Or did he believe that it was *diplomatically* impossible to demand the return of Hin-jin in light of the Chinese view of the treaties? A lesson seems to have been learnt from Chin-tae's case, but what lesson was it? Read in isolation, this scantily recorded incident says very little. But, as an instance of a wider pattern of legal practice, it suggests a nebulous colonial position on the extraditability of escaped fugitives.

A third incident confirms this air of legal imprecision. In May 1847, Hwang-a-kwan and two other domestic servants of Mr Wilson, a private resident of Hong Kong, reportedly stole $1,600 worth of Wilson's belongings and escaped to China. Wilson traced Hwang-a-kwan and his accomplices to their home village of Tunggan in Heangshan (Xiangshan), the Chinese county that also comprised Macau. Hwang-a-kwan's influential father blocked Wilson's inquiries, however, and the local authorities in Tunggan refused to intercede. Defeated, Wilson petitioned Davis, causing Davis to send Qiying a 'strong remonstrance'. In this remonstrance, Davis argued that it was 'a rule, that whenever an Englishman is injured, the Chinese authorities ought to give him redress immediately, without the slightest delay'.[45] But what did this rule entail? According to Davis:

> If Chinese officers ascertain that any villains have taken shelter at Hong Kong, these [villains] are instantly given up to them the moment a statement to that effect is made. Why should then in this instance, Hwang-a-kwan the principal thief and the others, with Hwang-méén-gan, the father of the former, who

abetted the robbery and is responsible for him, not be seized? ... *They must be seized, in order to carry out the provisions of the Treaty, and either be sent to this Colony to receive their punishment, or be punished at Heangshan. If this is not done, I cannot, as heretofore, deliver up any Chinese criminals who may be taken here.*[46]

Again, Davis' understanding of 'the Treaty' is obscure. His vague gesture to 'the provisions of the Treaty' was a far cry from the clause-by-clause analysis that Whitehall would conduct in later years. Ideas of reciprocity and territoriality pervaded his claims, but they amounted to little more than unconnected rhetorical dots. If China was not *required* to surrender Hwang-a-kwan and his accomplices, though it *may* do so in order to 'carry out' the treaties, then what was the scope of the Chinese obligation to surrender fugitives? Exactly what undertaking by China was the surrender of fugitives by Hong Kong supposed to reciprocate? If the bilateral agreement was merely a general agreement to do justice to the victims of crimes, as Davis seemed to imply that it was, then why were the treaties written so intricately, with multiple provisions appearing to specify different modalities of jurisdiction? *We* know that the answer to the latter question lies in the twists and turns of the Opium War peace process. As Chapter 1 has shown, the intricate provisions in Opium War treaties resulted from the contingencies of negotiation between parties of shifting and competing jurisdictional mindsets. But Davis, for his part, made no attempt even to read the treaties closely, so his approach demonstrates that the treaties were not interpreted in technical terms in the 1840s. Again, Davis seemed happy enough to let China assert a concurrent jurisdiction over Chinese subjects committing crimes in Hong Kong whenever this arrangement suited him.

Justice *was* ultimately done to Wilson, the victim of the theft, in Davis' opinion. In October 1847, the Chinese magistrate of Heangshan County, acting on Qiying's instructions, arrested the fathers of the three thieves after failing to locate the thieves themselves. The magistrate also put the entire property of the Hwang clan of Tunggan, including all its farms and ancestral temple, 'under sequestration' until Wilson was compensated. Senior members of the Hwang clan then sent Davis a petition, which Davis ignored, 'begging' him to entreat Qiying to keep only the property of the thieves' fathers sequestered, and to spare the extended Hwang clan from destitution.[47] Offended by this bypassing of the county authorities, Qiying wrote to Davis to denounce the Hwang clan's 'false and disgraceful representation ... indeed the worst instance of their wickedness and deceit'. In reality, said Qiying, the whole clan had 'screened the malefactors' from justice, so they deserved to be punished collectively: 'If the original stolen articles cannot be recovered, their possessions must be sold to make good the loss.'[48] Davis agreed. He published Qiying's letter in Hong Kong 'for the information' of its Chinese population, presumably to deter other servants from stealing from their employers; then, he reported his decision to London and closed the case.[49] Lost in these manoeuvres, once again, was the question of whether Britain could rightfully have insisted on the surrender of Hwang-a-kwan and his accomplices.

A Deadly Affray in Wong Ma Kok (1849–51)

The Hong Kong government's sloppy approach to bringing Chinese fugitives to justice was not sustainable. Things came to a head after two British officers, Captain Da Costa of the Royal Engineers and Lieutenant Dwyer of the Ceylon Rifles, were killed on 25 February 1849 near the village of Wong Ma Kok, about a mile away from their barracks at Chek Chu (the site of Chin-tae's boat robbery five years earlier). Da Costa and Dwyer were taking an afternoon walk, possibly drunk.[50] They entered Wong Ma Kok and barged into the home of a Chinese villager, Lo Yaong-shing. Next, one of them reportedly 'embraced' Lo Yaong-shing's daughter-in-law, Lo Chun-she. Lo Yaong-shing promptly told the officer to 'desist', only to be struck on the head with a walking stick.[51] Seven Chinese men intervened shortly afterwards, armed with spears. They were led by Chui A-po, a pirate chief and fugitive of some notoriety in Canton.[52] According to Lo Chun-she's husband, Lo A-kow, who witnessed these events, Chui A-po was 'the ringleader in the affray'. Joined sporadically by a few other villagers, Chui A-po's posse forced Dwyer and Da Costa to retreat, inflicting serious injuries on them. Then, when the British officers could no longer fight, they were 'slung on bamboos and carried down to the water side near the fishing nets and thrown into the water'.[53] Chui A-po, his followers, and an unknown number of villagers promptly fled to China. Two days later, Da Costa's body was found floating near the beach, presumably looted as a pocket watch and other valuables were conspicuously missing. Dwyer, on the other hand, was never found.[54]

A coroner's inquest into Da Costa's death commenced on 1 March 1849. After a four-day hearing, the coroner's jury recorded a verdict of murder against Chui A-po, his six followers, who were all named by witnesses, as well as 'others to the Jurors at present unknown'. The jury did not manage to establish whether any of the villagers who chose to remain in Wong Ma Kok – thus allowing themselves to be detained as suspects – had a hand in killing Da Costa. The main witnesses, Lo Yaong-shing and Lo A-kow, were careful to incriminate only Chui A-po and his followers, and other witnesses claimed total ignorance of the 'affray' of 25 February.[55]

Over the next seven months, Governor George Bonham wrote several letters to Xu Guangjin, Qiying's successor as Governor-General of Guangdong and Guangxi, to demand the surrender of Chui A-po for trial in Hong Kong. Unfortunately, these letters do not seem to have survived. Bonham later reported to the Colonial Office in November 1849 that he made a 'third or fourth repetition of my demand', to which Xu Guangjin gave a non-committal reply that, 'when taken, [Chui A-po] should assuredly suffer the extreme penalty of the law, that an example might be made of him'. Dissatisfied with this reply, Bonham 'immediately quoted to [Xu] the language of the Treaties with reference to our tenure of the Island [of Hong Kong], and reminded him that our Government had always duly attended to the formal requisitions of China for criminals taking refuge here'. Bonham noted that Xu 'rejoined however that the criminal in question being a Chinese, we [the British] were bound to deliver him up, even if we took him prisoner'. As Bonham explained, this remark by Xu 'seemed to me indicative of ignorance or disregard of our right' – that is, 'our right to try any person of any nation, here residing or found, if guilty of any breach of our law at the time of his residence'. Bonham put it to Xu 'that the Treaty obliged our two nations to a mutual surrender of criminals, formally demanded; that this stipulation had been always observed by us, and always would be'; so, Bonham said to Xu that he 'trusted' China to also observe the stipulation.[56]

Bonham's arguments fell flat, as Xu maintained 'that the punishment of a robber and murderer seemed to him an object desirable in itself, irrespectively of the territory in which he might be taken'.[57] Further discussions were then side-tracked when Chinese policemen from Xin'an County were discovered in Hong Kong with warrants for the arrest of certain Chinese fugitives. The uninvited presence of Chinese law enforcement was nothing new. Bonham's predecessors, Davis and Pottinger had pressured Chinese officials to concede on several occasions that only British personnel could arrest people in Hong Kong, even for crimes only justiciable in China. In other words, the early governors of Hong Kong had asserted that the scope of Britain's judicial authority to try people and executive authority to arrest people were two different issues.[58] Now, Bonham made the same argument, citing earlier correspondence between Davis and Qiying. This appeal to precedent paid off: Xu agreed that 'according to Treaty, Chinese criminals escaping to Hong Kong must be formally demanded of the British authorities'. However, Xu did not circle back to Chui A-po's case at this point. Crucially, Bonham also decided not to refocus their discussion. For Bonham, Xu's reply was 'satisfactory as an admission of the inviolability of our territory'; so, Bonham 'thought it prudent to abstain for the present from further discussion upon the other part of our exclusive right'.[59] Bonham felt that this move was 'prudent' because he believed, probably correctly, that any further demand for Chu A-po would only have crumbled against China's unwillingness to surrender Chinese subjects. As Bonham explained:

> If we persist in our inquiries, we shall be told that [Chui A-po] was killed in resisting lawful authority, or some other subterfuge will be employed to prevent the necessity of surrendering a Chinese to a foreign power; which is the construction that would doubtless be put by the [Chinese] people at large upon this act of their officers, should they fulfil the Treaty stipulation in this respect.[60]

Bonham's argument that the British claim to Chui A-po embodied 'the other part of our exclusive right [of territorial sovereignty]' clearly shows the inchoateness of extradition discourse in 1840s Hong Kong. Again, questions of extradition collapsed in Hong Kong into questions of jurisdiction and sovereignty. Again, the British right to retrieve escaped fugitives was not understood as a distinct treaty right but rather as a vague facet of British sovereignty.

In January 1850, the Colonial Office and Foreign Office approved Bonham's decision not to press for the surrender of Chui A-po. However, both ministries rejected Bonham's legal reasoning. After 'a careful reference' to the Treaty of the Bogue (1843), officials agreed that the relevant provision, Article 9, only 'regulates the question concerning the restoration of persons who have committed offences *against their own government*'.[61] A Senior Clerk at the Colonial Office, Arthur Blackwood, noted that 'there is no provision in the Treaty for the surrender of a Chinese subject, amenable to colonial jurisdiction, for an offence committed in Hong Kong or elsewhere, who may have escaped to China'.[62] The Permanent Secretary at the Colonial Office, Herman Merivale, agreed that 'the Treaty obliges the Chinese to surrender *English* offenders, but certainly not *Chinese* offenders as Gov. Bonham seems to imagine'.[63] Finally, the Foreign Secretary, Palmerston wrote in a despatch to Bonham:

> that according to international law, unless it be otherwise stipulated by Treaty, the government of one country is not bound to give up any of its subjects who, having committed a crime in another country, have returned to the Country of their Birth and Allegiance. The Chinese Authorities therefore are not bound to give up to you any Chinese subject who, having committed a crime in Hong Kong, has fled into the Chinese Territory.[64]

This interpretation of the law was more faithful to the wider British idea of extradition than anything officials in Hong Kong had articulated so far. Palmerston's despatch reflected the dominant British view that sovereign states were not bound to extradite fugitives in the absence of treaty arrangements, and that treaty arrangements also determined the scope of any such obligation.[65] This positivist view had eclipsed older views that extradition was a legal duty under the law of nations; though, as contemporary scholars such as Charles Egan and Travers Twiss observed, even the older, natural law account was contested by other jurists, who regarded extradition beyond formal treaties only as a matter of international 'comity' or goodwill.[66] In any case, Article 9 of the Treaty of the Bogue clearly referred only to 'subject[s] of the Crown of England [who] shall … desert, fly, or escape into the Chinese territory'; so, Whitehall concluded that China was not legally obliged to surrender Chinese subjects.

The imperial interpretation of the law was clear and careful. However, it had no immediate effect because it was not accompanied by any concrete instruction to Bonham. Despite applying different reasoning, the colonial and imperial governments agreed on the practical point that Chui A-po was presently beyond the reach of British justice. Subsequent events then steered the colonial discourse back towards ambiguity. In February 1851, a group of Chui A-po's own followers gave him up to the crew of the East India Company ship, *Phlegethon*, at the port of Canton.[67] Chui A-po's men were answering a £100 bounty that Bonham had put up back in March 1849. The Colonial Office had approved this measure, though Bonham had, of course, not discussed it with Xu Guangjin.[68]

Chui A-po was thus brought to Hong Kong and tried before the Supreme Court on 10 March 1851 for the murder of Captain Da Costa. He was given an attorney, William Gaskell, at government expense, as Bonham wanted to avoid allegations of an unfair trial. Gaskell raised two arguments that revisited the question of British jurisdiction in Hong Kong. He argued, first, that Clause 13 of the General Regulations of Trade, appended to the Treaty of Nanjing (1842), denied the Supreme Court jurisdiction over Chinese subjects. Clause 13 was the provision that entrenched the right of British subjects to be disciplined by British officers in treaty-port China; now Gaskell argued, 'upon the ground of reciprocity', that the Clause also 'stipulated that Chinese Criminals should be handed over for trial and punishment to their own authorities'. But the Chief Justice, John Hulme, decided to the contrary that 'the clause had reference solely to crimes committed within the Chinese territory', so it did not apply to the murder of Da Costa in Hong Kong. Gaskell's second jurisdictional argument addressed the unusual circumstances of Chui A-po's arrest: the attorney contended 'that the prisoner had not been fairly apprehended by his own authorities and handed over to ours, but had been treacherously waylaid and kidnapped within Chinese territory'. This argument was also rejected. Hulme decided that the legality of the arrest was a diplomatic question 'to be decided between Her Majesty's Plenipotentiary [Bonham] and Governor-General [Xu]' – the court 'had the prisoner in the dock, and would try him'.[69]

Bonham and Xu never did discuss Chui A-po's 'kidnapping' because Bonham had no reason to do so – no reason to dredge up the fruitless talks of 1849 now that Hong Kong needed nothing more from China. Meanwhile, Chui A-po was convicted of manslaughter. A conviction for murder was avoided because Hulme directed the jury that the defence of provocation applied, so the jurors should either return an acquittal or a verdict of manslaughter if they were satisfied that Chui A-po was provoked by Da Costa and Dwyer's molestation of Lo Chun-she. Evidential concerns also influenced Hulme's direction. Lo Chun-she and her husband Lo A-kow were made to testify to events from two years ago, so the attorney, Gaskell argued for that and other reasons that their testimonies were unreliable and did not prove that Chui A-po had malice aforethought. These concerns led Hulme to remind the jury that 'if the slightest doubt existed, such doubt should go in favour of the accused'. Manslaughter, then, was the jury's verdict.[70] Hulme finally sentenced Chui A-po to transportation for life – this was a few years before Hong Kong abolished penal transportation – but this sentence was never carried out because Chui A-po, who did not wish to be transported, hanged himself in Victoria Gaol on 27 March 1851.[71]

The story of *The Queen* v. *Chui A-po* has been told before, but never as an episode in the making of extradition law. Scholars have focused instead on how this case strained the British commitment to impartial justice and the rule of law.[72] This is for good reason: the case became a cause célèbre after receiving extensive coverage in the colonial press, as its visceral facts divided public opinion. Some observers felt that the conduct of the Chinese villagers of Wong Ma Kok was understandable because the loutishness of Da Costa and Dwyer would equally have provoked Englishmen into violence. Others saw the killing of the two officers as an outrage that was too leniently punished by the conviction of one man for manslaughter. Nevertheless, scholars have overlooked the fact that none of this public controversy inflected *official* discussions between Hong Kong and London. While the public debated the moralities of the affray in Wong Ma Kok, the Crown focused only on its jurisdictional position under the Chinese treaties, suggesting that, in its eyes, *Chui A-po* had a very different significance. Notably, the official discourse explored the technical question of the British treaty right to retrieve fugitives from China, but only fleetingly and tentatively. Officials would address this question more fully in the 1860s, when its tendency to provoke dispute proved too persistent to ignore.

'A Kind of Balanced One-Sidedness' in the Treaty of Tianjin

The Hong Kong government suspended its demands for fugitives when bilateral relations deteriorated in the 1850s, leading to the

Arrow War. Britain and China then signed the Treaty of Tianjin (1858) in an attempt to restore peace, and, after a resumption of hostilities during 1858–60, affirmed an amended version of the Treaty of Tianjin at the Convention of Beijing (1860).[73] The Treaty of Tianjin magnified earlier ambiguities involving fugitives escaping Hong Kong. Consequently, later efforts to address these ambiguities retrospectively imbued the Treaty with technical meanings that it originally carried only obliquely and imperfectly.

The Provisions of the Treaty of Tianjin: Signs of Conceptual Baggage

Article 1 of the Treaty of Tianjin 'renewed and confirmed' the Treaty of Nanjing of 1842, but it declared that the 'Supplementary Treaty [of the Bogue, of October 1843] and General Regulations of Trade [of July 1843] are hereby abrogated', 'the substance of their provisions having been incorporated in this Treaty [of Tianjin]'. This convoluted approach to modifying the Opium War treaties of 1842–43 was intended to preserve the cession of Hong Kong (Treaty of Nanjing, Article 3) as well as the basic legal structure of the treaty port system (Treaty of Nanjing, Articles 2 and 5). The Treaty of Tianjin was designed to do all that while providing for the opening of more treaty ports, the opening of Beijing to resident diplomats, and the right of British subjects to travel in the Chinese interior, among other concessions that Whitehall wanted the Earl of Elgin, the British negotiator at Tianjin, to obtain from China. Parts of the Treaty of the Bogue and General Regulations of Trade – the parts that Whitehall deemed important – were therefore rewritten and 'incorporated' into the Treaty of Tianjin, as elements of what was now a much more wide-ranging treaty system.

Foremost among the old treaty provisions was Clause 13 of the General Regulations of Trade, on the exemption of British subjects from Chinese jurisdiction. In 1857, the Foreign Secretary, the 4th Earl of Clarendon, reminded Elgin that he must 'not omit in any new Treaty with China to obtain a full confirmation of the right of jurisdiction at present enjoyed by Her Majesty in the Chinese dominions'.[74] This emphatic instruction resulted in Article 16 of the Treaty of Tianjin:

Chinese subjects who may be guilty of any criminal act towards British subjects shall be arrested and punished by the Chinese authorities, according to the laws of China. British subjects who may commit any crime in China shall be tried and punished by the Consul, or other public functionary authorized thereto, according to the laws of Great Britain. Justice shall be equitably and impartially administered on both sides.

Like the old, now-abrogated Clause 13, the new Article 16 provided for Chinese and British authorities to wield personal jurisdiction 'in China', without specifying whether Hong Kong would come under a different principle. The Hong Kong question was never formally settled bilaterally, as this book has shown. That old ambiguity was now perpetuated by Article 16 of the Treaty of Tianjin. Next, Article 21 of the Treaty of Tianjin specified that:

If criminals, subjects of China, shall take refuge in Hong Kong, or on board the British ships there, they shall, upon due requisition by the Chinese authorities, be searched for, and, on proof of their guilt, be delivered up. In like manner, if Chinese offenders take refuge in the houses or on board the vessels of British subjects at the open ports, they shall not be harboured or concealed, but shall be delivered up, on due requisition by the Chinese authorities, addressed to the British Consul.

This article effectively replaced Article 9 of the Treaty of the Bogue, governing the mutual surrender of criminals between China and Hong Kong. Unlike the now abrogated Article 9, however, Article 21 of the Treaty of Tianjin was not expressly reciprocal: it continued to require Hong Kong to surrender fugitives to China, but it was silent on the Chinese obligation to surrender fugitives to Hong Kong.

Historians have never explained how Article 21 of the Treaty of Tianjin came to take this form. Elgin's voluminous correspondence with the Foreign Office appears to provide no assistance as questions of extradition barely rated a mention in it.[75] Silence can sometimes speak volumes, however. Heard against the interwar discourse described in this chapter, this particular silence suggests that the British right to retrieve fugitives from China, specifically for crimes committed in Hong Kong, was still only an inchoate idea in the late 1850s. The Foreign Office – and, by extension, Elgin – did not push for this right because the idea of it had been obscured or diluted by more general ideas of the British exemption from Chinese jurisdiction and British sovereignty in Hong Kong. Only Chui A-po's case had caused Whitehall to read Article 9 of the Treaty of the Bogue in isolation, as entrenching a distinct British right to retrieve British fugitives from China *for crimes committed in Hong Kong*. Chui A-po was a Chinese subject, however, and Whitehall took the view that Hong Kong had no right to his surrender for that reason. It seems likely, therefore, that this negative precedent, so to speak, was simply not striking enough to cause the British right in Article 9 to register in the minds of officials as a right in and of itself. So, the answer to the question of why Britain seems to have given up or neglected to renew a treaty right at Tianjin is that this is the wrong question to ask. The better question is whether the officials who interpreted and practised the law in the 1840s and 1850s believed that the treaty established this right in the first place. Their words and actions suggest that they did not; so, from their point of view, they did not fail to renew any earlier right.

Conversely, Article 21 of the Treaty of Tianjin expressly provided for the *Chinese* right of extradition because the idea of the Chinese right was more well formed in the British official mind. The Colonial Office acknowledged as early as in February 1843, when the legal status of Hong Kong was still under debate, that 'according to the law as declared in the *Creole* case ... once [Hong Kong] has become a British Colony the executive authorities will have no power of extradition' in the absence of legislation.[76] After consulting the same Law Officers who had advised the Crown in the *Creole* case of 1841, Whitehall decided that the enactment of suitable legislation could be left to legislators in Hong Kong, and that an Act of Parliament was not required.[77] This decision was largely consistent with what Trinidad was later allowed to do during 1846–47: the Legislative Council of Trinidad was allowed to enact an ordinance empowering its governor to surrender fugitives to Venezuela. But, whereas the Trinidad Ordinance codified reciprocal extradition on the basis of *locus delicti* – that being the informal agreement between Trinidad and Venezuela – the corresponding law in Hong Kong, the Rendition Ordinance of 1850, contained no such formulation because the underlying agreement between Britain and China was much murkier. Indeed, the Rendition Ordinance effectively did nothing more than to give legal cover for the colonial surrender of Chinese fugitives to China. Still, this was enough to raise the imperial profile of the colonial practice. Whitehall's attention was drawn in the 1850s and early 1860s to the eagerness of the Hong Kong government to enforce the Rendition Ordinance, as Chapter 3 has shown. The British delegation at Tianjin was likely led to believe, as a result, that this particular modality of jurisdiction was an important element of the Opium War treaties of 1842–43 – a part worth 'incorporating' into the Treaty of Tianjin.

Retrospective Rationalisation: The Construction of a Treaty Omission

The complex origins of Article 21 of the Treaty of Tianjin meant that it did not *immediately* create a hole in the net of British justice. The idea that Article 21 gave Britain absolutely no right of extradition was constructed retrospectively, in the mid-1860s. We know this because a pivotal dispute in 1865 rehashed the ambiguities of the interwar years, and the officials who took the most literal reading of Article 21 had to contend with competing interpretations that still did not regard extradition as a distinct treaty mechanism. The interaction between Article 21 (on fugitive surrenders) and Article 16 (on the exemption of British subjects from Chinese jurisdiction) was particularly contested in this period, even among British officials; so, a conceptually precise understanding of the British legal position in China definitely did not exist when the Treaty of Tianjin was signed in 1858.

In July 1865, Acting Governor William Mercer of Hong Kong informed the Colonial Office about the Chinese refusal to surrender the accused perpetrators of three robberies, who had all escaped to China. The robberies were committed in December 1864 at an unspecified location in Hong Kong, in February 1865 at the Central Bank of Western India in Victoria City, and in May 1865 at the Hotel d'Europe, also in Victoria. Mercer sent several letters to Viceroy Ruilin (Jui-Lin), the Governor-General in Canton, to request the surrender of these fugitives, but Ruilin either ignored these requests or denied them with reference to Article 16 of the Treaty of Tianjin.[78] In relation to one fugitive, Chung A-kiao, Ruilin argued that it was 'provided by Article XVI that Chinese subjects who may be guilty of any criminal act towards British subjects shall be arrested and punished by the Chinese authorities'. 'Now,' Ruilin declared, 'Chung A-kiao is a Chinese subject who, having committed a robbery in Hong Kong, fled back to the interior where he has been arrested by the Chinese authorities whose duty it is, in accordance with the Treaty, to punish him themselves, conformably with Chinese law.'[79] Mercer disagreed, minuting in response that 'the Chinese still persist in their right to try offences committed in the Queen's dominions and to refuse to surrender such criminals to be tried by the Queen's Tribunals, misquoting also the very Treaty to which they appeal'.[80] In Mercer's opinion, Article 16 had 'no bearing on the question as [the article referred] only to crimes committed within Chinese jurisdiction'. Mercer believed for this reason that it was important for Britain to 'protest against [this] denial of The Queen's supremacy on British soil'.[81]

Mercer's dispute with Viceroy Ruilin covered well-trodden ground. It followed a similar pattern as the bilateral disputes over Chin-tae (1844) and Chui A-po (1849): the Hong Kong government requested the surrender of certain fugitives, and the Chinese government denied the request on the basis that British courts had no jurisdiction over Chinese subjects. As we have seen, Chui A-po's case prompted Palmerston to put it to Governor Bonham that Article 9 of the Treaty of the Bogue did not give Britain any right to demand the surrender of Chinese subjects. Now, the three robberies of 1864–65 brought Chui A-po's case back to the fore, as the British chargé d'affaires in Beijing, Thomas Wade, cited Palmerston's despatch to Bonham in an attempt to persuade Mercer that Britain still had no such right.[82]

It is telling that Mercer was not persuaded. He countered, alluding to Article 16 of the Treaty of Tianjin, that 'in the case of British offenders no reservation is made [by China] as to the place of the offence, and a delivery of a British offender is made by the Chinese even if the crime be committed in Chinese territory'. Here, Mercer was referring to the principle of personal jurisdiction – jurisdiction according to the subjecthood of criminals – which Chinese officials had followed since 1842. This, according to Mercer, was 'surely a greater concession than the delivery of a criminal, no matter what his nation, whose crime has been committed in British territory'.[83] In other words, Mercer believed that Britain's right to retrieve fugitives of all nationalities for crimes committed in British territory was included in its 'greater' right to retrieve British fugitives regardless of *locus delicti* – a right that China did not dispute. This argument confirms that Mercer conflated Articles 16 and 21 of the Treaty of

Tianjin in his own way; and, like earlier governors, he had a capacious idea of British sovereignty and an undistilled idea of extradition.

The Attorney General of Hong Kong, Julian Pauncefote, was more restrained and also more inclined to take the words of the treaty seriously. Pauncefote agreed with Mercer that Viceroy Ruilin had misread Article 16. For Pauncefote, Ruilin's claim that Article 16 governed crimes committed in Hong Kong was clearly untenable: it was 'too extravagant to be entertained'. Pauncefote argued, specifically, that 'the assumption by the Vice Roy of a jurisdiction over [Chinese subjects in Hong Kong] by virtue of Article XVI, and *a fortiori* of an exclusive jurisdiction, should in my opinion be protested against'.[84] However, Pauncefote confined his objection to the '*a fortiori*' Chinese claim under Article 16: he clarified that 'the Chinese Authorities may *by their Code of Laws* have the power to arrest and punish when found within their jurisdiction Chinese Criminals who have committed offences in Hong Kong, and as *there is no clause by which we can demand the rendition of such Criminals* it is well that they are liable to punishment in their own Country'.[85] By making this subtle but crucial clarification, Pauncefote cautioned the Crown against overstating its legal position. He meant to suggest that China was perfectly entitled to withhold the perpetrators of the three robberies of 1864–65, and that China was also entitled to punish them in China – just not for the reason that Viceroy Ruilin had given.

The Colonial Office effectively agreed with Pauncefote. Its decision, in the pithy words of Frederic Rogers, was that 'Mercer is wholly in error' in his demands for the Chinese fugitives.[86] Rogers later explained himself in a memorandum of August 1866, which put the matter to rest by laying out a definitive interpretation of Articles 16 and 21 of the Treaty of Tianjin – an interpretation that the Foreign Office also shared.[87] Rogers disentangled the two articles by analysing their impact on Chinese and British rights separately, and by assuming nothing more than the relatively uncontroversial principle (at least among British officials) that the courts in Hong Kong were competent to try persons of all nationalities for crimes committed in colonial territory. This was also where Rogers recorded his crucial conclusion that 'there is a kind of balanced one-sidedness' in Articles 16 and 21. In Rogers' view, the two articles stood for the principles that:

1. Chinese authorities are not bound to deliver up British criminals taking refuge in China. Therefore, the extradition [clause in Article 21] is one-sided in favor of China. This appears to be a mere omission.
2. Chinese committing crimes in Hong Kong are not to be delivered up to Chinese authorities for trial. Therefore, the exclusive jurisdiction clause [in Article 16] is onesided in favor of England. This of course is designed.[88]

For Rogers and Whitehall at large, the absence of a British right of extradition – the absence of a right to retrieve fugitives *for crimes committed in British territory* – was an unavoidable consequence of making everything else fit. The absence of that right was the logical conclusion of adopting the most plausible interpretation of the Treaty of Tianjin, which not only bore the closest resemblance to the British imperial idea of extradition, but also vindicated British territorial jurisdiction in Hong Kong *and* British allegiance-based jurisdiction at the Chinese treaty ports. Whitehall's conclusion was simple when all was said and done: it was one thing for a sovereign state to exercise jurisdiction in foreign territory, and another for the state to retrieve fugitives from foreign territory. Part of this subtle distinction had peeked through the imperial analysis of Chui A-po's case, as we have seen. But it was only now, after another war, another treaty, and sixteen long years, that Whitehall managed to assemble every piece of this jurisdictional puzzle.

Implications: Impunity for British Fugitives?

The British review of the Treaty of Tianjin during 1865–66 had the comical implication that, although China was willing to surrender British subjects regardless of *locus delicti* (as Mercer had surmised, and British diplomats in Beijing also verified), Britain now took the position that it would not make requests for escapees from Hong Kong.[89] In this strangely amicable impasse, neither side would accept the other side's jurisdictional concession for fear of undermining their own interpretation of the treaty.

It was, to an extent, easy for Britain to forgo the right of extradition, properly so called. This was because it was virtually unheard of for British subjects of European descent to escape to China after committing crimes in nineteenth-century Hong Kong. What seems to be the only known case of this kind is documented in J. W. Norton-Kyshe's

History of the Laws and Courts of Hong Kong (1898). In January 1863, 'three European convicts named Jordan, Irving and Kelly' escaped Victoria Gaol. The three convicts were believed to have 'crossed over to Kowloon and walked a considerable distance inland', likely into Chinese territory. But they survived only eleven days before hunger compelled them to turn back and surrender to the colonial police.[90] Even as a counterexample, therefore, this story illustrates the unattractiveness of China as a refuge for fugitives who could not pass as Chinese.

The problem faced by fugitives like Jordan, Irving, and Kelly was that they had no one to turn to and nowhere to hide. The movement of Western subjects in Chinese territory was tightly controlled under Chinese law and treaty law, even after 1860. Anyone caught beyond the treaty ports without consular papers, or 'passports', or otherwise in violation of treaty arrangements, was liable to be arrested and given up to their consular authorities.[91] British subjects who were safely in consular custody were then liable under British legislation to be sent to Hong Kong to stand trial for any crime cognisable by the colony's Supreme Court.[92] This procedure for relocating accused criminals for trial resembled international extradition but was not so understood because the relocation was conducted exclusively by British authorities. Indeed, this procedure was more analogous to the procedure in the Apprehension of Offenders Act 1843, the imperial statute that regulated the delivery of accused felons between constituent parts of the sovereign British Empire.[93] Since people of European and other non-Chinese descent could rarely pass as Chinese, their chances of disappearing in China would have been slim, or at least much slimmer than if they fled elsewhere. Likely for this reason, the records of the Colonial Office suggest that the 'loss' of the British treaty right to the extradition of non-Chinese British subjects was politically inconsequential. If the records are accurate, Hong Kong did not make a single request for China to surrender such fugitives before 1865 – before Whitehall formed the view that such requests were no longer treaty compliant.

The fate of British subjects of Chinese descent was more complex. Again, the British records do not seem to reveal any colonial request for such 'Chinese British' fugitives before 1865. More precisely, the records do not reveal any colonial attempt to retrieve

Chinese-descended fugitives *as British subjects*: the cases examined in this chapter all involved people that the Chinese government regarded as Chinese subjects with the tacit concurrence of the Hong Kong government. The most logical explanation for this trend is the small size of Hong Kong's native-born population during the mid-nineteenth century, especially in proportion to its exploding population of first-generation Chinese immigrants. These demographics left very little room for colonial officials to position fugitives of Chinese descent as British subjects – little room, as a result, for Whitehall to explore the legalities of Chinese British subjecthood.

Officials had encountered similar questions of subjecthood in an adjacent context, however. In their capacity as Chief Superintendents of British Trade in China, Governors Davis and Bonham had given protection to a small number of Straits-born Chinese sojourners at the treaty port of Amoy, in Fujian Province – sojourners born in the Straits Settlements, the dependency of the Bengal Presidency until 1867 and a Crown colony thereafter. Since many of these Straits Chinese were of Southern Fujian extraction, many of them started trading or working in Amoy after the Opium War. In some cases, they infringed Chinese law by engaging in smuggling, the coolie trade, and secret society activity, hence their appeals for British protection.[94] Now, the treaty status of Chinese British subjects was still a live issue when imperial officials interceded in the bilateral dispute that arose from the three robberies of 1864–65 – the dispute over the extraditability of fugitives escaping Hong Kong. Like Pauncefote, the Attorney General of Hong Kong, no one at Whitehall doubted the Chinese right to discipline Chinese subjects in China under Chinese law. Imperial officials believed, instead, that difficulties only arose when Chinese subjects were also British subjects under British law. In November 1865, the Foreign Secretary, the Earl of Clarendon, reminded the Minister to China, Rutherford Alcock, that:

> We must be very careful to insist upon the British nationality of Anglo-Chinese in Hong Kong, notwithstanding their celestial [i.e. Chinese] origin. We can never allow them to be amenable to Chinese jurisdiction under any circumstances whatever. Tried and punished they must be in Hong Kong, if tried and punished anywhere, and though the Chinese under the terms of the treaty [of Tianjin] as they now stand may not be bound to give them up, they have no right to restrain or punish them in China, for offences committed in Hong Kong or anywhere else. The 16th Article of the Treaty covers them.[95]

This passage clearly shows that questions of extradition were now intersecting questions of extraterritoriality. Moreover, the conceptual decoupling of these two treaty mechanisms had now caused imperial officials to believe that, if forced to choose between two unpleasant options, they would rather see Chinese British fugitives go unpunished than abandon them to Chinese justice. Exemplified in Clarendon's letter to Alcock, this remarkable attitude would have been quite literally unthinkable just a few years ago, when the British understanding of British jurisdiction in China was not yet so strictly defined by *locus delicti*. Put differently, Clarendon's latest vexation makes sense only in the wider context that this chapter has outlined – the context in which British officials believed that they had forgotten to renew their right of extradition in China, even though earlier officials had no clear idea of that right.

But there was one last complication: not every 'Anglo-Chinese' was actually regarded as entitled to protection in Chinese territory. The class of people contemplated by Clarendon had a 'double allegiance' or 'double nationality' under British law: they were British subjects by virtue of being born in British territory but also Chinese subjects by virtue of being born to Chinese parents. British law recognised the foreign nationality of the British-born children of foreigners as a matter of reciprocity, as British statutes conferred British subjecthood (under certain conditions) upon the foreign-born children and grandchildren of natural-born British subjects.[96] This principle of *jus sanguinis* or nationality by descent was not previously thought to have any effect on the rights of British-born Chinese sojourners in China.[97] However, doubts entered official minds during the sweeping review of the Treaty of Tianjin in 1865–66, likely because prominent imperial precedents now stood for the rule that dual nationals could *not* receive British protection in the territory of their foreign parents' country of birth. In 1864, for example, 'it was decided that the children of American citizens born in British territory, but being in American territory could not claim the protection of Her Majesty's Government to exempt them from American military service'.[98] This particular account of the law may have been influenced by the British policy of neutrality in the American Civil War, but other dual nationals residing or sojourning in the country of their foreign nationality were also denied protection during 1865–66. For example, a British–Colombian resident of Colombia and a British–Hamburgian resident of Hamburg both failed to obtain British protection against miliary conscription.[99] So, it was in this context that Whitehall reviewed the Treaty of Tianjin. In December 1865, the Permanent Secretary at the Foreign Office, Edmund Hammond noted, with Clarendon's approval and the concurrence of the Law Officers of the Crown, that:

> Children born in Hong Kong of Chinese parents, subjects of the Emperor [of China], though regarded generally as British subjects by reason of their place of birth, could not be held to be British subjects against the Chinese Govt. as to secure when in China the privileges of British subjects.[100]

This policy would remain in place until 1904.[101] At the point of its inception in late 1865, it seemed to render most ethnic Chinese residents of Hong Kong liable to Chinese jurisdiction, were they to escape to China as fugitives. This, at least, was the theoretical implication of the imperial restatement of the law. The true fate of fugitives who escaped Hong Kong after 1865 is obscure because official discussions on this issue fizzled out after the colony was told, in January 1866, that the Foreign Office would attempt to insert a British right of extradition in a revised Treaty of Tianjin.[102] But, as it happened, subsequent negotiations for revising the treaty did not produce this result. This was for two simple reasons: first, it quickly became clear that China would never agree to surrender fugitives of Chinese descent, whatever their status under British law;[103] second, as Chapter 5 will show, the How Yu-teen scandal of 1865 diverted Whitehall's attention towards the more urgent problem of the unclarified scope of the *Chinese* right of extradition.[104] For these reasons, the Hong Kong government was left in a permanent limbo, unable to make extradition requests and unable to do much else about fugitives escaping to the Chinese mainland. The colony's inability to make extradition requests meant, in turn, that opportunities did not arise for officials to resolve the dilemma that Clarendon had identified – the dilemma between impunity for British fugitives in China and the erosion of the cherished British immunity from Chinese jurisdiction.

*

Between 1843 and 1866, Britain went from having an inchoate right of extradition in China to having no right at all. This process of legal transformation involved a stuttering official effort to reconcile the contested Chinese treaties with wider British ideas and practices of sovereignty and jurisdiction. The process gave rise in the end to the idea that Britain had assumed a one-sided obligation to extradite Chinese fugitives in exchange for a one-sided right of extraterritoriality, hence Frederic Rogers' ostensibly paradoxical but actually revealing diagnosis of the 'balanced one-sidedness' in the Treaty of Tianjin. It cannot be emphasised enough that Rogers proffered an *emergent* interpretation of the treaty: his highly technical interpretation was not foreseen or negotiated for, let alone agreed bilaterally. The distinction between extradition and extraterritoriality was also meaningless, even absurd, to many Chinese officials who continued to understand jurisdiction purely in terms of subjecthood. Nevertheless, this distinction is historically significant because it demonstrates the centrality of Hong Kong in the British self-understanding of the legal foundations of the entire British Empire in China. This self-understanding was not static: it evolved over time, becoming more intricate and analytical as officials explored the jurisdictional junctions of subjecthood and *locus delicti*.

The Treaty of Tianjin also made a mark on British jurisprudence as a rare precedent for unilateral extradition. It was the only such treaty known to the officials who testified at the hearings of the Select Committee on Extradition (1868), where questions of reciprocity loomed large. The Select Committee was concerned that the paradigm of reciprocity had caused treaty negotiations to break down over differences between British and foreign laws, such that the Crown was often left without any power to extradite foreign fugitives even in accordance with British legal standards. In addressing this problem, Edmund Hammond of the Foreign Office proposed to the Select Committee that Parliament should enact a general statute setting out, as comprehensively as possible, the conditions under which Britain would perform extradition. Hammond proposed to tell foreign states that, if they wanted to retrieve their fugitives from Britain, then they must 'come into' the proposed British regime and take it for what it was worth ('*quantum valeat*'). Hammond argued that if foreign states took issue with British laws, then they were perfectly free not to make reciprocal promises, or to impose their own conditions on the surrender of fugitives to Britain. In Hammond's opinion, Parliament should authorise the Crown to extradite foreign fugitives all the same, since 'it is of no advantage to us to keep a foreign criminal in this country'.[105]

In his testimony, Hammond cited the 'extradition article in the treaty with China, which is rather a one-sided article in terms; we undertake to give up Chinese criminals, but the Chinese are not bound to give up criminals to us'.[106] The Legal Adviser to the Colonial Office, Henry Holland (later Lord Knutsford) also testified, when asked whether Britain had 'ever obtained any criminals from the Chinese', that his office had 'no record of any case' of this kind. Indeed, there *were* no cases. Yet, as Holland intimated, Britain was surrendering Chinese fugitives to China all the same, in accordance with Hong Kong's Rendition Ordinance 1850. Accordingly, Holland agreed with Hammond that it was 'very desirable, taking the lowest point of view, to get rid of the foreign criminals, if the foreign country desires to have them', even 'without reciprocity'.[107]

Holland's and Hammond's testimonies disclosed the Crown's relative indifference to retrieving fugitives from foreign countries – relative, at least, to its anxiousness to clarify and codify its own powers of extradition. This parochial attitude was vindicated in the final outcome of the Select Committee's recommendations, the Extradition Act 1870. The Extradition Act 1870 enabled the Crown to obtain powers of extradition by applying the Act, by Order in Council, to any formal 'arrangement' with a foreign state, reciprocal or otherwise.[108] As it happened, the treaties that Britain signed after 1870 were still broadly reciprocal. Notably, however, the Extradition Act enabled the Foreign Office to push through a treaty with Switzerland, which required Britain to surrender British subjects for crimes committed in Swiss territory without requiring Switzerland to surrender Swiss nationals for crimes committed in British territory.[109] Perhaps the British government would have agreed to this somewhat unequal arrangement (in 1880) even without drawing on its experience in Hong Kong: British officials had few reservations about the fairness of Swiss legal procedures. Even so, it was in Hong Kong that Britain first practised unilateral extradition. Perhaps more tellingly, *reciprocal* provisions for extradition were later included in a Sino-British Convention for regulating the Sino-Burmese frontier (1894), as well as in a British treaty with Siam (1883), another country in which British subjects claimed extraterritorial rights. Signed at various stages during the British conquest of Upper Burma, these treaties clearly distinguished reciprocal extradition from British extraterritorial jurisdiction.[110] Again, this technical approach to framing treaty mechanisms did not come out of nowhere: decades of jurisprudence and experimentation preceded it.

5

Founding Alsatia

The extradition law of Hong Kong entered a new era of stringency and formality between 1865 and 1873. The colonial practice of subjecting fugitives to 'rendition' was transformed in this period from a loosely regulated practice into one that was bound by intricate rules written in imperial despatches and case law. The rule against surrendering fugitives for 'political offences' was enforced. So was the rule that came to be known as 'double criminality' – that fugitives should only be surrendered for crimes punishable under the laws of both countries in the transaction – and, likewise, an early version of the 'speciality' rule, requiring fugitives to be surrendered upon official guarantees that they would only be punished for the crimes for which they were surrendered and not for any other crimes.

These and other exacting rules were laid down during and after two pivotal incidents. First, the Colonial Office opened an inquiry into the rendition of How Yu-teen (Hou Yutian) after the Chinese authorities in Canton executed him by the violent method of *lingchi*, or 'slicing', and news of this outcome shocked the British Parliament in 1865. Then, in 1871, the abolitionist Chief Justice of Hong Kong, John Smale, issued two writs of habeas corpus to block the rendition and also the trial of Kwok-a-Sing, an indentured migrant who mutinied on board a ship that was bound for Peru. On a historic appeal by the Crown, the Judicial Committee of the Privy Council issued a judgment that, while partially reversing Smale's controversial decisions, heavily circumscribed Hong Kong's rendition regime.

This process of regulatory tightening in Hong Kong coincided with law reform in the British imperial metropole. In 1868, Parliament appointed the Select Committee on Extradition to answer growing calls for a coherent imperial policy on foreign fugitives. In studying how haphazardly the Crown had dealt with fugitives in earlier decades, the Select Committee recorded How Yu-teen's case alongside other colonial and imperial precedents as proof of the pressing need to codify the political offence exception and other legal safeguards.[1] The result of the Select Committee's recommendations, the Extradition Act 1870, quickly influenced official and judicial decisions in *Kwok-a-Sing*; so, although the imperial Act did not formally govern the surrender of fugitives to China, it was indirectly folded into the colonial law of Hong Kong and, indeed, into the laws of other colonies with local extradition regimes. The Privy Council's decision in *Kwok-a-Sing* laid, in turn, the doctrinal foundations for the Chinese Extradition Ordinance 1889, the imperially compliant law of Hong Kong that remained in force, substantially unamended, until the end of British rule in 1997.

The new legal climate was resistant to claims of colonial exceptionalism. Post-*Kwok-a-Sing*, officials in Hong Kong could no longer tie the legalities of Chinese extradition to the needs of colonial governance. All fugitives were regarded as having substantial rights, even if this raised the ire of China, and even if some fugitives were never brought to justice. The new rules were so strict that Governor George Bowen reported a widely held belief in 1883, that 'Hong Kong will become more of an Alsatia than it even now is for the disorderly classes of Southern China' – Alsatia, like the historically contested province of Alsace, which straddled France and Germany, and more pertinently its namesake, a friary in Whitefriars, London, which sheltered debtors from prosecution until the eighteenth century.[2] Whitehall understood the colonial concern, but its newfound rigidity was driven by even bigger concerns than the reputation of Hong Kong among Chinese people or the Chinese government. As this chapter will show, officials in London were quite willing to stomach the cavalier treatment of Chinese fugitives in the absence of direct pressure from judges and politicians for closer oversight. The quiet, negotiable, and executive-led regulation of Chinese rendition was still viable even after the How Yu-teen scandal, if only barely. But the Privy Council's judgment in *Kwok-a-Sing* proved too conspicuous to ignore or overrule through legislation amid the zeitgeist of the Extradition Act 1870. *Kwok-a-Sing* thus resulted in a complete and irreversible abandonment of flexible rendition.

Early Constraints on Extradition (1842–65)

In October 1862, the Hong Kong government received a request for two Chinese fugitives on charges of 'conspiracy against the Imperial Government in Canton'. Both men were detained under the Rendition Ordinance 1850. Although they were quickly discharged by a magistrate for lack of evidence, Acting Governor William Mercer reported the case to London because he wanted to know if similar requests should be entertained in future.[3] Mercer initiated this query against the backdrop of the Taiping Rebellion (*c.* 1850–64), the civil war in China that killed over twenty million people by one account.[4] This catastrophic conflict was rooted in ethnic unrest, the gradual decline of the Qing dynasty, and the socially disruptive introduction of Christianity in China, as Philip Kuhn has argued.[5] Britain was officially neutral, though British, French, and American military officers intervened strategically to prevent Taiping forces from capturing the commercially important city of Shanghai.[6] In Hong Kong, a local ordinance of 1855 made it a crime, punishable by a fine and up to two years' imprisonment, for residents of the colony to 'assist' any faction in the Chinese conflict.[7]

Mercer understood the British aversion to extraditing political offenders, but he noted that neither the Rendition Ordinance nor Article 21 of the Treaty of Tianjin seemed to restrict the type of crimes for which fugitives may be surrendered.[8] The Colonial Office responded with caution. First, the Law Officers were consulted. They advised that it was indeed lawful for Hong Kong to surrender fugitives to China for all crimes against Chinese law, including those which 'in Europe would be described as "political offences"'.[9] Then, the Permanent Secretary, Frederic Rogers requested the Foreign Office to 'assume the responsibility' for this extraordinary legal opinion. For Rogers, 'this is a very singular state of things for which the Foreign Office is wholly responsible'. This was because it was under the Foreign Office's direction that Britain had 'adopted in respect of the barbarous

Govt. of China obligations which we scruple to miss in respect to the more civilized nations of Europe'.[10] The Foreign Office endorsed the Law Officers' opinion despite Rogers' concerns, so the Colonial Office conveyed the legal opinion to Hong Kong in April 1863.[11]

This ominous discussion alluded to how Britain had 'scrupled' to avoid problematic treaty obligations. The 'political offence exception', as it would come to be known, was a continental European innovation of the early nineteenth century. Revolutionary France was the first country to use it in treaties, and Belgium codified it domestically in 1833.[12] Britain, by contrast, did not formally recognise this legal doctrine until 1870, despite welcoming political refugees with open arms. This was because the British Crown was long regarded as powerless to remove people from the realm without express legislation, and legislation was only enacted sparingly, to implement narrowly formulated international agreements.[13] When the British government negotiated extradition with France and the United States during 1842–43, it chose to account for potentially problematic cases in an indirect way, by limiting its obligations to short lists of extraditable crimes. For example, larceny or theft was omitted from the Anglo-American Webster–Ashburton Treaty because fugitive slaves were known to steal horses and other property while escaping to freedom.[14] In January 1842, the colonial government of Upper Canada surrendered Nelson Hackett to Arkansas for stealing a pocket watch from one of his master's neighbours – an item that did not facilitate his escape from slavery.[15] Hackett's case unsettled Whitehall, but the question of whether abolitionist Britain would surrender fugitive slaves for larceny was quickly sidestepped because the Webster–Ashburton Treaty omitted larceny, restricting extradition to cases of murder, assault with intent to murder, piracy, arson, robbery, forgery, and the 'utterance' or knowing delivery of forged documents.[16] The same technique of carefully enumerating extraditable crimes was used in the 'colonial' extradition regimes of the 1840s to 1860s – colonial ordinances authorising extradition to certain countries, notably Venezuela, with whom treaties were not signed at the imperial level. Meanwhile, arrangements to extradite fugitives to other countries were either not made at all or treaties were signed but not implemented domestically; so, again, the rule against extraditing political offenders was not explicitly written down.[17]

The rise of the political offence exception was also hindered by the oblique resolution of some politically sensitive cases on technical points of procedure or jurisdiction. The cases of How Yu-teen and Kwok-a-Sing would both follow this pattern to a degree. But perhaps the most prominent earlier case of this kind was that of John Anderson, the fugitive slave from Missouri whose extradition was blocked in 1861 by the Upper Canada Court of Common Pleas. In this case, the court discharged Anderson for the technical reason that his warrant of commitment stated the vague charge of 'felonious killing' instead of the extraditable charge of murder (i.e. killing with malice aforethought). Anderson had killed a man, Seneca Diggs, who was exercising his power under the law of Missouri to apprehend fugitive slaves. It was thus difficult for anyone to make the substantive argument, without an express exception for slaves or political offenders, that Anderson's act was not murder under the Webster–Ashburton Treaty and implementing statute. Indeed, the Court of Common Pleas only reviewed Anderson's case after the Queen's Bench in Toronto had decided, controversially, that he was extraditable for murder even as a fugitive slave.[18]

Similarly, the Queen's Bench in London discharged Patrick Ternan and two other self-styled agents of the Confederate States of America in 1864, blocking their extradition to the United States on jurisdictional grounds. Ternan and his associates had hijacked the United States schooner, *Joseph L. Gerrity*, after boarding it as passengers. Since the hijacking took place on the high seas, the court decided that it amounted to piracy *jure gentium* instead of piracy within the meaning of the Webster–Ashburton Treaty. In the court's opinion, the treaty encompassed only 'piracy ... within the *exclusive* jurisdiction of the United States'.[19] So, by resolving the case in this way, the court avoided the political question of whether neutral Britain should extradite the supporters of one side of the American Civil War to the government of the other side.[20]

The early inchoateness of the political offence exception was exactly why the empire pursued statutory reform: it was a major impetus for the Select Committee of 1868. The so-called 'rule' of the exception animated legal practice, to be sure. Versions of it appeared in legal treatises, court submissions, and even abortive treaties with France (1852) and Prussia (1864).[21] But the rule was not entrenched in legislation or case law, and its boundaries were unclear because the overarching British strategy had been to 'scruple to miss' inconvenient obligations, as Frederic Rogers put it so lucidly, and this strategy had set the parameters of legal practice. Among the evidence that was presented to the Select Committee, the clearest invocation of the political offence exception *as a legal rule* occurred in a case from Trinidad. The case involved José Gregorio Monagas, son of the former Venezuelan president of the same name. The younger Monagas escaped to Trinidad in 1858 after a military coup toppled his family's political dynasty. The new government of Venezuela requested his surrender on charges of murder, but Governor Robert Keate decided that this request was politically motivated. In Keate's view, the Trinidad Ordinance of 1847 for surrendering fugitives to Venezuela was 'never intended to apply to political offenders'. By taking this position, Keate read an implied restriction into the Ordinance of 1847. To strengthen his position, however, Keate also took care to ground his decision to refuse the Venezuelan request in the Trinidad law officers' opinion that the evidence against Monagas was 'mere hearsay' and insufficient for extradition.[22]

What about the arrangement with China? The British negotiators of the Opium War and Arrow War treaties did not attempt to restrict the British obligation to surrender fugitives to China, but this was because that obligation had a substantially different origin. It was part of a complex system for dividing jurisdiction over British and Chinese subjects, as this book has shown. This treaty system was only interpreted after the fact as containing an extradition agreement. Also, officials in Hong Kong were so eager to surrender Chinese subjects for piracy and other crimes committed at sea, often without prior request from China, that they simply did not consider if some of those prisoners could have claimed political asylum.[23] Preoccupied with keeping the colonial peace, officials in Hong Kong overlooked the fact that, as Robert Antony has argued, piracy was understood in Qing China as a 'serious crime linked to treason'.[24] The Chinese view was shaped over centuries by the threat that large and heavily armed pirate fleets often posed to imperial Chinese authority, especially in times of political or economic turmoil.[25] In 1805, for example, 50,000 to 70,000 seafarers plundered Guangdong at the end of a civil war in neighbouring Annam (Vietnam), a nominal tributary state of Qing China.[26] The Opium Wars and Taiping Rebellion triggered a similar resurgence in maritime violence between the 1840s and 1860s, though this was partly counteracted by the ascendant China Station of the British Royal Navy.[27] In this context, British diplomats later admitted to being unsure if pirates were being punished in China as rebels or only as ordinary criminals who attacked people at sea 'for the sake of some free cash'.[28] These questions were raised from the mid 1860s, but not before.

In short, Whitehall was ill-equipped in 1862–63 to answer Acting Governor Mercer's question about the legality of extraditing Chinese political offenders. The uncertain state of the law was exactly why the Colonial Office hesitated to circulate the Law Officers' opinion that the political offence exception did not apply to Chinese fugitives, relenting only when the Foreign Office endorsed this course of action. The Foreign Office's decision would prove to be a mistake, as the How Yu-teen scandal broke out only two years later.

Piracy, Rebellion, and the Execution of How Yu-teen (1865)

How Yu-teen was tried and executed in Canton shortly after being extradited in May 1865. This caused a scandal in London mainly because the mode of the execution shocked the British public: it was *lingchi*, 'slicing', or 'lingering death', the ancient Chinese method that was still used in the nineteenth century for the most serious crimes in Chinese law, notably rebellion and patricide.[29] Edmund Hammond of the Foreign Office expressed the popular view that *lingchi* was akin to the medieval English punishment of hanging, drawing, and quartering – a 'practice of a barbarous age', abandoned 'as we advanced in knowledge, and became more humane'.[30] To make matters worse, British observers in Canton had wrongly identified How Yu-teen as 'Mo Wang' or 'Mo Wong', a Taiping leader who had actually died in Suzhou in 1863.[31] The *lingchi* of the misidentified 'Mo Wong' was thus reported in newspapers in Hong Kong and London. Details and embellishments were added along the way, including a key assertion that 'Mo Wong' was extradited for piracy but punished for rebellion.[32] Picking up on this point, the Liberal MP, W. H. Sykes publicly accused Acting Governor Mercer of failing to protect people who 'sought refuge under the British flag' and falling for a 'trumped up ... story of Mo-Wong being a pirate'. Sykes sympathised with the Taiping rebels owing to their Christian faith and willingness to resist Manchu oppression. He was widely known, in particular, to abhor the British government's refusal to openly support the Taiping cause.[33] So, in Sykes' view, Mercer was 'in dereliction of the solemn duty imposed upon him by the 21st Article of the Treaty [of Tianjin]'. This was supposedly because 'Mo-Wong, being a political refugee, did not, according to the usual relations between European States, fall within the category of the 21st Article at all'.[34]

The Colonial Office took action in August 1865. Mercer was told to address Sykes' allegations, and to stop surrendering Chinese subjects on piracy charges until further notice.[35] He was also told a few weeks later, before he could respond, generally to surrender prisoners to China only if he had 'ample reason for knowing' that they would not suffer 'inhumane' treatment.[36] The emphasis that these instructions placed on piracy over political offences reflected the character of the prevailing jurisprudence in Hong Kong. Whereas the rendition of Chinese political offenders had only been discussed in hypothetical terms, the rendition of Chinese pirates was an established practice that the Colonial Office had just reaffirmed in April 1865.[37] The rules of that practice had always been purely jurisdictional: Hong Kong was only prevented from using the Rendition Ordinance against Chinese pirates in cases that involved British subjects, property, or territory, as Chapter 3 has shown. Now, the fact that the first instinct of the Colonial Office was to suspend this practice suggests a newfound belief that it was the root cause of the present scandal. By exposing the *ling-chi* of How Yu-teen, Sykes probably reminded Whitehall that the legal practice in Hong Kong was in tension with the recent decision of the English Queen's Bench in *Ternan* (1864), the case of the Confederate hijackers. The Secretary of State for the Colonies, Edward Cardwell notably minuted in response to Sykes' allegations that 'it seems the Treaty of Tientsin does not apply to Pirates'.[38] Cardwell had ignored *Ternan* just four months before Sykes' exposé, when he reaffirmed the legality of Hong Kong's rendition practices in April 1865.[39]

Cardwell's latest focus on the extraditability of pirates was out of touch with public opinion, but it created space for Mercer to justify his conduct. In September 1865, Mercer argued in a report that Sykes' allegations were unfounded because 'Mo Wong' was actually How

Yu-teen, and his crime was 'not piracy but robbery from a boat within the dominions of the Emperor of China'.[40] According to the English translation of the rendition request, which Mercer received from China, How Yu-teen was charged with 'larceny and robbery' on a river near Shanghai, specifically for plundering over 3,000 silver taels from a boat chartered by a merchant, Chan Tsun-kit. How Yu-teen was also alleged to have held Chan Tsun-kit captive, though the rendition request was not framed around that particular crime.[41] As far as Sykes' allegations were concerned, therefore, Mercer explained that How Yu-teen was surrendered on a non-political charge of robbery under Chinese law. Mercer added for good measure that 'had [the crime] been piracy, we should have been forced to take cognisance of it in our own Courts, and should not have been justified in the criminal's rendition'. Again, this was not the prior practice in Hong Kong, but it was a credible view to espouse now that the prior practice was suspended. Mercer knew that his report might be made public. Indeed, he requested Whitehall to give it 'equal publicity' to Sykes' allegations against him.[42]

Mercer drew no attention to local disagreement about the nature of How Yu-teen's crime, though he did enclose a copy of the rendition proceedings in the Magistrates Court of Hong Kong. According to the proceedings, the victim of the robbery, Chan Tsun-kit, testified that How Yu-teen was 'the head of a band of pirates' who had robbed him and held him for ransom. How Yu-teen's barrister argued in response that Chan Tsun-kit's testimony disclosed only piracy, a crime justiciable in Hong Kong: he argued that there was no evidence that How Yu-teen had violated *municipal* Chinese law. This argument effectively invoked the rule in *Ternan* – that extradition was unlawful where British courts had jurisdiction to try fugitive pirates under international law. In the case of How Yu-teen, the magistrate rejected this argument for reasons that were not recorded, though he probably based his ruling on a factual finding that the robbery was committed exclusively in Chinese territorial waters (whereas the events in *Ternan* took place on the high seas). This, at least, was Mercer's understanding of the rendition hearing.[43]

Mercer's report allowed Whitehall to diffuse the scandal in London by demonstrating the factual inaccuracy of the 'Mo Wong' story. The report was presented to Parliament in early 1866, together with copies of correspondence showing that Mercer had followed due process and the Treaty of Tianjin.[44] These papers also implicitly countered Sykes' allegation that officials in Hong Kong had surrendered a political refugee. As Rogers observed at the Colonial Office, 'before them there was simply evidence of robbery on a Chinese river, without any allegation or appearance that the robbery had anything of a political character about it'. 'So,' Rogers concluded, 'I do not see that the Governor and his advisers had any alternative' – that is, any choice but to go through with the rendition. The Secretary of State, Cardwell decided for this reason to 'acquit [Mercer] of any blame in this matter'.[45]

But there was still the problem of the *lingchi*, which demonstrated that the Hong Kong government could follow the law and still be complicit in the judicial torture of a political offender. How did this happen? Jenny Day has shown in an illuminating new work that How Yu-teen was in fact a Taiping rebel, though he was not Mo Wong. Indeed, he became a leading member of the Taiping Rebellion in the 1850s, and he was commanding a rebel fleet when he attacked Chan Tsun-kit's boat in 1862, two years before the Taiping capital of Nanjing fell to the imperial Chinese army. How Yu-teen later settled in Hong Kong in 1864. So did Chan Tsun-kit. After a chance meeting with How Yu-teen, Chan Tsun-kit filed a complaint against him in Canton. Chan Tsun-kit thus gave the Chinese provincial government in Canton a golden opportunity to retrieve How Yu-teen on a robbery charge, with a view to punishing him as a rebel once he was back on Chinese soil.[46]

What happened next was crucial. First, Chinese officials suppressed evidence of How Yu-teen's Taiping affiliation. Then, they submitted a seemingly innocuous rendition request to Hong Kong through D. B. Robertson, the British Consul in Canton, with his knowledge and tacit support. Robertson admitted this in a letter to the Foreign Office of October 1865, five months after the *lingchi*.[47] The Foreign Office decided then to withhold this information from Parliament, likely because it would have cast the diplomatic service in a bad light. The records suggest that the Colonial Office also supported this decision, at least implicitly, even though the Hong Kong government was, by all indications, genuinely oblivious to the conspiracy. How Yu-teen's barrister was probably also oblivious, as he was reported to have tried but failed to elicit evidence of How Yu-teen's background while cross-examining witnesses.[48] This barrister had some experience keeping the Hong Kong government in check: he was none other than Edward Pollard, the Queen's Counsel who had helped to prevent the Peruvian coolie trafficker, Juan Pastor, from being handed over to China in 1861.[49] It seems likely, therefore, that How Yu-teen chose to conceal his own identity in what may have been a fatal miscalculation of his legal position.

Apart from clearing Mercer's name, Cardwell despatched new instructions that were tailored to protect officials in Hong Kong – and, by extension, the Crown – from future manipulation. First, the political offence exception was expressly laid down. The new governor, Richard Graves MacDonnell, was told that 'no offender is to be given up who is charged with an offence of a purely political kind'.[50] MacDonnell was informed that earlier instructions to the contrary were rescinded, as officials recalled that they had given Mercer a general permission to surrender political offenders back in 1863. Mercer never used this permission (at least, not knowingly), and Westminster also knew nothing about it, but Cardwell preferred to 'openly repudiate' it anyway.[51] Secondly, and relatedly, Governor MacDonnell was told 'not to deliver up any offender without ascertaining from the Consular or diplomatic officer through whom the requisition is presented, that the [offender] will have a fair trial, and that there is no ground for apprehending that being demanded upon one charge he will really be tried for another'.[52] This was a clear enunciation of the 'speciality' rule. It served to safeguard against the kind of conspiracy that sparked the 'Mo Wong' scandal.

Cardwell's third instruction was that the Governor of Hong Kong should have 'no cause for fearing that [any fugitive] will be subjected to torture or to any barbarous form of death'.[53] This instruction addressed *lingchi*, of course – the traitor's death in China. Again, the Governor was to liaise with the diplomat through whom the rendition request was made. The Governor was, in that sense, required to deter British diplomats from lying by omission, as Consul D. B. Robertson had done. This warning was not expressed so blatantly, but the implication was there. Next, the Governor was not to consider himself bound by any local magistrate's decision to commit an accused person for rendition. The Governor should, instead, give 'due weight to the authority of the Court on one side, and on the other to the probable consequences to the accused person'.[54] This instruction stressed the primacy of executive discretion in extradition: it stressed the imperial view that judges and magistrates had no power to compel the Crown to extradite anyone, as their proper role was rather to prevent extradition when it was legally unjustified. Finally, the Colonial Office clarified that the surrender of accused pirates to China was still suspended: all pirates were still to be tried in Hong Kong until further notice.[55]

Interlude: Towards a New Normal (1866–70)

The new restrictions on Hong Kong's rendition practice were imposed between December 1865 and January 1866. They were originally meant to be temporary because the Foreign Office had simultaneously instructed the Minister to China, Rutherford Alcock, to approach Beijing about revising the treaty provision for fugitive surrenders, Article 21 of the Treaty of Tianjin, particularly to exempt fugitives from judicial torture.[56] Alcock's negotiations failed, however: they dragged on for so long that Article 21 was never actually revised, so the temporary restrictions of 1865–66 were never revoked. Officials in Hong Kong ended up making do with the restrictions until events were overtaken by the proceedings of the 1868 Select Committee on Extradition, and by the dramatic unfolding of Kwok-a-Sing's case during 1870–71.

The Foreign Secretary, the Earl of Clarendon, recognised at the outset that Alcock's mission was a tall order. The existing Article 21 was favourable to China. Also, in seeking to renegotiate Article 21, Alcock could not risk 'any positive declaration to the Chinese government which might be construed by them into a breach of our treaty engagements'.[57] In Clarendon's view, Alcock might suggest to the Chinese that a new Article 21 would serve their interests as much as it would serve British interests. Clarendon observed, for example, that pirates captured by the Royal Navy and brought to Hong Kong did not 'take refuge in Hong Kong' under Article 21, so Britain was technically not obliged to give them up. Hong Kong had in fact given up many such pirates in previous years. But Article 21 was unclear, nonetheless. It was arguable, therefore, that 'the Article as it now stands, considered in a Chinese point of view, is inadequate for the purposes for which the Chinese government in all probability procured its insertion in the Treaty'. Clarendon surmised that, if China could be made to see this point, then it might agree to revise the article, and Alcock could then press for a guarantee against 'torturous or inhuman punishment'. This was only an idea, however. The tone of Clarendon's instructions to Alcock suggests that he realised how little Britain had to offer in exchange for what it wanted. This was so not least because the Foreign Office also had other items on its wish list, as Clarendon informed Alcock. The imperial Law Officers had suggested that a revised Article 21 should incorporate the speciality rule and the rule of double criminality, and Clarendon himself wanted Britain to have a reciprocal right of extradition – a right that Article 21 did not provide.[58]

The difficulty of Alcock's mission was also compounded by a political question that divided British officials: was it prudent or legitimate for Britain to 'interfere' with Chinese criminal procedures? Consul Robertson argued, in his usual sympathy with China, that 'it is a question how far any right exists to interfere with the legal Institutions of a Country or dictate to a Government in what mode Prisoners surrendered under Treaty stipulations shall be dealt with'.[59] But Clarendon and his Permanent Secretary, Edmund Hammond, countered that 'we do not seek to interfere with capital punishment in cases where, by the laws of China, a culprit is liable to it; but we protest against the mode of applying the punishment, and against *our* being made, by *our* surrender of criminals, partaker in practices which are repugnant to *our* customs, feelings and religion'.[60] British officials and parliamentarians had taken the same parochial attitude towards Western states, too. Although the obstacles to British cooperation with the likes of France or Prussia were not as striking as *lingchi*, Britain was no stranger to shying away from extradition treaties on account of incompatibilities in legal procedure. In the case of China, the key difference was that there was already a treaty – a treaty that, as we know, came about under different circumstances – but this was exactly why the Foreign Office wanted to revise the Chinese treaty. Clarendon argued, furthermore, that the problem of 'interference' was overblown because *lingchi* was a relatively rare punishment, and 'it is surely within the power of the Emperor of China to mitigate degrees of punishment'. For Clarendon, 'it can hardly be supposed that the Chinese Government would deny the existence of this power, or would assert the determination of the Emperor to disregard the representation of a friendly nation pleading for its exercise on behalf of the very few criminals, judging from passed experience, when it might, by their surrender, expose [them] to a cruel death'.[61]

Clarendon was correct, to a point. In May 1866, the legation in Beijing reported that Prince Gong (Kung), the former Prince Regent of China and founder of the Chinese Board of Foreign Affairs, the *Zongli Yamen*, would see to the exemption of extradited fugitives from *lingchi*. Gong would instruct provincial officials to remit cases of *lingchi* to Beijing, so that the *Zongli Yamen* could 'undertake in all such cases … to move the Emperor to commute the sentence of *ling-chih* to summary decapitation'.[62] This concession was given in response to Alcock's representation that the British government was 'most anxious to guard itself against participation in proceedings the issue of which is at variance with the laws of humanity as understood by Christian States'.[63] Alcock stressed that Prince Gong's concession amounted to taking Chinese convicts 'out of the jurisdiction of the Board of Punishments, or High Court of Justice, to which they properly belong, and [to] place them under the control of the *Yamen* of Foreign Affairs and the Throne'.[64] Alcock took pains to stress this point because Gong had not promised to suspend other practices of torture, especially as part of China's interrogation of accused persons. British officials had long known about those practices, but they had shut their eyes to them when the surrender of fugitives to China was not being scrutinised in London – when the surrender procedure was not clearly and consistently understood as extradition.[65] Now that this issue was unavoidable, Alcock felt obliged to justify his decision not to push Prince Gong about it. Surmising that interrogative torture was fundamental to Chinese law, Alcock argued that it was 'impossible to insist upon the whole of their judicial machinery and legal processes being set aside … in order to meet the views of a Foreign Government'.[66]

It happened that this issue was already looming on the ground, as Hong Kong strove to enforce the existing rendition regime under the new imperial restrictions. In April 1866, Governor MacDonnell received a request for a fugitive, Chow A-kwok, alias

Kwok Leong-hee, on a charge of robbing a pawnshop in the city of Shun Tak (Shunde), near Canton.[67] This request was handled very carefully. A hearing on 1 May led to a committal for rendition. However, MacDonnell reopened the case after Kwok Leong-hee engaged a barrister, Mitchell, who argued that his client was entitled to cross-examine the witnesses for the prosecution.[68] Two witnesses were recalled from China with Consul Robertson's assistance, and other witnesses were also summoned for a re-hearing. A witness from Shun Tak then deposed that he had known Kwok Leong-hee for many years, and that Kwok Leong-hee had 'frequented the City as a Gambler'. This and other depositions persuaded the Magistrate, John Whyte, and the Attorney General, Julian Pauncefote, that Kwok Leong-hee was not a political refugee.[69] For his part, MacDonnell also obtained a clear guarantee that Kwok Leong-hee would 'receive a fair and equitable trial ... and that neither before nor after sentence will he suffer any kind of torture or cruel punishment whatever'.[70] MacDonnell requested Robertson to obtain a revised guarantee from the Chinese Viceroy, Ruilin, after deciding that an initial guarantee by Ruilin was not a sufficiently 'comprehensive pledge'. Only after taking these meticulous steps did MacDonnell surrender Kwok Leong-hee on 5 June 1866.[71]

The Colonial Office approved MacDonnell's decision: officials agreed that he had 'fully acted up to his instructions as to rendition'.[72] This respectable precedent was dearly bought, however. In August 1866, MacDonnell learnt from Robertson that Kwok Leong-hee was still under detention and had not been convicted because he had not confessed. After receiving no further news, MacDonnell wrote to Minister Alcock in February 1867 to protest that 'the object of Her Majesty's Government was simply to prevent a refugee on British soil from being made the victim of any inhuman torture or punishment.' According to MacDonnell, 'it was never intended that notorious Criminals like Kwok Leong-hee should not merely escape all punishment for atrocious crimes, but should be enabled by withholding confession of their guilt to obtain free quarters for life at the expense of the Government whose laws they had outraged'.[73] MacDonnell was frustrated because Kwok Leong-hee was charged with a serious crime: the robbery in Shun Tak was a gang robbery, and the gang took hostages and fired at soldiers in evading arrest.[74]

Kwok Leong-hee's case demonstrated, then, that the new restrictions on rendition might yield unsatisfactory results, even though everyone implicitly agreed that they would rather see fugitives go scot-free than be complicit their torture or cruel execution. In other words, British officials would rather surrender a host of Kwok Leong-hees than a single How Yu-teen.

Alcock took more than a year to address MacDonnell's concerns because he encountered difficulties gathering information on confessions in Chinese law. He finally reported in May 1868 that he had 'arrived at the truth': under Chinese law, confessions were 'essential, and cannot be dispensed with except in very rare cases where offenders are caught red-handed in the commission of some atrocious crime, or in crimes against the Sovereign power and in active rebellion'.[75] This finding persuaded Alcock that Britain could not demand an absolute guarantee against torture in a revised Article 21 of the Treaty of Tianjin. That, for Alcock, 'would be equivalent to a Foreign power insisting that we should dispense with all evidence on oath, that is our guarantee for truth; and torture is now, as it was not so long ago in most European countries, regarded by the Chinese as the best test of truth'. Alcock argued that as 'superior' as British procedures may be, 'it is hardly possible to graft them upon the Chinese system by a treaty clause'. Such a 'dangerous experiment' would only create a legal system that was neither Chinese nor British: it would be a 'hybrid system made up of contradictory elements ... wanting in all the conditions essential to the administration of justice in either the one or the other'. Alcock argued for these reasons that Britain should accept Prince Gong's extra-treaty concession on exempting fugitives from *lingchi*, abandoning further attempts to 'interfere' with Chinese legal procedures.[76]

The Foreign Office suspended the revision of Article 21 at this stage.[77] But it would likely have done so even without Alcock's exhortation, as the Select Committee on Extradition had convened on 1 May 1868 and treaty negotiations with other countries were already on hold. Furthermore, the Select Committee hearings threw up the possibility that Britain would stop signing extradition treaties altogether. This was because the Select Committee considered a proposal, made by Hammond of the Foreign Office, to authorise the Crown to extradite fugitives without treaty arrangements, under universally applicable rules that Parliament would lay down – rules that would include the political offence exception.[78] Hammond's proposal to dispense with treaties was ultimately not taken up. Enacted in August 1870, the Extradition Act 1870 required the Crown to make international 'arrangements' for extradition, and then to apply the Act to each 'arrangement' by Order in Council.[79] Still, Parliament's intentions were unclear during 1868–69, so this was almost certainly why the Foreign Office did not do anything concrete about Article 21 of the Treaty of Tianjin.

The Foreign Office would have noticed, too, that the Select Committee put Article 21 directly in conversation with other extradition agreements. The case of How Yu-teen, or 'Mo Wong', was examined alongside other politically sensitive cases, including *Monagas* (1859), *Anderson* (1861), and *Ternan* (1864), all of which demonstrated the need for imperial reform. From the cases from the Western world, the Select Committee discovered that the political offence exception was at most 'implied' in each treaty, as Hammond admitted, 'because the crimes for which we can give persons up are specified, and a crime committed for a political motive is not included in the specification'.[80] From *How Yu-teen*, by comparison, the Select Committee learnt that the Treaty of Tianjin was even more poorly drafted. Henry Holland of the Colonial Office testified that the British obligation to surrender Chinese fugitives was unlimited 'upon the face of the treaty'. In practice, as Holland observed, all restrictions were 'left entirely to the Colonial Government [of Hong Kong]' to enforce according to informal instructions from the Colonial Office.[81] The precariousness of all these existing practices prompted the Select Committee to favour legislative clarity and uniformity, hence its recommendation for a comprehensive imperial statute. All told, it was clear where the winds of legal change were blowing: a bespoke approach to Chinese extradition was becoming less viable by the day.

Mutiny, Piracy, and the Two Arrests of Kwok-a-Sing (1871)

Barely had the Extradition Act 1870 been enacted, when Kwok-a-Sing and around forty other Chinese indentured emigrants, or coolies, mutinied on the French ship, *Nouvelle Pénélope*, five days into its voyage from Macau to Callao, Peru. The *Nouvelle Pénélope* had left Macau on 30 September 1870 with a crew of eighteen. It was carrying 310 coolies, a third of whom would later claim that they were coerced or deceived into signing contracts of indenture. The mutineers killed the ship's captain, chief mate, and seven other crewmen on 4 October. They made the remaining crew turn the ship around, looted the ship, and finally abandoned it near Tien Pak (Dianbai) in Guangdong, 180 miles west of Macau. The people who were still on the ship were then rounded up by Chinese officers assisted by the French Consul in Macau. Most of these survivors were set free, but a few were sent to Hong Kong with instructions to report any fugitive mutineers to the local authorities. This was how Kwok-a-Sing was found. As one of several leaders of the mutiny, he was easy to identify. Witnesses had seen him on the poop deck of the *Nouvelle Pénélope*, giving orders in the dead captain's clothes.[82]

Kwok-a-Sing's case would soon entwine every strand of jurisprudence that Britain had spun over thirty years to deal with crimes committed by Chinese subjects. Events began when one of Kwok-a-Sing's co-mutineers, Chun A-sing, was detained in early January 1871 under the Rendition Ordinance of 1850 on a charge of murder under Chinese law. The Rendition Ordinance was still in force because the Extradition Act 1870 had left the law of Hong Kong untouched: the Extradition Act had repealed and replaced the imperial statutes that governed Britain's empire-wide treaties of extradition with the United States, France, and Denmark, but Parliament had opted to let the Crown decide how 'colonial' regimes of extradition should be harmonised with the new imperial framework.[83]

It was, as a result, pursuant to the Rendition Ordinance that Chun A-sing was brought before a magistrate on 13 January 1871 and delivered to Canton the next morning.[84] The Lieutenant Governor of Hong Kong, Henry Whitfield, duly authorised the rendition, but the speed of these proceedings startled John Smale, the colony's liberal and abrasive Chief Justice.[85] Smale reminded officials privately about 'the case of Mo-Wong' while impressing upon them that the *Nouvelle Pénélope* mutiny raised 'very many points of law', which 'ought to be discussed on a Habeas Corpus'. Smale argued, crucially, that the *Nouvelle Pénélope* 'engaged in the Macao Coolie *Slave* Trade', so 'every man coerced in her had an inalienable right to seek by any means (even by killing men) his liberty'.[86] Smale urged officials to bring Chun A-sing back from Canton, but he was told curtly that this was impossible.[87]

Information on Kwok-a-Sing emerged five days later, amid this simmering quarrel over the political and procedural boundaries of extradition. Wary of Smale's scrutiny, the colonial government detained Kwok-a-Sing initially for being 'dangerous to the peace and good order of the Colony', pursuant to a security ordinance of 1857.[88] This ordinance authorised the deportation of Chinese detainees to China. It was a powerful and all-purpose instrument of colonial ordering, as Chapter 2 has shown. Then, only after China requested his rendition for murder, specifically for killing Captain le Vigoureux of the *Nouvelle Pénélope*, did the colonial government pivot to detaining Kwok-a-Sing under the Rendition Ordinance. France also lodged a request, but Lieutenant Governor Whitfield understood that the French Consul in Macau wanted China to deal with Kwok-a-Sing. Whitfield noted that the French request was only meant to 'facilitate' the Chinese request, or to serve as a backup in case the Chinese request fell through.[89]

An extradition hearing was therefore held between late January and early February 1871 – a more thorough hearing this time around. The magistrate, Charles May, questioned witnesses and heard the arguments of Kwok-a-Sing's attorneys, Edmund Sharp and J. J. Francis. Sharp was first engaged by the local Chinese community to represent Kwok-a-Sing, but Francis took over after Sharp joined the colonial government as Crown Solicitor. The government later discovered that Chief Justice Smale had taken it upon himself to brief Sharp, telling him, privately, that this was 'eminently a case for a Habeas Corpus'. Sharp conveyed Smale's sentiments to Francis, so Francis applied for the writ after Kwok-a-Sing was (predictably) committed to Victoria Gaol on 7 February to await rendition to China.[90]

The case became very complicated at this stage. While Kwok-a-Sing's rendition to China stood on a knife-edge, Whitfield made preparations for an alternate proceeding: he assessed the legality of surrendering Kwok-a-Sing to France instead of China. The Colonial Office had last approved a similar course of action in 1850 in response to the coolie mutiny on the French ship, *Albert*. Then, as we saw in Chapter 3, another mutiny on the American ship, *Robert Bowne*, caused the imperial Law Officers to advise in 1852 that any mutineer on a ship on the high seas could lawfully be surrendered to the ship's flag country.[91] This legal opinion was still on file in Hong Kong, but Whitfield was unsure if it was still valid in light of the conflicting authority of *Ternan* (which held that high-seas mutineers were pirates *jure gentium* and therefore not extraditable).[92]

Whitfield was also unsure if the 1843 extradition treaty with France was still active. This was a reasonable apprehension because France had almost terminated the treaty during the winter of 1865–66 on the grounds that it was ineffectual. At the time, the Foreign Office mollified the French government by getting Parliament to enact a temporary statute making authenticated copies of French depositions admissible at British extradition hearings without oral evidence.[93] This statute expired after twelve months, but the French crisis later blew over when the Extradition Act made foreign depositions permanently admissible: the perceived risks of this procedural concession were now offset by the political offence exception and speciality rule.[94] Having not received news that the Extradition Act had saved the French treaty, Whitfield consulted Whitehall on 21 February 1871, while also inquiring about the tension between the *Robert Bowne* and *Ternan* precedents.[95]

Whitfield obtained a reply in a month by making use of the new telegraph station in Singapore, which had just become operational in 1870.[96] A telegraph cable would later reach Hong Kong in June 1871, enabling near instant communication with London whenever the expense was justified.[97] Whitfield's telegram of 21 February was quite elliptical, however. It did not reveal that Kwok-a-Sing was still being detained for rendition to China, nor did it mention Smale's political views on the coolie trade.[98] These omissions caused the Colonial Office to misjudge the situation until further details got through by regular post. The Colonial Office's telegraphic reply was equally fragmented: it did not mention that *Ternan* no longer applied to treaties implemented under the Extradition Act. The imperial law had changed because the Extradition Act had made 'piracy by the law of nations' extraditable, while clarifying more generally that any concurrent British jurisdiction over an extraditable crime was no bar to extradition.[99] The Colonial Office did not mention this: officials telegraphed, instead, only that the French treaty was 'still in force' and the Law Officers' opinion on the *Robert Bowne* case was 'doubtful if [the] crime was piracy, correct if murder'.[100] Much like Whitfield's initial query, this message was vague and misleading. Nevertheless, it embodied the complexity of the unfolding dispute, showing how Kwok-a-Sing's case was centred on two intersecting questions, both of which had strong political overtones. First, the case raised the question of how mutinies should even be framed in law; second, it raised the question of whether the rendition of fugitives to China was or ought to be governed by the same rules as the extradition of fugitives to France and the United States.

The habeas corpus application against Kwok-a-Sing's rendition to China was argued at the Supreme Court of Hong Kong in February and March 1871. Smale granted the writ: the *Hong Kong Daily Press* published his judgment on 29 March.[101] The most controversial part of this judgment was Smale's opinion that Kwok-a-Sing had committed no crime at all. Smale compared Kwok-a-Sing's case to the cases of *Anderson* (1861) and the *Creole* (1841), deciding on that basis that Kwok-a-Sing was not liable to rendition as he was 'under unlawful coercion', so he had 'a right to take life to free himself from such constraint on his personal liberty'. In Smale's opinion, it was immaterial that Kwok-a-Sing did not claim to have been coerced or deceived into boarding the *Nouvelle Pénélope*, unlike some other people on the ship. This was because no one could 'become a slave even by his own consent', and slaves included 'all persons holden in servitude as pledges for debt'.[102] This radical ruling impugned the legality of the entire coolie trade. Coolie ships were still heavily dependent on Hong Kong for food and nautical supplies in 1871.[103] The Chinese Passengers Act 1855 (discussed in Chapter 3) prohibited the crews of coolie ships from installing cages and other coercive fittings within British territory; however, it was still British policy that mere indentured servitude, entered voluntarily and unattended by mistreatment, was not a form of slavery, and any abuses perpetrated in Macau and elsewhere were beyond British control.[104] Smale challenged this policy in his judgment. In doing so, he challenged the empire itself.

The colonial government had a different view. Where Smale saw only slaves fighting for freedom, Lieutenant Governor Whitfield and his Attorney General, Julian Pauncefote, saw possible criminals exploiting the coolie trade for personal gain.[105] This was because the

British consulate in Canton had received intelligence suggesting that the mutiny on the *Nouvelle Pénélope* might really have been an organised hijacking. There was evidence, at least, that several mutineers went back to Macau. They were later arrested in a coolie barracoon, 'which they had re-entered for the purpose of being reshipped'. One detainee even confessed to having staged two other mutinies by posing as a coolie: the *Nouvelle Pénélope* was apparently his third conquest.[106] It was possible, therefore, that Kwok-a-Sing was involved in a scheme of this kind. Officials in Hong Kong were likely concerned, either way, about the wider problem of hijackings at sea. This problem had emerged in the late 1860s as a side effect of the suppression of traditional piracy by British and Chinese forces. Britain and China had agreed to 'concert measures' for suppressing piracy under the Treaty of Tianjin, and China had done its part by assembling a fleet of steam warships in Guangdong by 1869.[107] This Chinese fleet pulled its weight in anti-piracy operations, while the Royal Navy continued to make its presence felt.[108] The piratical gangs of Guangdong were increasingly pushed off the open seas as a result, but they also launched more covert attacks in substitution – mutinies and hijackings, which no amount of naval power could defeat.[109] The evolving problem of Chinese piracy was likely why the intelligence on the *Nouvelle Pénélope* troubled officials in Hong Kong. It was why officials regarded Smale's abolitionist narrative of the mutiny as reckless and naïve.

Smale, for his part, also gave other reasons for discharging Kwok-a-Sing – reasons that hewed closer to legal orthodoxy than his ruling on the coolie trade. First, he addressed the contested framing of the mutiny. He decided that Kwok-a-Sing's crime, 'if anything', was piracy *jure gentium*, so Kwok-a-Sing was not extraditable to China according to *Ternan*. Smale regarded this as a secondary issue, but it would prove decisive on appeal, as we shall see. Second, and finally, Smale decided that the Rendition Ordinance 1850, under which Kwok-a-Sing was detained, was 'inoperative' because it implemented the 1843 Treaty of the Bogue, but that treaty had been replaced by the 1858 Treaty of Tianjin. Since the rendition clause in the new treaty (Article 21) was not implemented under any other legislation, Smale decided that the Governor of Hong Kong was powerless to surrender fugitives to China. Smale believed that this conclusion cohered with the Extradition Act 1870, which specified that any Order in Council applying the Act to an international arrangement 'shall not remain in force for any longer period than the arrangement [itself]'.[110] Smale added, notably, that 'the principles and provisions of the Extradition Act ... are such that if the Treaty of 1858 were now for the first time to be carried into effect by Order in Council under that Act, the provisions would be very different from those of [the Rendition Ordinance 1850]'.[111] 'Very different,' indeed, because the times had changed and the law of Hong Kong had clearly not caught up.

Smale discharged Kwok-a-Sing on 18 April 1871, prompting an immediate response from the colonial government.[112] Whitfield activated his backup plan: he had Kwok-a-Sing rearrested 'within a gunshot' of the Supreme Court, upon a warrant issued under the Extradition Act, with a view to extraditing him to France.[113] Whitfield was able to use the Extradition Act because it vested the same executive powers of extradition that British Secretaries of State wielded in England in the governors of all overseas British dependencies.[114] Meanwhile, the Attorney General, Pauncefote prepared an ordinance 'to remove Doubts as to the Application of [the Rendition Ordinance 1850]'.[115] This declaratory ordinance was later enacted in May 1871 to little fanfare. It formally applied the Rendition Ordinance to Article 21 of the Treaty of Tianjin, thus overruling Smale's judgment on this issue, at least for future cases.[116]

A major dispute between the government and Supreme Court of Hong Kong was now well under way. The government endeavoured to bring Kwok-a-Sing to justice, but the chief justice maintained that he was a fugitive slave. Events took another turn on 25 April, when the French Vice Consul in Hong Kong, C. L. de la Forest, withdrew his extradition request. Having read Smale's judgment on the Chinese request, de la Forest explained that he would not pursue an unfavourable case just to invite another round of 'unjust conclusions' against the *Nouvelle Pénélope*.[117] Pauncefote then decided to charge Kwok-a-Sing with piracy *jure gentium*, following Smale's decision that Kwok-a-Sing's conduct amounted to this crime 'if it amounted to any crime at all'.[118] Kwok-a-Sing was accordingly kept under detention while Pauncefote travelled to Macau to collect evidence for a piracy trial. The Portuguese governor of Macau, Antonio Sergio de Souza, was happy to assist because his own reputation was on the line: he promised to furnish witnesses and documents 'to prove the incorrectness of the Statement that the Coolies were kidnapped'.[119]

But Smale refused to try Kwok-a-Sing for piracy. When Kwok-a-Sing's attorney, J. J. Francis applied for another writ of habeas corpus, Smale seized the opportunity to discharge Kwok-a-Sing for a second time on 22 May. Francis argued, and Smale agreed, that Kwok-a-Sing had been detained twice for 'the same felonious acts', so his second detention violated the Habeas Corpus Act 1679.[120] Smale decided that, although the charge of piracy differed from that of murder, both charges were framed around nearly identical facts surrounding the death of Captain le Vigoureux.[121] In discharging Kwok-a-Sing on this basis, however, Smale also issued another sweeping dictum accusing British officials of turning a blind eye to the suffering of Chinese 'slaves'. An El Salvadoran coolie ship, *Dolores Ugarte* (also known as *Don Juan*) was destroyed in early May in a fire at sea, not far from Macau, after a failed mutiny.[122] As news trickled in that several hundred coolies had perished, Smale used this incident to bolster his ruling that all indentured migrants were slaves under English law. 'Being prisoners,' he declared once again, 'they have a right to regain their freedom by any means in their power.'[123]

The dispute in Hong Kong finally spiralled out of control in the summer of 1871. As Kwok-a-Sing slipped through the colonial government's fingers, he brought an action against Pauncefote for damages of £500 for unlawful detention, pursuant to the Habeas Corpus Act. Furious at this move, Pauncefote speculated that the sum of £500 was chosen to prevent an appeal to the Privy Council, since any larger sum would have triggered an automatic right of appeal.[124] But the underlying problem was that this action for damages was also in Smale's jurisdiction, and Pauncefote and Whitfield were now convinced that Smale was dangerously partisan. Whitfield even pleaded with the Colonial Office to suspend Smale in June, not only to save Pauncefote from a potentially ruinous verdict, but also to enable Kwok-a-Sing to be tried for piracy.[125] The Colonial Office had no time to react. The action against Pauncefote went to trial in July, and Smale confirmed the government's suspicions of his partiality: he tried to bully the jury into finding against Pauncefote.[126] This backfired, however, as the jury dismissed the case and Whitfield interpreted Smale's unprofessional behaviour as further proof that he was unfit to be Chief Justice.

After gathering some hearsay evidence that Smale had gone so far as to instigate Kwok-a-Sing's attorney, Francis, to sue Pauncefote in the first place, Whitfield repeated his request for an imperial inquiry into Smale's conduct.[127]

The Colonial Office would eventually decide not to discipline Smale, partly because it was never proved that he had conspired with Francis, and partly for the arbitrary reason that he was difficult to replace at short notice.[128] Nevertheless, the Law Officers of the Crown were consulted in July 1871 about the viability of appealing Smale's decisions to discharge Kwok-a-Sing.[129] In taking this path, the Colonial Office was swayed by Pauncefote and Whitfield's frustration with Smale's forceful activism, and also by its own fear that Smale's judgments would set Hong Kong up as a 'safe refuge' for mutineers of every stripe. The Parliamentary Under-Secretary, E. H. Knatchbull-Hugessen, noted that Smale's 'doctrine' equating the coolie trade with slavery was 'not a proposition which can be maintained, even although we may admit that much illegality and cruelty probably goes on under cover of a legitimate trade'.[130] By August, it was also clear to Knatchbull-Hugessen that the events in Hong Kong had 'the seeds of a great row' and only an appeal to the Privy Council could restore order to the colony.[131] Other officials agreed that their priority was not to put Kwok-a-Sing on trial, but rather to address the controversial issues raised by Smale.[132] Indeed, all indications were that Kwok-a-Sing had absconded. But the Secretary of State, the 1st Earl of Kimberley, decided to press on with appealing Smale's habeas corpus decisions after the Law Officers advised that the Crown was well placed to do so.[133] Kimberley intimated that a colonial judge could not be allowed to dictate imperial policy on the Macau coolie trade. 'We must clear up the question of law,' he noted, 'before we deal with the question of policy, which is quite another matter. I think it will turn out that Mr Smale has confounded the two questions.'[134]

Imperial Appeal (1873)

Attorney General of Hong Kong v. *Kwok-a-Sing* was the ninth appeal from the Supreme Court of Hong Kong to the Judicial Committee of the Privy Council. It was the first to involve a Chinese person, as earlier appeals had only revolved around European settlers and corporate litigants.[135] *Kwok-a-Sing* was thus a milestone in the deepening of British rule over Hong Kong, in the sense that issues affecting the colony's large Chinese population were finally being addressed by judges in the metropole. It is also significant that earlier disputes over the Chinese rendition agreement did not produce any formal case law. Kwok-a-Sing was the first China-bound fugitive to be discharged on habeas corpus, so his case was the first true test of Crown practice in open court. In 1861, by contrast, Smale's predecessor, William Adams declined to discharge the Peruvian coolie trafficker, Juan Pastor. Chief Justice Adams opted to raise his doubts about Pastor's extraditability to China privately with Governor Robinson, allowing Robinson to remit the question to London while keeping Pastor in detention. Pastor was still discharged in the end, as we saw in Chapter 3. But he was discharged by executive discretion and not by judicial decree. Not so for Kwok-a-Sing, hence the legal milestone.

The Privy Council granted leave to appeal in February 1872, heard arguments in May 1873, and gave its judgment in June 1873.[136] First, the Privy Council upheld Smale's decision to discharge Kwok-a-Sing from his detention under the Rendition Ordinance 1850. But the Privy Council decided this point only on the narrow grounds that the charge against Kwok-a-Sing, for 'the murder of a Frenchman on board a French ship ... on the high seas', fell beyond the scope of the Rendition Ordinance. Speaking for the Privy Council, Lord Justice George Mellish noted that the Rendition Ordinance was difficult to interpret in light of the 'extreme generality' of its provision for fugitives to be surrendered for 'any Crime or Offence against the laws of China'. 'Some limitation must be placed upon the meaning of [these] words,' said Mellish. Otherwise, 'every Chinese who had done something which the law of China treats as a political offence, or ... anything which the law of China treats as criminal, though the law of all European countries treats as it as innocent, might be given up'.[137]

Mellish reasoned that Article 21 of the Treaty of Tianjin was intended to deter 'ordinary' criminals, rather than political offenders, from taking refuge in Hong Kong; so, in implementing Article 21, the Rendition Ordinance 'ought to be confined to those ordinary crimes and offences which are punishable by the laws of all nations, and which are not peculiar to the laws of China'. Now, any law of China that penalised Chinese subjects for killing people on foreign soil or foreign ships also struck the Privy Council as 'peculiar' in this sense. For the purposes of rendition, Chinese extraterritorial laws were 'peculiar' because 'the general principle of criminal jurisprudence is that the quality of the act done depends on the law of the place where it is done'. If British officials were to depart from this principle – if they were to surrender anyone to China under an extraterritorial law of China – then that might expose the person to punishment not countenanced by the law of the *locus delicti*. In Kwok-a-Sing's case, it might cause him to be punished in ways that French law would not permit. In other cases, Chinese law might effectively be allowed to override English law. For the Privy Council, this was unacceptable because it might be tantamount to exposing people to political persecution or other proceedings repugnant to English law.[138]

The Privy Council's decision to exclude political and extraterritorial crimes from the Rendition Ordinance is interesting because it was accompanied by a decision to tiptoe around the politics of the coolie trade. Since the Privy Council was already affirming Smale's ruling that Kwok-a-Sing was not extraditable to China, it decided that it 'need not give any opinion' on the rest of Smale's first judgment (of 29 March 1871). Mellish simply noted that 'their Lordships do not agree ... that the *Nouvelle Pénélope* was a slave ship, and that Kwok-a-Sing and the other coolies, who acted with him, were justified in killing the captain and the French sailors'.[139] This was for evidential reasons, as Mellish foregrounded the evidence that most if not all of the *Nouvelle Pénélope* mutineers were willing emigrants. Smale, of course, had disregarded this evidence since he equated slavery with indentured servitude. By ignoring Smale's capacious idea of slavery, the Privy Council implicitly discredited it, while steering clear of a wider assessment of the coolie trade.

It is also interesting, in the same vein, that the Privy Council refused to decide whether the Rendition Ordinance had duly implemented Article 21 of the Treaty of Tianjin. The Crown argued that although the Rendition Ordinance referred only to the abrogated Treaty of the Bogue (1843), that old treaty was 'in reality included in the new treaty'. In any case, the Crown argued that any ambiguity was settled by the 'declaratory' ordinance that was enacted after Smale issued his first judgment. In response, Mellish tried pushing back, arguing that if enforced retrospectively against Kwok-a-Sing, the declaratory ordinance was 'substantially an Act of Attainder': a legislative pronouncement of Kwok-a-Sing's guilt without judicial due process. In Mellish's view, unelected colonial legislators had no jurisdiction to make such an oppressive law, as even the Queen could not enact certain colonial laws without Parliament's consent. 'She cannot give a power which deprives English subjects of their rights,' Mellish suggested. 'She cannot give a power, for instance, to make torture lawful in Hong Kong' – only Parliament could. The Law Officers of the Crown countered, however, that '[w]e are not prepared to say she cannot, unless you find an Act of the Imperial Legislature cutting short that power'.[140]

The Law Officers' rationale was that the Crown's legislative power in colonies without elected legislatures was subordinate only to the will of Parliament. Since Parliament had not legislated on the Chinese rendition agreement, all relevant ordinances enacted by Crown-appointed legislators in Hong Kong were legally valid. In this way, this discussion at the Privy Council threatened to turn the appeal into a constitutional dispute. It threatened to provoke an adjudication on colonialism itself – on the embarrassing situation that the Crown was often able to make colonial laws that offended metropolitan sensibilities simply because Parliament was inattentive. The messy rendition law of Hong Kong was a case in point – the *lingchi* scandal of 1865 was still in recent memory – but the constitutional cause of this legal mess was even more juridically inconvenient. It is not surprising, therefore, that the Privy Council avoided this issue in its judgment. The Privy Council certainly seemed unwilling to over-decide the question of Kwok-a-Sing's liability to rendition to China.

Having affirmed but tempered Smale's first decision to discharge Kwok-a-Sing, the Privy Council proceeded to overrule his second decision – his decision to prevent Kwok-a-Sing from being tried in Hong Kong for piracy. In the Privy Council's opinion, Smale was wrong to decide that the second arrest of Kwok-a-Sing violated the Habeas Corpus Act. This was because the Act only applied 'when the second arrest is substantially for the same cause as the first, so that the return to the second writ raises ... the same question with reference to the validity of the grounds of detention as the first'.[141] So, the validity of the first arrest of Kwok-a-Sing depended on the ambit of the Rendition Ordinance: the first arrest was *unlawful* because the Ordinance was not used correctly. But the validity of the second arrest depended on different factors: the second arrest was *lawful* because piracy *jure gentium* was justiciable in Hong Kong and there was enough evidence to commit Kwok-a-Sing for trial. There was, specifically, enough prima facie evidence of 'a felonious, that is a piratical, intention ... on the part of Kwok-a-Sing fit to be left to a jury'; so, by this logic, Smale was wrong to block the piracy trial. This decision of the Privy Council was consistent with its opinion that Kwok-a-Sing was not liable to rendition to China for piracy *jure gentium* since that offence was 'not an offence against the law of China within the meaning of the [Rendition] Ordinance'. As Mellish explained, 'if [Kwok-a-Sing] is punishable by the law of China, he is only so punishable because he has committed an act of piracy which, *jure gentium*, is justiciable everywhere'.[142]

By resolving *Kwok-a-Sing* in this way, the Privy Council brought the law on China-bound fugitives closer to the standards of the imperial Extradition Act 1870. The political offence exception was read tactfully into the inconveniently superficial Rendition Ordinance. The wider ruling that the Rendition Ordinance only applied to crimes 'punishable by the laws of all nations' also mirrored the codified rule of double criminality in the Extradition Act. These pronouncements supplemented and formalised the ad hoc restrictions that Whitehall had imposed on Hong Kong after the *lingchi* scandal of 1865. They ushered in a new era of colonial practice, in which metropolitan standards of extradition reigned supreme.

Aftermath: Formalisation and Harmonisation (1873–89)

Kwok-a-Sing spurred Whitehall into pursuing further legislative reforms. The coolie trade was the first order of business: the Colonial Office directed the new Governor of Hong Kong, Arthur Kennedy (1872–77), to explore further measures for protecting Chinese migrants in 1872, even before the Privy Council heard the appeal. This move embodied the intention of the Secretary of State, the Earl of Kimberley, not to conflate the rectification of the law and policy of the British involvement in the Macau coolie trade. Stakeholders in Hong Kong were invited to make suggestions, as Whitehall considered all options short of prohibition – short of seizing all coolie ships and prosecuting their crews as slavers (which, predictably, was the preferred solution of Chief Justice Smale).[143] Further discussions led in 1873 to the enactment of two colonial ordinances, which subjected coolie ships visiting Hong Kong to higher standards of passenger welfare.[144] More importantly, a third ordinance prohibited colonial residents and British subjects from supplying coolie ships in any way, effectively cutting off the coolie traders' only reliable source of supplies for transpacific voyages.[145] Meanwhile, Britain and China pressured Portugal into purging the root causes of coolie mutinies by ending the Macau coolie trade altogether: this was achieved by March 1874.[146] China, in particular, had long opposed the Portuguese facilitation of indentured emigration at Macau, but Portugal finally gave in after the British reforms of 1873 deepened its diplomatic isolation and eroded its economic incentive to preserve the legal status quo.[147] Attorney General Pauncefote's view of *Kwok-a-Sing* was thus vindicated, as he had argued in 1871 that the Macau coolie trade should be 'abolished by legitimate means' – through legislation and diplomacy – and not by 'hold[ing] out Pirates and Murderers to public commendation'.[148]

As for the law of extradition, Whitehall took stock of it in 1874. *Kwok-a-Sing* did not settle everything, even as a landmark precedent. The Hong Kong Rendition Ordinance still lacked a list of extraditable crimes, for a start. The Privy Council had no choice but to take a 'blacklist' approach of excluding certain types of crimes from the Rendition Ordinance, but Pauncefote proposed the enactment of a schedule of extraditable crimes in the style of the Extradition Act. Crimes listed in such a schedule would be defined according to English law, so the scope of Chinese rendition would no longer be indefinite. Indeed, Pauncefote proposed to apply the Extradition Act directly to the Treaty of Tianjin by Order in Council, though he also noted, in the alternative, that a colonial bill to amend the Rendition Ordinance would permit the imposition of even stricter rules than those in the imperial Act. Pauncefote mooted the latter, 'colonial' option because he believed that magistrates in Hong Kong were rarely able to detect perjury in extradition hearings. Surmising that this increased the risk of scandals, he suggested replacing public rendition hearings in Hong Kong with closed-door hearings before the colony's Executive Council.[149] As it happened, the Colonial Office rejected this idea for lack of precedent. But the rest of Pauncefote's report planted a seed of enthusiasm for codification, which later germinated into the Chinese Extradition Ordinance 1889.[150]

Things moved quickly in 1875, after Governor Kennedy reported the arrest of two Chinese subjects for hijacking a British steamer, *Spark*, in Chinese territorial waters. The hijackers seized the ship between Canton and Macau, killing several crewmen in the process. They were arrested in Hong Kong and committed for trial on charges of piracy *jure gentium*. The magistrate, Charles May, who was also the magistrate in *Kwok-a-Sing*, decided that the judgment of the Privy Council prevented him from issuing warrants of committal under the Rendition Ordinance.[151] The piracy trial of the *Spark* hijackers later collapsed after the Chinese government, claiming jurisdiction of the case, refused to send witnesses to testify in Hong Kong.[152] Nevertheless, Kennedy wanted to know if the case was handled correctly, as a matter of law. Kennedy's query thus reached the desk of the ubiquitous Pauncefote, who was now an Assistant Undersecretary at the Colonial Office.[153] Pauncefote had just completed a stint as Chief Justice of the Leeward Islands: his work in Hong Kong had served him well, so well that he would later be appointed Legal Adviser at the Foreign Office, then Permanent Secretary at the Foreign Office, then Ambassador to the United States.[154] In March 1875, he agreed that the *Spark* hijackers were not extraditable in light of *Kwok-a-Sing*, though he argued that they should have been tried for robbery and murder under British law and not piracy *jure gentium*. Pauncefote made this argument because he believed that the Governor of Hong Kong should ideally be allowed to extradite fugitives to China for piracy *jure gentium*. He also believed that the colony's Legislative Council should overrule *Kwok-a-Sing* on the issue of concurrent jurisdiction, just as Parliament had overruled *Ternan* with the Extradition Act. In other words, Pauncefote had identified yet another loose thread from *Kwok-a-Sing*, which he believed needed tying up.[155]

Pauncefote's opinion on the *Spark* case triggered imperial instructions for the Hong Kong government to draft a new Chinese Extradition Ordinance. This instruction was carried out by the new Attorney General of Hong Kong, John Bramston, in August 1875. Bramston's draft ordinance imported key features of the Extradition Act – legal ideas now well accepted throughout British officialdom.

The draft contained a provision authorising extradition in cases of concurrent jurisdiction, a schedule of extraditable crimes, as well as provisions for the political offence exception and rule of double criminality.[156] When assessing Bramston's draft ordinance for 'conformity' with the Extradition Act, Whitehall also directed legislators in Hong Kong to include two other safeguards, which, again, were now imperial doctrine: the speciality rule and a guarantee that fugitives would have at least fifteen days to apply for habeas corpus from the date of their committal for extradition.[157]

These developments demonstrate that, by 1876, there was no more scope for Hong Kong to revive its flexible practice of rendition. Imperial anxiety over the deviance of the Chinese rendition regime had now snowballed into a rigid expectation of conformity – an expectation that did not tolerate counterarguments premised on concerns of substantive justice or diplomatic practicality. All this is clear because Bramston's draft ordinance of 1875 was eventually enacted in 1889 with only a few amendments: Whitehall did not reverse its policy of legal harmonisation in the intervening fourteen years. Incidentally, the fourteen-year delay between 1875 and 1889 was caused by an administrative oversight. After being reviewed in London during 1875–76, Bramston's draft ordinance was forwarded to the British legation in Beijing with a view to obtaining the Chinese government's views on it. However, this copy of the draft was 'never again heard of', and no one followed up on the matter.[158] As a result, the Hong Kong government relied on the authority of *Kwok-a-Sing* to answer several Chinese extradition requests in the 1880s, and officials forgot about the draft ordinance until Governor William Des Voeux brought it to imperial attention in 1888.[159]

Des Voeux's intention was actually to modify the draft ordinance in favour of more permissive extradition. In a sixty-five-page despatch to the Colonial Office, he argued that the forthcoming Chinese Extradition Ordinance should dispense with the rule of double criminality, and also that it should provide a simplified extradition procedure for Chinese fugitives of less than two years' residency in Hong Kong. Recent immigrants should not have the benefit of extradition hearings at all, argued Des Voeux: they should be extraditable solely upon official Chinese assurances of their guilt, coupled with promises that they were not indentured servants or political offenders. Des Voeux proposed these retrograde reforms because he felt that the 'expensive precautions' taken in Hong Kong since 1865 were 'really useless' at evaluating extradition requests, even as they irritated the Chinese government whenever fugitives were discharged. In Des Voeux's view, the result was a failure of justice and diplomacy. A stringent Chinese Extradition Ordinance was likely to 'render Hong Kong a safe refuge for the criminals of all China', he argued. It was likely to create 'an Alsatia, an unfit residence for other than criminals, and a standing nuisance to the neighbouring Empire', all while risking the 'permanent alienation of ... a valuable ally'. For Des Voeux, Britain did not have 'any right to evade the obligation which we have incurred by Treaty, unless we are prepared to openly denounce that Treaty'.[160]

Proffered in 1888, Governor Des Voeux's arguments were all too familiar. His fear of founding a Chinese Alsatia – a haven for fugitives – harked back to when pirates flooded Hong Kong in the 1850s, and his unwillingness to be seen as breaching the Treaty of Tianjin echoed imperial sentiments that predated the *lingchi* scandal of 1865. However, Des Voeux's arguments cut no ice with the former Legal Adviser to the Colonial Office, Henry Holland, who was now Lord Knutsford and Secretary of State for the Colonies. For Knutsford, the forthcoming Chinese Extradition Ordinance was little more than a means of 'assimilating' the law of Hong Kong with imperial law.[161] Other officials agreed, as they summarily dismissed Des Voeux's arguments in ways that revealed how radically imperial priorities had shifted. Notably, Des Voeux's proposal to partially abolish extradition hearings was criticised as 'startling', 'lazy', and 'unjustifiable' because it made light of imperial law.[162] An Assistant Undersecretary, Edward Wingfield, noted that, as the same rules now applied to all British extradition regimes, there was no longer any basis for a looser enforcement of the Treaty of Tianjin. 'However important it might be to Hong Kong to be rid of Chinese criminals,' said Wingfield, 'it would be quite inadmissible to waive in the case of China the requirement [for extradition hearings] which is enforced by Act of Parliament in the case of all civilized nations with whom we have Extradition Treaties.' Knutsford agreed that any circumvention of extradition hearings 'cannot be entertained'.[163]

The upshot of these discussions was a Chinese Extradition Bill that respected the spirit of Bramston's draft ordinance of 1875 – the draft that applied the hard-earned lessons of *Kwok-a-Sing*. Only a few final amendments were made to the Bill in 1889, when Governor Des Voeux presented it to the Legislative Council of Hong Kong. These final amendments placed yet more restrictions on extraditing fugitives to China: depositions taken in China were made inadmissible in Hong Kong, and long-term residents of the colony were given additional protections not enjoyed by other Chinese subjects.[164] These amendments were introduced by Legislative Councillors who, though also unelected, were more attuned than Des Voeux to the colonial Chinese fear of persecution by the Chinese government.[165] Des Voeux accepted this point of view after it was made known to him. In July 1889, he noted in his defence that he had 'previously no idea of the terror of the Mandarins which pervades all classes of Chinese [people]' in Hong Kong. Contrary to his earlier position, therefore, Des Voeux now agreed that 'however desirable it may be to get rid of our criminals, it is still more desirable not to lessen the security of person and property now felt by the law-abiding Chinese, and which is so extremely important a factor in the prosperity of the Colony'.[166] Satisfied, the Colonial Office quickly approved the Chinese Extradition Ordinance in September 1889, showing, for its part, that it was more eager to enforce a minimum imperial standard for extradition than to second-guess the further demands of colonial legislators.[167] This, then, was how the mature law of extradition took shape in Hong Kong; this was how the idiosyncratic Chinese rendition regime of earlier decades was consigned to history.

*

The transformation of the extradition law of Hong Kong between 1865 and 1873 was, in a sense, a uniquely dramatic instance of a wider imperial phenomenon. The law of the whole British Empire was reformed in this period, though only in Hong Kong was the Crown accused of complicity in the torture of a political refugee. Also, only in Hong Kong were the stakes so high that the Crown appealed to the Privy Council. British practices of extradition were untidy everywhere, but the Treaty of Tianjin was particularly under-regulated. So, as the catalysts of law reform on that front, *How Yu-teen* and *Kwok-a-Sing* embodied the dangers of legal ambiguity across the empire. The two scandals exposed the embarrassing consequences of the British reluctance, before the late 1860s, to state in legislation and case law that British officials would not extradite political refugees, and that they reserved the right to decide whether the outcome of any British extradition proceeding was a breach of treaty. The British attitude to extradition certainly became more candid and unilateral from the late 1860s. Nowhere was this shift more apparent than in Hong Kong.

Viewed on its own terms, this period of legal change in Hong Kong also shows how extradition law was made through the rise of Crown accountability to the imperial Parliament and judiciary. Officials in Hong Kong, as in other territories, were motivated to extradite fugitives for two main reasons: to do substantive justice and to maintain friendly relations with foreign countries. Pushing against those motivations were the dictates of public opinion and the rule of law. These being the main tensions of extradition, it is telling that Whitehall chose to keep giving Hong Kong a long leash in the early 1860s despite realising by that time that this policy might raise serious objections. It is telling that this was done in a colony with no 'responsible government' – a colony whose officials were not accountable to locally elected legislators – and where judges were not previously accustomed to championing the rights of alien persons.

It is telling, too, that things suddenly changed when the Crown was called to account from 1865; that, in initiating overdue reforms, imperial officials concealed the awkward truth of their earlier willingness to surrender political offenders to China; and, finally, that officials accepted the Privy Council's double-edged judgment in *Kwok-a-Sing*, after lodging the appeal in order to tame the maverick Chief Justice Smale. The Victorian Crown despised political activism by colonial judges who served without tenure, as John McLaren has argued: 'Conciliation maybe, but single-minded dedication to reformist change, no!'[168] In *Kwok-a-Sing*, Smale's criticism of the indefinite scope of the Rendition Ordinance 1850 was tolerably conciliatory, but his crusade against the Macau coolie trade was obnoxiously reformist. The Crown responded by bringing Smale in line, but also by taking key parts of his judgments seriously, rectifying the law of Hong Kong – acting, above all, to curtail its governor's power of rendition, turning it into a modern, limited power of extradition.

Conclusion

Legacies of Extradition

The British law of extradition was not exactly made in Hong Kong, but it was remade there between 1842 and 1873. As this book has shown, judges, lawyers, and officials debated the rights and liabilities of Chinese subjects living and sojourning in Hong Kong, concluding, in the end, that they could only be surrendered to China and other countries under strict rules that bound the whole British Empire. Some of those rules predated the founding of Hong Kong, at least in some form: mandatory hearings before magistrates, for example, and the rule of double criminality. Other rules crystallised later, shaped at times by events in Hong Kong, and shaping them in turn: the speciality rule and political offence exception. But, above all, extradition was gradually distinguished in Hong Kong from other modalities of criminal jurisdiction – other methods of dealing with accused criminals, namely discretionary rendition, summary deportation, and trial and punishment under territorial or extraterritorial laws. The development of extradition in Hong Kong thus went beyond technical rulemaking, as it involved changes in how legal actors understood official acts of moving or not moving people around as prisoners. As we have seen, the scope and premises of British jurisdiction were so deeply contested that officials framed and rationalised their actions in inconsistent ways, complicating local jurisprudence until pressures for legal harmonisation emanated from London.

It was no coincidence that the emerging law and language of extradition also brought Hong Kong deeper into the fold of British sovereignty: legal harmonisation ran parallel to the intensification of formal imperialism. In 1843–44, inchoate ideas of extradition enabled British officials to make initial claims of territorial jurisdiction, sidestepping the difficulties of regarding the Chinese residents of Hong Kong as naturalised British subjects. Next, Hong Kong bore many trappings of British sovereignty during 1844–65, but its legal status was blurred by the systematic removal of Chinese subjects through poorly regulated procedures – practices that detracted from official promises to bring everyone in the colony under the equal protection of British law. By 1873, by contrast, the mature law of extradition impeded those practices, hardening the international border between Hong Kong and China. The application of imperial standards of extradition bound Hong Kong more closely to Trinidad, Canada, and other British territories of clearer jurisdictional boundaries – territories also governed by strict regimes of extradition. Indeed, Hong Kong was likened to Britain itself, where British territorial sovereignty was not disputed. Entrenched in new legislation and case law, these imperial affinities were a world away from the messy aftermath of the Opium War. In puzzling over the jurisdictional implications of the Chinese cession of Hong Kong, James Stephen of the Colonial Office lamented in 1843 that 'all ordinary analogies seem to fail in their application to the case of China'.[1] Not so by 1873.

Ideas of extradition altered the legal status of China, too, albeit more subtly. The hard border around Hong Kong cut both ways, preventing the colony from retrieving fugitives from China as much as the other way around. In fact, British officials concluded in 1865 that China was not required to extradite anyone to Hong Kong on charges of crimes committed there. In their view, this was because the Treaty of Tianjin (1858) did not impose such an obligation, though it obliged China to hand British subjects over to British consuls on charges of crimes committed in Chinese territory. As explained in Chapter 4, this interpretation of the treaty was grounded in the idea that a state's obligation to extradite fugitives was a very specific kind of obligation, and China's obligation to accommodate British extraterritorial jurisdiction was not quite the same thing. In this view, China had, as a territorial sovereign, given up some but not all of its rights. China was thus in a similar position as France, the United States, and Britain's other extradition partners. In British eyes, these countries were all obliged to relinquish control of people in their territory only to the extent that treaties mandated such procedures. Again, the law of extradition provided an intellectual framework for drawing productive analogies among the different frontiers of the sovereign British Empire. Retrospectively layered over the Treaty of Tianjin, this framework legitimised Chinese sovereignty in a way that ran counter to wider patterns of British and other Western coercion.

The origins of British imperialism in China begin to look quite different when these reverberations of extradition are factored into the historical analysis. Specifically, the legal shifts described in this book reveal a close intellectual connection between British views of Hong Kong and the extraterritorial British Empire on the Chinese mainland. This connection is obscured if the Opium War treaties of 1842–43 are portrayed, as they almost always are, as codifying ready-made mechanisms of extraterritoriality and extradition. I have argued that these mechanisms emerged over time, through official deliberations about British jurisdiction over British and alien fugitives moving in and around British Hong Kong. The provisions of the Opium War treaties supplied only a vague starting point for more precise interpretations to be made with reference to evolving ideas of sovereignty and subjecthood. Refinements in some aspects of the treaties then had knock-on effects on others, imbuing the whole treaty system with new meaning. Above all, the escalating exercise of British territorial jurisdiction in Hong Kong put the 'territoriality' in 'extraterritoriality'. The British claim to the right to control every inhabitant of Hong Kong made their refusal to let China do the same thing in Chinese territory seem much more unfair to China than when the negotiators of the Treaty of Nanjing spoke more neutrally (and non-territorially) about putting all fugitives in the hands of their own authorities.

It is important that these legal transformations were largely the products of unilateral British action. The scholarly and popular narrative of Western states imposing 'unequal treaties' on non-Western states emphasises the role of gunboat diplomacy, but many of the law-making processes tracked in this book unfolded in British courtrooms and colonial correspondence, far from all channels of diplomacy.[2] Chinese officials were not compelled to accept the outcomes of these proceedings: they often did not accept them at all. To be sure, British officials realised early on that their physical occupation of

Hong Kong gave them enough leverage to interpret the treaties without consulting their Chinese counterparts, even in relation to contested issues of jurisdiction. In 1843, one of Henry Pottinger's translators, Robert Thom, minuted candidly that Hong Kong 'being now English ground and Sir Henry being Governor of it, he may do with the people on it just as he likes ... Why have any further correspondence on the matter?'[3] Sure enough, later British officials never saw the need to obtain China's formal consent to the trial, punishment, or detention of Chinese subjects by British authorities in Hong Kong. These moves were certainly arrogant. Nevertheless, they amounted to a retrospective and improvised approach to claiming treaty rights, adopted by actors with changing ideas of jurisdiction and sovereignty. All this was more than gunboat diplomacy. It was more than the kind of premeditated exaction of concessions that Western states are often said, in sweeping terms, to have inflicted upon Qing China. In other words, the early history of Hong Kong shows that the processes that shaped Sino-British treaty relations were more imperial and less international than usually assumed. The processes were just as reflective of domestic British constitutionalism as international legal positivism, if not even more so.

In a similar vein, British officials responded mostly to domestic pressures for legal change. It is undeniable that they were influenced by 'orientalist' ideas of the barbarousness and infirmity of Chinese law – racialised and exaggerated ideas that, as Li Chen has argued, Westerners had invoked to justify rejecting Chinese jurisdiction since the eighteenth century.[4] This book has shown, however, that even speculations about Chinese practices of judicial torture did not stop early officials from handing over hundreds of Chinese prisoners from Hong Kong. This later changed from 1865, not because British officials became even more orientalist, but because their conduct towards alien fugitives came under closer scrutiny by judges and parliamentarians capable of embarrassing the Crown publicly. More generally, we have seen that officials in London and Hong Kong cared less about protecting fugitives per se, than about defending their own actions against formal challenges and informal inquiries. Most officials simply wanted to be seen as acting within their powers and not complicit in any wrongdoing. Beyond that, they were generally indifferent to how China treated its own people – and, indeed, anyone who was not a British subject. This was true in *Kwok-a-Sing* (1871–73), *How Yu-teen* (1865), *Juan Pastor* (1861), the case of the assaulters of Constable Hall (1846), and other cases that defined what the colonial government of Hong Kong could or could not do to aliens accused of crimes.

In short, we cannot explain the British treatment of Chinese subjects without tracking the practices and discourse that embodied the internal restructuring of British legal authority. To make sense of British conduct, we must see that the British jurisprudence on alien persons followed its own internal logic, which was evolving along its own trajectory. This logic – the logic of extradition – was not inherently derisive of foreign justice, though, if it came to it, foreign claims of jurisdiction were readily rejected, effectively as the collateral damage of British ordering. Ultimately, what occupied British minds were parochial questions about the limits of the Crown's discretion to discipline aliens in different ways. Gradually articulated and enforced in Hong Kong, these limits enfolded the colony in a semblance of the rule of law – a trace of an idea that Chinese subjects had legal recourse against unlawful detention, punishment, and removal, not in spite of their alien status but precisely because of it. The Crown was still immensely powerful, obviously, as its control over the Legislative Council of Hong Kong enabled it to create and maintain potent regimes of deportation until well into the twentieth century. However, even those regimes were at least nominally reviewable by judges under legal precedents that dated to the formative mid nineteenth century. The writ of habeas corpus signified limited government in the long tradition of the common law. Confirmed by the Privy Council in *Kwok-a-Sing*, the availability of the writ to Chinese subjects was a key facet of Hong Kong's constitutional maturation.

All told, jurisdictional and constitutional transformations make up the story of *Extradition and Empire*. Although Hong Kong was just one colony, its early history perfectly connects the origins of the British law of extradition to the imperial transition from Georgian jurisdictionalism to Victorian territoriality – the transition from an empire of British subjects (broadly defined) to one that systematically protected and disciplined alien persons of non-European allegiance and descent. Over time, the jurisprudence of alienage remained relevant in demographically fluid colonies like Hong Kong, where most people were either aliens or dual nationals under the intersecting principles of *jus soli* and *jus sanguinis*. In this context, the law of the place became arguably the only constant, the only reliable anchor in a sea of jurisdictional conflict and complexity. Though often harsh and never democratic, the colonial *lex loci* of Hong Kong could at least be trusted to be its own entity, free from Chinese and other foreign influence. As such, it was an enticing prospect for hundreds of thousands of migrants who wanted a new life for one reason or another.

Ideas of extradition actuated local, territorial, and limited common law government in mid nineteenth-century Hong Kong. They set Hong Kong apart from China in idea and practice. So, it is not surprising that similar ideas have fuelled the modern undoing of this colonial legacy amid China's gradual reabsorption of the territory. In 2019, nearly 2 million people took to the streets of the Hong Kong Special Autonomous Region (SAR) to protest a legislative bill that sought to enable the ad hoc surrender of accused fugitives to any country, including the mainland People's Republic of China, in the absence of permanent agreements implemented under local legislation.[5] Later withdrawn by the SAR government, this so-called 'extradition bill' was widely perceived as eroding the substantial autonomy that the territory was (and is) supposed to retain for fifty years after its return to Chinese rule on 1 July 1997 – its famous 'handover' from Britain pursuant to the Sino-British Joint Declaration of 1984.[6]

In the view of many people in Hong Kong, the bill of 2019 threatened to prematurely assimilate the SAR into mainland China. This was not only because it was tabled without much public consultation, but also because it did not provide sufficient means for local judges and officials to make independent decisions as to the fate of accused fugitives. Indeed, even moderate critics argued that the proposed system of ad hoc rendition would inevitably have operated within the 'asymmetrical relationship' between the SAR and the mainland.[7] Being 'constitutionally subordinate to Beijing', the SAR government would have been practically powerless to reject rendition requests that formally complied with the procedural safeguards specified in the proposed legislation, even if the social or political circumstances of particular cases gave officials pause.[8] Furthermore, the bill would have allowed Beijing to render cases non-justiciable in Hong Kong, simply by issuing 'directives' declaring that they concerned matters of foreign affairs or national defence. The Basic Law of Hong Kong (essentially its written constitution) states that these matters fall beyond the scope of its autonomy from Beijing; so, in theory, anyone could have been given up to the mainland without possibility of judicial review.[9]

Again, orientalism reared its head. The old Western distrust of Chinese justice, now shared by many Chinese-descended residents of Hong Kong, engendered fears that a lax system of rendition would expose them to unfair trials and even torture on the mainland. Partly grounded in endless accounts of China's persecution of political detractors and ethnic minorities – credible reports and baseless rumours alike – these fears also stemmed from the fact that no system of rendition or extradition had tied Hong Kong to China since 1997. The colonial Chinese Extradition Ordinance of 1889 had fallen into disuse since 1949, as the People's Republic of China refused to participate in proceedings that legitimised what it regarded as the unequal and unlawful Treaty of Tianjin.[10] In preparing for the handover of July 1997, legislators in colonial Hong Kong later enacted a Fugitive Offenders Ordinance in April 1997, creating a local version of the British Extradition Act 1989, the successor to the Extradition Act 1870. The Ordinance of 1997 did not authorise rendition to the People's Republic, hence the popular view that the 'extradition bill' of 2019 represented an unacceptable departure from decades of established practice.[11]

Again, however, the true stakes of the 'extradition bill' were the constitutional status and identity of Hong Kong. In July 2019, several hundred radical protestors made this very clear by storming the premises of the Legislative Council, vandalising them and draping the blue ensign of the old British colony over the red-and-white bauhinia that adorns the wall of the Council chamber – the emblem of the modern SAR. Coupled with numerous rallies for civil rights and universal suffrage, some of which descended into violent clashes with armed police, these acts of resistance illustrate the intertwining of the 'anti-extradition movement' with wider struggles against the political, social, and economic 'mainlandisation' of Hong Kong, as scholars have argued.[12] For many residents of Hong Kong, opposing extradition was about much more than avoiding persecution in mainland China. Their whole way of life was and is changing, intolerably, in ways that often defy easy articulation. But these changes are most conspicuous when their own government appears to serve the interests of Beijing, or of China as a whole, over the interests of the local community.

The government of Hong Kong finally withdrew the 'extradition bill' in September 2019 amid persistent criticism and civil unrest. Rattled by these events, however, Beijing foisted a new National Security Law on the SAR in 2020, bypassing its Legislative Council entirely. The full implications of this legislation remain unclear, but its sharp end comprises blanket prohibitions against, among other things, acts of 'secession', 'subversion', and 'collusion' with foreign entities towards certain objectives, including the promotion of 'hatred' towards the governments of Hong Kong or China.[13] Crucially, the Chief Executive of Hong Kong is authorised to decide which judges will 'handle' national security trials, and judges are disqualified if they have 'behaved in any manner endangering national security'. And, if the government of Hong Kong is unable to enforce this National Security Law in any particular case, or if 'a major and imminent threat to national security has occurred', then the mainland authorities may assume jurisdiction. This will be done through a new Office for Safeguarding National Security (OSNS), located in Hong Kong. OSNS personnel are exempted in their official capacities from liability under local laws.[14] As international observers are well aware, dozens of people have already been arrested under these terms, which seem to impose ad hoc rendition in another guise – mainlandisation in a most potent and proximate form. Unable to resist these measures, and fearing for their safety, hundreds if not thousands more people have fled Hong Kong to seek refuge in the United Kingdom, United States, and other Western countries.[15] These émigrés are rejecting not only Chinese law, but also a place that, from their point of view, is increasingly indistinguishable from other Chinese territories.

The parallels with the nineteenth century are unmistakable. After playing a crucial role in the establishment of a frontier British colony, ideas of extradition are now implicated in the former colony's contested and even violent reassimilation into its historical hinterland. The processes of historical colonialism are now operating in reverse, as extended processes of decolonisation. Or perhaps they are still the same processes, merely expressed in a different register and overseen by a different hegemonic power. The lessons of law and government seem to be the same, either way. International treaties of cession and retrocession may signal that a population's legal status is about to change, but only domestic processes can give these treaties real meaning. When statuses and rights are contested, what matters is how governments and officials, claiming jurisdiction or sovereignty, move to control the legal framing and practical execution of whether, how, and why people are disciplined, locally or remotely. Through these manoeuvres – these malleable and evolving components of extradition – lives are transformed and empires are made.

Notes

Introduction

1. Song-Chuan Chen, *Merchants of War and Peace: British Knowledge of China in the Making of the Opium War* (Hong Kong: Hong Kong University Press, 2017).
2. Robert Bickers, *The Scramble for China: Foreign Devils in the Qing Empire, 1832–1914* (London: Allen Lane, 2011).
3. Jürgen Osterhammel, 'Semi-Colonialism and Informal Empire in Twentieth-Century China: Towards a Framework of Analysis', in Wolfgang J. Mommsen and Jürgen Osterhammel, eds., *Imperialism and After: Continuities and Discontinuities* (London: Allen and Unwin, 1986, 290–314); John Gallagher and Ronald Robinson, 'The Imperialism of Free Trade', *Economic History Review (New Series)* 6, no. 1 (1953): 1–15.
4. 'Treaty between Her Majesty and the United States of America, signed at Washington, August 9, 1842', C. (1st series) 424, UK House of Commons Command Papers LXI.1 (1843); 'Convention between Her Majesty and the King of French, for the Mutual Surrender, in Certain Cases, of Persons Fugitive from Justice, signed at London, February 13, 1843', C. (1st series) 444, UK House of Commons Command Papers LX.487 (1843).
5. Extradition Act, 33 & 34 Vict. c. 52 (1870), supplemented by the Extradition Act, 33 & 34 Vict. c. 52 (1873), and repealed and replaced by the Extradition Act 1989. For an overview of these statutes, see Alun Jones and Anand Doobay, *Jones and Doobay on Extradition and Mutual Assistance* (London: Sweet and Maxwell, 2005), 14–34.
6. Extradition barely rates a mention in most studies of British imperialism in Qing China. A notable exception is Emily Whewell, 'British

Extraterritoriality in China: The Legal System, Functions of Criminal Jurisdiction, and its Challenges, 1833–1943', PhD dissertation, University of Leicester (2015), 62–8. The wider phenomenon of Sino-British extradition during the nineteenth and twentieth centuries has also received little scholarly attention. Only now is this gap being filled by Jenny Huangfu Day, *Transborder Fugitives, Extradition, and Political Crimes in Modern China* (Cambridge University Press, in press). More tangential studies include Christopher Munn, '"Our Best Trump Card": A Brief History of Deportation in Hong Kong, 1857–1955', in Michael Ng and John D. Wong, eds., *Civil Unrest and Governance in Hong Kong: Law and Order from Historical and Cultural Perspectives* (London: Routledge, 2017), 2–20; Janice M. Brabyn, 'Extradition and the Hong Kong Special Administrative Region', *Case Western Reserve Journal of International Law* 20 (1988): 169–94.

7. See, for example, John K. Fairbank, *Trade and Diplomacy on the China Coast: The Opening of the Treaty Ports, Volume 1: 1842–1854* (Cambridge, MA: Harvard University Press, 1953), 121; William L. Tung, *China and Some Phases of International Law* (New York, NY: Oxford University Press, 1940), 79–84; G. W. Keeton, *The Development of Extraterritoriality in China* (New York, NY: Longmans, Green and Co., 1928), 152; Francis Piggott, *Exterritoriality: The Law Relating to Consular Jurisdiction and to Residence in Oriental Countries* (London: Butterworth, 1907), 19.
8. 'Treaty between Her Majesty and the Emperor of China, signed, in the English and Chinese Languages, at Nanking, August 29, 1842', C. (1st series) 521, UK House of Commons Command Papers LI.327 (1844); 'Supplementary Treaty between Her Majesty and the Emperor of China, signed at Hoomun-Chae, October 8, 1843', C. (1st series) 534, UK House of Commons Command Papers LI.341 (1844).
9. Charles Egan, *The Law of Extradition Comprising the Treaties Now in Force between England and France, and England and America* (London: W. W. Robinson, 1846). Scholars have identified Egan's book as 'the first English book' on extradition: V. E. Hartley Booth and Peter Sells, *British Extradition Law and Procedure: Including Extradition between the United Kingdom and Foreign States, the Commonwealth and Dependent Countries and the Republic of Ireland, Volume 1* (Alphen aan den Rijn: Sijthoff and Noordhoff, 1980), v.
10. Turan Kayaoğlu, *Legal Imperialism: Sovereignty and Extraterritoriality in Japan, the Ottoman Empire, and China* (Cambridge: Cambridge University Press, 2010); Anthony Anghie, *Imperialism, Sovereignty and the Making of International Law* (Cambridge: Cambridge University Press, 2004); Gerrit W. Gong, *The Standard of 'Civilization' in International Society* (New York, NY: Clarendon Press, 1984).
11. Henry Wheaton, *Elements of International Law* (London: B. Fellowes, 1836). On the rise of Eurocentric positivism in international legal thought

from the mid nineteenth century, see Jennifer Pitts, *Boundaries of the International: Law and Empire* (Cambridge, MA: Harvard University Press, 2018), 148–84. On earlier Western narratives of Chinese law between the late eighteenth and early nineteenth centuries, see Li Chen, *Chinese Law in Imperial Eyes: Sovereignty, Justice, and Transcultural Politics* (New York, NY: Columbia University Press, 2016); Song-Chuan Chen, 'Strangled by the Chinese and Kept "Alive" by the British: Two Infamous Executions and the Discourse of Chinese Legal Despotism', in Richard Ward, ed., *A Global History of Execution and the Criminal Corpse* (New York, NY: Palgrave Macmillan, 2015), 199.

12. Daniel S. Margolies, Umut Özsu, Maïa Pal, and Ntina Tzouvala, eds., *The Extraterritoriality of Law: History, Theory, Politics* (Oxford: Routledge, 2019), 2.
13. The historical contingency of territorial jurisdiction is explored, among other works, in Jordan Branch, *The Cartographic State: Maps, Territory, and the Origins of Sovereignty* (Cambridge: Cambridge University Press, 2014); Douglas Howland and Luise White, *The State of Sovereignty: Territories, Laws, Populations* (Bloomington, IN: Indiana University Press, 2009); Shaunnagh Dorsett, 'Mapping Territories', in Shaun McVeigh, ed., *Jurisprudence of Jurisdiction* (Oxford: Routledge-Cavendish, 2007), 137–58; Richard T. Ford, 'Law's Territory (A History of Jurisdiction)', *Michigan Law Review* 97 (1999): 843–930.
14. Lisa Ford, *Settler Sovereignty: Jurisdiction and Indigenous People in America and Australia, 1788–1836* (Cambridge, MA: Harvard University Press, 2010), 25, 36–40.
15. P. G. McHugh, *Aboriginal Societies and the Common Law: A History of Sovereignty, Status, and Self-Determination* (Oxford: Oxford University Press, 2004), 117–214; P. G. McHugh, 'A Comporting Sovereign, Tribes, and the Ordering of Imperial Authority in Colonial Upper Canada of the 1830s', in Martti Koskenniemi, Walter Rech, and Manuel Jiménez Fonseca, eds., *International Law and Empire: Historical Explorations* (Oxford: Oxford University Press, 2017).
16. P. G. McHugh, '"A Pretty Gov[ernment]!": The "Confederation of United Tribes" and Britain's Quest for Imperial Order in the New Zealand Islands during the 1830s', in Lauren Benton and Richard J. Ross, eds., *Legal Pluralism and Empires, 1500–1800* (New York, NY: New York University Press, 2013), 236.
17. McHugh, *Aboriginal Societies and the Common Law*, 63. See also Shaunnagh Dorsett, 'Sovereignty as Governance in the Early New Zealand Crown Colony Period', in Shaunnagh Dorsett and Ian Hunter, eds., *Law and Politics in British Colonial Thought: Transpositions of Empire* (New York, NY: Palgrave Macmillan, 2010), 209–28.
18. For an early version of this argument, see Ivan Lee, 'British Extradition Practice in Early Colonial Hong Kong', *Law & History* 6, no. 1 (2019): 85–114.

19. The Thirteen Colonies in America were an exception because they became independent before assimilating indigenous tribes. On the general European practice of using treaties to legitimise the dismantling of 'indigenous sovereignties', see Saliha Belmessous, ed., *Empire by Treaty Negotiating European Expansion, 1600–1900* (New York, NY: Oxford University Press, 2015).
20. Shaunnagh Dorsett, *Juridical Encounters: Māori and the Colonial Courts, 1840–1852* (Auckland: Auckland University Press, 2017).
21. Pär Cassel, 'Extraterritoriality in China: What We Know and What We Don't Know', in Robert Bickers and Isabella Jackson, eds., *Treaty Ports in Modern China: Law, Land and Power* (New York, NY: Routledge, 2016), 24–5.
22. Cassel, 'Extraterritoriality in China', 24; Pär Kristoffer Cassel, *Grounds of Judgment: Extraterritoriality and Imperial Power in Nineteenth-Century China and Japan* (New York, NY: Oxford University Press, 2012), 17. On Qing Chinese legal practices of border control, see also R. Randle Edwards, 'Imperial China's Border Control Law', *Journal of Chinese Law* 1 (1987): 33–62.
23. Cassel, *Grounds of Judgment*, 15–22.
24. Bradley Miller, *Borderline Crime: Fugitive Criminals and the Challenge of the Border, 1819–1914* (Toronto: University of Toronto Press, 2016), 4–6.
25. Miller, *Borderline Crime*, 4. See also Benjamin Hoy, 'Dispensing Irregular Justice: State Sponsored Abductions, Prisoner Surrenders, and Extralegal Renditions along the Canada–United States Border', *Law and History Review* 35, no. 2 (2017): 321–50.
26. For a similar argument that nineteenth-century sovereign states signed extradition treaties to address the 'problem' that '[l]aws stopped at the border, but people did not', see Katherine Unterman, *Uncle Sam's Policemen: The Pursuit of Fugitives across Borders* (Cambridge, MA: Harvard University Press, 2015), 3.
27. For a recent study that, albeit without problematising the idea of extradition, analyses extradition-like practices as evidence of the instability of British 'paramountcy' in India, see Priyasha Saksena, *Sovereignty, International Law, and the Princely States of Colonial South Asia* (Oxford: Oxford University Press, 2023), especially 31–7. On the pervasiveness of jurisdictional pluralism in early modern colonial empires, see Lauren Benton and Richard J. Ross, eds., *Legal Pluralism and Empires, 1500–1800* (New York, NY: New York University Press, 2013); Lauren Benton, *A Search for Sovereignty: Law and Geography in European Empires, 1400–1900* (New York, NY: Cambridge University Press, 2010). On the British Empire, in particular, see Lauren Benton and Lisa Ford, *Rage for Order: The British Empire and the Origins of International Law, 1800–1850* (Cambridge, MA: Harvard University Press, 2016).

28. Christopher Munn, *Anglo-China: Chinese People and British Rule in Hong Kong, 1841–1880* (Hong Kong: Hong Kong University Press, 2001), 4. Compare with the argument that 'colonial expansion in Hong Kong was made possible with Chinese cooperation throughout the early history of the colony', in John M. Carroll, *Edge of Empires: Chinese Elites and British Colonials in Hong Kong* (Cambridge, MA: Harvard University Press, 2005), 187.
29. Munn, *Anglo-China*, 1–18; Christopher Munn, 'The Rule of Law and Criminal Justice in the Nineteenth Century', in Steve Tsang, ed., *Judicial Independence and the Rule of Law in Hong Kong* (Hong Kong: Hong Kong University Press, 2001).
30. Peter Wesley-Smith, 'Anti-Chinese Legislation in Hong Kong', in Ming K. Chan, ed., *Precarious Balance: Hong Kong Between China and Britain, 1842–1992* (Armonk, NY: M. E. Sharpe, 1994); Michael Ng, *Political Censorship in British Hong Kong: Freedom of Expression and the Law (1842–1997)* (Cambridge: Cambridge University Press, 2022).
31. Elizabeth Kolsky, *Colonial Justice in British India: White Violence and the Rule of Law* (Cambridge: Cambridge University Press, 2010), 69–107, 142–84.
32. Adam M. McKeown, *Melancholy Order: Asian Migration and the Globalization of Borders* (New York, NY: Columbia University Press, 2011), 192–4; Paul Maylam, *South Africa's Racial Past: The History and Historiography of Racism, Segregation, and Apartheid* (Aldershot: Ashgate, 2001), 115–42.
33. McKeown, *Melancholy Order*, 194–210; Renisa Mawani, *Across Oceans of Law: The Komagata Maru and Jurisdiction in the Time of Empire* (Durham, NC: Duke University Press, 2018).
34. Hannah Weiss Muller, *Subjects and Sovereign: Bonds of Belonging in the Eighteenth-Century British Empire* (New York, NY: Oxford University Press, 2017).
35. Some scholars have suggested that the Treaty of Nanjing *did* confer British subjecthood on the pre-cession Chinese inhabitants of Hong Kong and that British officials simply failed to take this legal doctrine seriously. Chapter 1 of this book will show, to the contrary, that the doctrine itself was contested. See Steve Tsang, *A Modern History of Hong Kong: 1841–1997* (London: I. B. Tauris, 2007), 45; Munn, *Anglo-China*, 54–5.
36. Palmerston, Memorandum of 28 April 1850, FO 27/954, cited in Nicholas Adams, 'British Extradition Policy and the Problem of the Political Offender (1842–1914)', PhD dissertation, University of Hull (1989), 44–5.
37. Studies on the historical status of aliens and dual nationals under British law have largely focused on developments in Britain and continental Europe. See, for example, Rieko Karatani, *Defining British Citizenship: Empire, Commonwealth, and Modern Britain* (London: Frank Cass, 2003); Andreas Fahrmeir, *Citizens and Aliens: Foreigners and the*

Law in Britain and the German States, 1789–1870 (New York, NY: Berghahn Books, 2000); Ann Dummett and Andrew Nicol, *Subjects, Citizens, Aliens and Others: Nationality and Immigration Law* (London: Weidenfeld and Nicolson, 1990). For a recent analysis of the imperial politics of British-Chinese subjecthood (which does not discuss extradition), see Alexander Thompson, 'The British State at the Margins of Empire: Extraterritoriality and Governance in Treaty Port China, 1842–1927', PhD dissertation, University of Bristol (2018).

38. The modern legal literature on extradition is vast. Representative works that distinguish extradition from adjacent practices include David A. Sadoff, *Bringing International Fugitives to Justice: Extradition and Its Alternatives* (New York, NY: Cambridge University Press, 2016); Suzanne Egan, *Extraordinary Rendition and Human Rights: Examining State Accountability and Complicity* (London: Palgrave Macmillan, 2019); M. Cherif Bassiouni, *International Extradition: United States Law and Practice*, 6th ed. (New York, NY: Oxford University Press, 2014); Geoff Gilbert, *Transnational Fugitive Offenders in International Law: Extradition and Other Mechanisms* (The Hague: Kluwer Law International, 1998); Michael Forde, *The Law of Extradition in the United Kingdom* (Dublin: Round Hall Press, 1995). In the United States of America, international 'extradition' is also commonly distinguished from domestic, interstate 'rendition'. This usage seems to date at least to the 1890s. See, for example, John Bassett Moore, *A Treatise on Extradition and Interstate Rendition, Volume 1* (Boston, MA: The Boston Book Company, 1891), 819: 'The use of the term "extradition" to describe the rendition of fugitives from justice from one State of the Union to another is convenient and firmly established, but it is nevertheless inaccurate and misleading.' Compare with Samuel T. Spear, *The Law of Extradition: International and Inter-state*, 2nd ed. (Albany, NY: Weed, Parsons and Company, 1884), 283.
39. Accounts of this treaty usually draw on S. Langdon and Alan H. Gardiner, 'The Treaty of Alliance between Hattusili, King of the Hittites, and the Pharaoh Ramesses II of Egypt', *Journal of Egyptian Archaeology* 6, no. 3 (1920): 179–205.
40. It is unclear with whom the treaty of 1828 was signed: Albert Billot, *Traité de l'extradition* (Paris: Plon, 1874), 34.
41. Christopher L. Blakesley, 'The Practice of Extradition from Antiquity to Modern France and the United States: A Brief History', *Boston College International and Comparative Law Review* 4, no. 1 (1981): 39–60, 50–2; I. A. Shearer, *Extradition in International Law* (Manchester: Manchester University Press, 1971), 1–21.
42. Blakesley, 'The Practice of Extradition', 40.
43. Act of Congress of 12 August 1848, c. 167, 9 Stat. 302, and Extradition Act, 33 & 34 Vict. c. 52 (1870), cited in Shearer, *Extradition in International Law*, 12.

44. Paul O'Higgins, 'The History of Extradition in British Practice, 1174–1794', in T. S. Rama Rao, ed., *The Indian Year Book of International Affairs, 1964, Volume XIII, Part II* (Madras: University of Madras, 1964).
45. Habeas Corpus Act, 16 Cha. I c. 10 (1640). See generally Paul D. Halliday, *Habeas Corpus: From England to Empire* (Cambridge, MA: Harvard University Press, 2010).
46. 'By the law of the land no man can be exiled, or banished out of his native country, but either by authority of Parliament or in case of abjuration for felony by the common law': Edward Coke, *The Second Part of the Institutes of the Laws of England* (London: E. & R. Brooke, 1797), 47, cited in O'Higgins, 'The History of Extradition in British Practice', 109.
47. 31 Cha. II c. 2, ss. 11–12; Christopher H. Pyle, *Extradition, Politics, and Human Rights* (Philadelphia, PA: Temple University Press, 2001), 8–11; O'Higgins, 'The History of Extradition in British Practice', 110–15. O'Higgins suggests that jurists were unsure whether section 11 of the Habeas Corpus Act 1679 protected aliens, but Halliday has shown more generally that aliens routinely used the writ to escape various forms of detention in the eighteenth century: Halliday, *Habeas Corpus*, 203–8.
48. The Jay Treaty was named after Chief Justice John Jay, who negotiated it for the United States. On Anglo-American relations during the French Revolutionary Wars (*c.* 1792–1803), a conflict in which the United States kept an uneasy neutrality, see Bradford Perkins, *The First Rapprochement: England and the United States, 1795–1805* (Philadelphia, PA: University of Pennsylvania Press, 1955).
49. Treaty of Amity Commerce and Navigation, between His Britannick Majesty and the United States of America, signed at London on 19 November 1794.
50. Neil Boister, 'A History of Double Criminality in Extradition', *Journal of the History of International Law* 25, no. 2 (2023): 218–57.
51. Pennsylvania was one of the first American states to introduce degrees of murder by way of reforming the English categories of murder and manslaughter: Lawrence M. Friedman, *A History of American Law*, 4th ed. (New York, NY: Oxford University Press, 2019), 263–4.
52. Treaty with United States Act, 37 Geo. III c. 97 (1797), s. 26.
53. Jay Treaty, Article 27. On bills of indictment and pre-trial criminal proceedings in early modern England, see John H. Langbein, *The Origins of the Adversary Criminal Trial* (New York, NY: Oxford University Press, 2003), 40–7.
54. Treaty with United States Act 1797, s. 26.
55. The Jay Treaty was highly controversial, as critics in the United States felt that it favoured British interests: Jerald A. Combs, *The Jay Treaty: Political Battleground of the Founding Fathers* (Berkeley, CA: University of California Press, 1970).

56. Namely, in the Anglo-American treaty, murder, assault with intent to murder, piracy, arson, robbery, forgery, and the 'utterance of forged paper' (i.e. knowing delivery of forged documents); and, in the Anglo-French treaty, murder, attempted murder, forgery, and fraudulent bankruptcy.
57. Act of 6 & 7 Vict. c. 75 (1843), s. 4; Act of 6 & 7 Vict. c. 76 (1843), s. 4.
58. Egan, *The Law of Extradition*; Robert Phillimore, *Commentaries upon International Law, Volume 1* (Philadelphia, PA: T. & J.W. Johnson, 1854); Travers Twiss, *The Law of Nations Considered as Independent Political Communities* (Oxford: Oxford University Press, 1861).
59. Edward Clarke, *A Treatise upon the Law of Extradition* (London: Steven and Haynes, 1867), 67.
60. James Fitzjames Stephen, *A History of the Criminal Law of England, Volume 2* (London: Macmillan and Co, 1883), 66.
61. *Calvin's Case* (1608) 7 Co. Rep. 1a; *Campbell* v. *Hall* (1774) 1 Cowp. 161. See B. H. McPherson, *The Reception of English Law Abroad* (Brisbane: Supreme Court of Queensland Library, 2007), 13–18.
62. The treaty with Denmark was implemented under the Act of 25 & 26 Vict. c. 70 (1862).
63. Caroline Shaw, *Britannia's Embrace: Modern Humanitarianism and the Imperial Origins of Refugee Relief* (New York, NY: Oxford University Press, 2015); Bernard Porter, *The Refugee Question in Mid-Victorian Politics* (New York, NY: Cambridge University Press, 1979).
64. Clarke, *A Treatise upon the Law of Extradition*, 111.
65. 'Report from the Select Committee on Extradition; Together with the Proceedings of the Committee, Minutes of Evidence, and Appendix', UK House of Commons Papers VII.129, No. 393 (1868).
66. Extradition Act, 33 & 34 Vict. c. 52 (1870). On the international history of the political offence exception, see Julia Jansson, *Terrorism, Criminal Law and Politics: The Decline of the Political Offence Exception to Extradition* (Oxford: Routledge, 2020); Christine van den Wijngaert, *The Political Offence Exception to Extradition: The Delicate Problem of Balancing the Rights of the Individual and the International Public Order* (Deventer: Kluwer, 1980).
67. Henry Chartres Biron and Kenneth E. Chalmers, *The Law and Practice of Extradition* (London: Steven and Sons, 1903), 156.

1 Improvising Sovereignty

1. Pottinger to Stanley, 9 December 1843, CO 129/2, fo. 381.
2. Frederic Wakeman Jr., 'The Canton Trade and the Opium War', in John K. Fairbank, ed., *The Cambridge History of China, Volume 10: Late Ch'ing 1800–1911, Part 1* (Cambridge: Cambridge University Press, 1978), 163–212.

3. Song-Chuan Chen, *Merchants of War and Peace: British Knowledge of China in the Making of the Opium War* (Hong Kong: Hong Kong University Press, 2017).
4. Paul A. van Dyke, *The Canton Trade: Life and Enterprise on the China Coast, 1700–1845* (Hong Kong: Hong Kong University Press, 2005).
5. Historians disagree whether Beijing approved of these local practices but it is clear that they flourished either way: R. Randle Edwards, 'Ch'ing Jurisdiction over Foreigners', in Jerome Alan Cohen, R. Randle Edwards, and Fu-Mei Chang Chen, eds., *Essays on China's Legal Tradition* (Princeton, NJ: Princeton University Press, 1981), 222–69; Pär Kristoffer Cassel, *Grounds of Judgment: Extraterritoriality and Imperial Power in Nineteenth-Century China and Japan* (Oxford: Oxford University Press, 2012), 40–3. Compare with Li Chen, *Chinese Law in Imperial Eyes: Sovereignty, Justice, and Transcultural Politics* (New York, NY: Columbia University Press, 2016), 54–5.
6. Edwards, 'Ch'ing Jurisdiction over Foreigners'.
7. Li Chen, 'Law, Empire, and Historiography of Modern Sino-Western Relations: A Case Study of the Lady Hughes Controversy in 1784', *Law and History Review* 27, no. 1 (2009): 1–53.
8. *Third Report from the Select Committee of the House of Commons, Appointed to Enquire into the Present State of the Affairs of the East-India Company* (London: J. L. Cox and Son, 1832), 526, cited in Chen, *Merchants of War and Peace*, 110.
9. George H. C. Wong, 'The Ch'i-Shan-Elliot Negotiations Concerning an Off-Shore Entrepot and a Re-evaluation of the Abortive Chuenpi Convention', *Monumenta Serica* 14 (1949–55): 539–73, 556.
10. J. W. Norton-Kyshe, *History of the Laws and Courts of Hong Kong, Volume 1* (London: T. F. Unwin, 1898), 4–5.
11. Norton-Kyshe, *History of the Laws and Courts of Hong Kong, Volume 1*, 4–5.
12. China Trade Act, 3 & 4 Will. IV c. 93 (1833), s. 6; Order in Council of 9 December 1833, in Lewis Hertslet, ed., *Hertslet's Commercial Treaties: A Complete Collection of the Treaties and Conventions, and Reciprocal Regulations, at Present Subsisting between Great Britain and Foreign Powers, Volume 4* (London: Butterworth, 1840), 84–7. See Philip Lawson, *The East India Company: A History* (New York, NY: Lawson, 1993), 156–9.
13. East India Company Charter Act, 53 Geo. 3, c. 155 (1813).
14. 9 Geo IV c. 31 (1828). The other statutes included the Acts of 33 Hen. VIII c. 23 (1541), 43 Geo. III c. 113 (1803), and 57 Geo. III c. 53 (1817). See C. R. Pennell, 'The Origins of the Foreign Jurisdiction Act and the Extension of British Sovereignty', *Historical Research* 83, no. 221 (2010): 465–85; W. Ross Johnston, *Sovereignty and Protection: A Study of British Jurisdictional Imperialism in the Late Nineteenth Century* (Durham, NC: Duke University Press, 1973), 32–6.

15. G. W. Keeton, *The Development of Extraterritoriality in China, Volume 1* (London: Longmans, Green and Co., 1928), 71; Edwards, 'Ch'ing Jurisdiction over Foreigners'.
16. Elizabeth Kolsky, *Colonial Justice in British India: White Violence and the Rule of Law* (Cambridge: Cambridge University Press, 2010).
17. *R* v. *Allen* (1837) 173 Eng. Rep. 291.
18. Order in Council of 9 December 1833, in Hertslet, ed., *Hertslet's Commercial Treaties, Volume* 4, 84–7.
19. Hosea Ballou Morse, *The International Relations of the Chinese Empire, Volume 1* (London: Longmans, Green and Co., 1910), 120–1.
20. Wong, 'The Ch'i-Shan-Elliot Negotiations', 557–8.
21. Dodson, Campbell, and Wilde to Palmerston, 12 August 1840, reproduced in Clive Parry, ed., *Law Officers' Opinions to the Foreign Office, 1793–1860, Volume 19* (Farnborough: Gregg International Publishers, 1970), 87–104. The Crown later did issue an Order in Council on 4 January 1843, 'transferring the Court of Justice from Canton to Hong Kong, for the trial of offences committed by British subjects in China'. But this Order was superseded in turn by instruments that enabled British sojourners in mainland China to be disciplined by consular officers stationed at the treaty ports opened under the Treaty of Nanjing. Meanwhile, the jurisdiction to try British subjects for crimes committed in Hong Kong was transferred to the Supreme Court of Hong Kong in August 1844. See Hertslet, ed., *Hertslet's Commercial Treaties, Volume 6* (1845), 228–9, 251–4, 276–9; Hong Kong Ordinance No. 15 of 1844.
22. Stanley to Addington, 30 January 1843, CO 129/3, fo. 22.
23. Order in Council of 9 December 1833, in Hertslet, ed., *Hertslet's Commercial Treaties, Volume* 4, 84–7.
24. Norton-Kyshe, *History of the Laws and Courts of Hong Kong, Volume 1*, 4–7; Christopher Munn, 'William Caine and the Hong Kong Magistracy', *Hong Kong Law Journal* 25 (1995): 213–38.
25. Peter Wesley-Smith, *The Sources of Hong Kong Law* (Hong Kong: Hong Kong University Press, 1994), 88, 209; D. J. Lewis, 'A Requiem for Chinese Customary Law in Hong Kong', *International and Comparative Law Quarterly* 32, no. 2 (1983): 347–79; D. M. Emrys Evans, 'Common Law in a Chinese Setting: The Kernel or the Nut', *Hong Kong Law Journal* 1 (1971): 9–32.
26. Robert Bickers, *The Scramble for China: Foreign Devils in the Qing Empire, 1832–1914* (London: Allen Lane, 2011), 82–3.
27. 'Treaty between Her Majesty and the Emperor of China, signed, in the English and Chinese Languages, at Nanking, August 29, 1842', C. (1st series) 521, UK House of Commons Command Papers LI.327 (1844).
28. Pottinger to Aberdeen, 19 July 1843, FO 17/68, fo. 62.
29. 'Supplementary Treaty between Her Majesty and the Emperor of China, signed at Hoomun-Chae, October 8, 1843', C. (1st series) 534, UK House of Commons Command Papers LI.341 (1844). Historians have

often conflated or confused the General Regulations of Trade with the Supplementary Treaty of the Bogue. For an account of the post-Nanjing treaty negotiations, which, by drawing on Chinese records, clearly shows that two separate supplementary instruments were prepared, see Mao Haijian, *The Qing Empire and the Opium War: The Collapse of the Heavenly Dynasty*, trans. Joseph Lawson, Craig Smith, and Peter Lavelle (Cambridge: Cambridge University Press, 2016), 446–7.

30. Treaty of Nanjing, Articles 2–7 and 10.
31. Mao, *The Qing Empire and the Opium War*, 450–1. Mao's account is corroborated on this point by the records of the British Foreign Office, FO 17/57–71 and FO 705/45.
32. Keying, Elepoo, and Newkien to Pottinger, 1 September 1842, FO 17/57, 335, 339–341.
33. Pottinger to Aberdeen, 3 September 1842 and Pottinger's Memorandum of 5 September 1842, FO 17/57, fo. 206, 345–349.
34. Pottinger's Memorandum of 5 September 1842, FO 17/57, fo. 348–349.
35. Pottinger to Keying, Elepoo, and Newkien, 17 September 1842, FO 17/58, fo. 125–126.
36. Keying, Elepoo, and Newkien to Pottinger, 27 September 1842, FO 17/58, fo. 131–134.
37. Patrick H. Hase, *Forgotten Heroes: San on County and Its Magistrates in the Late Ming and Early Qing* (Hong Kong: City University of Hong Kong Press, 2017).
38. Keying, Elepoo, and Newkien to Pottinger, 27 September 1842, FO 17/58, fo. 131–134.
39. Pottinger to Aberdeen, 16 October 1842, FO 17/58, fo. 102, 107, emphasis in original.
40. Woosnam's Minute of 21 January 1843, FO 17/66, fo. 141.
41. Elepoo, Kekung, and Liang to Pottinger, February 1843, FO 17/66, fo. 331, 335–336.
42. Pottinger to Elepoo, Kekung, and Liang, 20 February 1843, FO 17/66, fo. 338.
43. Kekung to Pottinger, 9 March 1843, FO 17/66, fo. 338–344.
44. Clause 13 of the General Regulations of British Trade should not be confused with Article 13 of the Treaty of the Bogue. The latter was a different provision for the customs clearance of merchant ships at the treaty ports.
45. General Regulations of British Trade appended to the Treaty of Nanjing, emphasis added.
46. Aberdeen to Pottinger, 4 January 1843, CO 129/3, pp. 34–41, cited in Frederick Madden and David Fieldhouse, *The Dependent Empire and Ireland, 1840–1900: Advance and Retreat in Representative Government (Select Documents on the Constitutional History of the British Empire and Commonwealth, Volume V)* (Westport, CT: Greenwood Press, 1991), 460.

47. By comparison, British consuls were appointed to the unceded treaty ports under authority of an Order in Council of 17 April 1844, issued under the British Subjects in China Act, 6 & 7 Vict. c. 80 (1843). See Hertslet, ed., *Hertslet's Commercial Treaties, Volume 6*, 251–4, 276–9. On the staffing of British consulates in treaty-port China, see generally P. D. Coates, *The China Consuls: British Consular Officers, 1843–1943* (New York, NY: Oxford University Press, 1988).
48. For example, Keying to Davis, 21 June 1844, CO 129/8, fo. 284–285; Keying to Davis, private letter received on 3 January 1845, CO 129/11, fo. 51.
49. For example, Bonham to Grey, 21 November 1849, CO 129/30, fo. 324–325; Bonham to Palmerston, 26 November 1849, FO 17/159, fo. 110–111; *China Mail*, 13 March 1851, CO 132/2, fo. 177.
50. Stephen to Addington, 22 February 1843, CO 129/3, fo. 94–96.
51. Addington to Stephen, 22 March 1843, CO 129/3, fo. 153.
52. Stephen's Minute of 23 March 1843, CO 129/3, fo. 165.
53. Stephen's Minute of 11 February 1843, CO 129/3, fo. 93.
54. Addington to Stephen, 22 March 1843, CO 129/3, fo. 153–156.
55. Legal Opinion of John Dodson, Frederick Pollock, and William Webb Follett, 18 March 1843, CO 129/3, fo. 166–170.
56. Stephen's Marginal Note, likely 24 March 1843, CO 129/3, fo. 168. Stephen also argued that the Chinese residents of Hong Kong 'have the *Jus Postliminii*'. This was a reference to the legal principle that, unless otherwise agreed in a treaty, the resumption of peace between warring states required them to return captured prisoners and territory. See the Legal Opinion of George Chalmers, 1814, reproduced in William Forsyth, ed., *Cases and Opinions on Constitutional Law and Various Points of English Jurisprudence* (London: Stevens and Haynes, 1869), 257–86 at 277.
57. On the four types of allegiance that the English Crown and later the British Crown could command – natural, legal, local, and acquired allegiance – see Keechang Kim, *Aliens in Medieval Law: The Origins of Modern Citizenship* (New York, NY: Cambridge University Press, 2000), 176–99; James H. Kettner, *The Development of American Citizenship, 1608–1870* (Chapel Hill, NC: University of North Carolina Press, 1978), 13–64.
58. Stephen's Minute of 12 July 1843, CO 129/3, fo. 219; *Calvin's Case* (1608) 7 Co. Rep. 1a.
59. *Campbell* v. *Hall* (1774), 1 Cowp. 161 at 171–204. See Rieko Karatani, *Defining British Citizenship: Empire, Commonwealth, and Modern Britain* (London: Frank Cass, 2003), 42.
60. Forsyth, ed., *Cases and Opinions on Constitutional Law*, 333–40.
61. Articles 4 and 9 of the Treaty of Paris (1763), reproduced in the House of Lords Sessional Papers, Volume 1 (1714–1805), 159–74. For later

analyses of this question, which arrived at different conclusions, see, for example, E. F. W. G. van Pittius, *Nationality within the British Commonwealth of Nations* (London: P. S. King & Son, 1930), 72; Clive Parry, *Nationality and Citizenship Laws of the Commonwealth and of the Republic of Ireland* (London: Stevens & Sons, 1957), 72–3.

62. Clive Parry, ed., *A British Digest of International Law, Volume 5* (London: Stevens and Sons, 1965), 142; Francis Piggott, *Nationality Including Naturalization and English Law on the High Seas and Beyond the Realm, Part 1: Nationality and Naturalization* (London: William Clowes and Sons, 1907), 88.
63. Legal Opinion of Campbell and Rolfe, 28 December 1838, reproduced in Forsyth, ed., *Cases and Opinions on Constitutional Law*, 326–8.
64. Hannah Weiss Muller, *Subjects and Sovereign: Bonds of Belonging in the Eighteenth-Century British Empire* (New York, NY: Oxford University Press, 2017), 166–208. See also Robert Travers, *Ideology and Empire in Eighteenth-Century India: The British in Bengal* (New York, NY: Cambridge University Press, 2007), 181–206.
65. *Mayor of Lyons* v. *East India Company* (1836) 1 Moo. P.C. 175. On the origins of the Judicial Committee, see P. A. Howell, *The Judicial Committee of the Privy Council, 1833–1876* (Cambridge: Cambridge University Press, 1979).
66. All aliens in Britain were finally allowed to hold and devise land (in line with continental European practices) after the enactment of the Naturalisation Act, 33 & 34 Vict. c. 14 (1870). See generally Andreas Fahrmeir, *Citizens and Aliens: Foreigners and the Law in Britain and the German States, 1789–1870* (New York, NY: Berghahn Books, 2000), 179.
67. *Lyons* (1836) 1 Moo. P.C. 175, 257–58.
68. *Lyons* (1836), 287, emphasis added.
69. *Lyons* (1836), 288–9.
70. Addington to Stephen, 22 March 1843, CO 129/3, fo. 156.
71. Stephen to Addington, 30 March 1843, CO 129/3, fo. 162.
72. As Governor John Bowring remarked in 1858, '[i]t may be doubted if there be an opulent native in Hong Kong who would refuse obedience to the authorities in China, or take the oath of allegiance to the Queen of Great Britain': Bowring to Lytton, 18 September 1858, CO 129/69, fo. 249.
73. Addington to Stephen, 22 March 1843, CO 129/3, fo. 151, 157–159.
74. Stephen's Minutes of 23–24 March 1843, CO 129/3, fo. 165.
75. Stephen's Minutes of 23–24 March 1843, CO 129/3, fo. 165.
76. Stanley's Minute of 27 March 1843, CO 129/3, fo. 165.
77. Charter of the Colony of Hong Kong, 5 April 1843, CO 381/35, reproduced in Madden and Fieldhouse, *The Dependent Empire and Ireland*, 463–4. The power of colonial legislatures to enact ordinances

to naturalise aliens was confirmed under the Naturalisation of Aliens Act, 10 & 11 Vict. c. 83 (1847): Karatani, *Defining British Citizenship*, 55.

78. On judicial subservience to the Crown in the dependent British Empire, see John McLaren, *Dewigged, Bothered, and Bewildered: British Colonial Judges on Trial, 1800–1900* (Toronto: University of Toronto Press, 2011), especially 34–55. On Hong Kong, specifically, see Steve Tsang, ed., *Judicial Independence and the Rule of Law in Hong Kong* (Hong Kong: Hong Kong University Press, 2001). See also Chapter 5 of this book, which explores the role of judicial activism in the development of extradition law.
79. Pottinger to Aberdeen, 17 March 1843, FO 17/66, fo. 221; Pottinger to Aberdeen, 13 June 1843, FO 17/67, fo. 263–265. In September 1842, Major Malcolm travelled to London on a fast steamer to deliver the British copy of the Treaty of Nanjing. To reward his work, the British government made him a lieutenant colonel in December 1842 and sent him back to China in January 1843 with further instructions for Pottinger: Aberdeen to Pottinger, 4 January 1843, FO 17/64, fo. 13–15.
80. Pottinger's Memorandum of 13 May 1843, FO 17/67, fo. 265.
81. Keying to Pottinger, undated letter of May 1843, CO 129/3, fo. 363.
82. Stephen's Minute of 9 November 1843, CO 129/3, fo. 356.
83. Aberdeen to Pottinger, 6 April 1843, FO 17/64, fo. 212.
84. Pottinger to Aberdeen, 27 July 1843, FO 17/68, fo. 231.
85. James Hayes, 'Hong Kong Island Before 1841', *Journal of the Royal Asiatic Society (Hong Kong Branch)* 24 (1984): 105–42.
86. Proceedings of *The Queen* v. *Lo A-tow and Others*, CO 129/2, fo. 389–396.
87. *The Queen* v. *Lo A-tow*, CO 129/2, fo. 389–396.
88. *The Queen* v. *Lo A-tow*, CO 129/2, fo. 389–390.
89. *The Queen* v. *Lo A-tow*, CO 129/2, fo. 396; Ordnance Survey of Hong Kong, 1845, 'Hong Kong and China 1' subseries of CO 700.
90. *The Queen* v. *Lo A-tow*, CO 129/2, fo. 393.
91. Caine to Lau, letter received on 22 August 1843, CO 129/2, fo. 424.
92. Caine to Lau, 4 September 1843, CO 129/2, fo. 430.
93. Lau to Caine, 30 August 1843, CO 129/2, fo. 424–426.
94. Translation of Warrant, CO 129/2, fo. 419.
95. *The Queen* v. *Lo A-tow*, CO 129/2, fo. 389.
96. Remarks on the Trial by the Chief Magistrate, 14 September 1843, CO 129/2, fo. 411–414.
97. Pottinger's Memorandum of 30 September 1843, CO 129/2, fo. 415–417.
98. See Chapter 5 of this book.
99. Pottinger's Memorandum of 30 September 1843, CO 129/2, fo. 415–417.

100. Pottinger to Stanley, 9 December 1843, CO 129/2, fo. 381.
101. Pottinger's Note of 30 September 1843, CO 129/2, fo. 415.
102. Aberdeen to Davis, 26 March 1844, CO 129/8, fo. 71–74.
103. Stephen and Stanley's Minutes of 8 March 1844, CO 129/2, fo. 384.
104. Will Peyton, 'John Francis Davis as Governor and Diplomat on the China Coast (1844–1848)', *International History Review* 39, no. 5 (2017): 903–26.
105. Aberdeen to Davis, 26 March 1844, CO 129/8, fo. 74.
106. Davis to Aberdeen, 23 May 1844, CO 129/8, fo. 253.
107. Munn, 'William Caine and the Hong Kong Magistracy'.
108. Davis to Stanley, 6 July 1844, CO 129/6, fo. 357–363.
109. Stephen to Addington, 22 February 1843, CO 129/3, fo. 94–96.
110. Lord Stanley caused Davis' report to be filed away by writing, quite simply, 'Put by.'
111. G. B. Endacott, *Government and People in Hong Kong: A Constitutional History* (Hong Kong: Hong Kong University Press, 2000), 32–5. Compare with Christopher Munn, *Anglo-China: Chinese People and British Rule in Hong Kong, 1841–1880* (Hong Kong: Hong Kong University Press, 2001), 53–5, 164; Frank Welsh, *A History of Hong Kong* (London: HarperCollins, 1993), 164; John K. Fairbank, *Trade and Diplomacy on the China Coast: The Opening of the Treaty Ports, volume 1: 1842–1854* (Cambridge, MA: Harvard University Press, 1953), 128–9.
112. Ordinance No. 15 of 1844, ss. 3 and 13, later repealed and replaced by the largely similar Ordinance No. 6 of 1845.
113. Ordinances No. 5 and 10 of 1844: Munn, *Anglo-China*, 116.
114. May Holdsworth and Christopher Munn, *Crime, Justice and Punishment in Hong Kong: Central Police Station, Central Magistracy and Victoria Gaol* (Hong Kong: Hong Kong University Press, 2020), 116–18; Munn, *Anglo-China*, 209–10.
115. Bonham to Grey, 21 November 1849, CO 129/30, fo. 324–325; Bonham to Palmerston, 26 November 1849, FO 17/159, fo. 110–111.
116. Davis to Keying, 4 January 1845, CO 129/11, fo. 53. On the later exclusion of Chinese migrants from British settler colonies and the United States of America, see Adam M. McKeown, *Melancholy Order: Asian Migration and the Globalization of Borders* (New York, NY: Columbia University Press, 2011); John Fitzgerald, *Big White Lie: Chinese Australians in White Australia* (Sydney: University of New South Wales Press, 2007).
117. Notably, the British jurist and future Queen's Advocate, Travers Twiss effectively reproduced Davis' argument in his treatise, *The Law of Nations Considered as Independent Political Communities* (Oxford: Oxford University Press, 1861), 224. On late-nineteenth and early twentieth-century positivist rationalisations of extraterritoriality, see generally Turan Kayaoğlu, *Legal Imperialism: Sovereignty and Extraterritoriality in Japan, the Ottoman Empire, and China* (Cambridge: Cambridge University Press, 2010).

2 Domesticating Mobility

1. Frank Welsh, *A History of Hong Kong* (London: HarperCollins, 1993), 137.
2. Blue Books of Statistics for the Colony of Hong Kong, CO 133/7 (1850), fo. 74, and CO 133/17 (1860), fo. 95.
3. For the wider argument that 'Hong Kong bridged formal and informal empire' in different ways, serving military, diplomatic, commercial, and legal functions that ebbed and flowed over time, see Robert Bickers, 'The Colony's Shifting Position in the British Informal Empire in China', in Judith M. Brown and Rosemary Foot, eds., *Hong Kong's Transitions, 1842–1997* (London: Macmillan, 1997), 33–61.
4. Davis to Aberdeen, 5 July 1844, CO 129/8, fo. 359–362.
5. See Chapter 1 of this book.
6. Davis to Aberdeen, 5 July 1844, CO 129/8, fo. 361–362.
7. Lauren Benton and Lisa Ford, *Rage for Order: The British Empire and the Origins of International Law, 1800–1850* (Cambridge, MA: Harvard University Press, 2016), 90.
8. Amanda Nettelbeck, *Indigenous Rights and Subjecthood: Protection and Reform in the Nineteenth-Century British Empire* (New York, NY: Cambridge University Press, 2019); Lisa Ford, 'Protecting the Peace on the Edges of Empire: Commissioners of Crown Lands in New South Wales', in Bain Attwood, Lauren Benton, and Adam Clulow, eds., *Protection and Empire: A Global History* (New York, NY: Cambridge University Press, 2018), 175–93; Alan Lester and Fae Dussart, *Colonization and the Origins of Humanitarian Governance: Protecting Aborigines across the Nineteenth-Century British Empire* (Cambridge: Cambridge University Press, 2014), 173–225.
9. J. W. Norton-Kyshe, *History of the Laws and Courts of Hong Kong, Volume 1* (London: T. F. Unwin, 1898), 4–5.
10. Elliot to Auckland, 1 May 1841, FO 17/51, fo. 319, cited in Christopher Munn, *Anglo-China: Chinese People and British Rule in Hong Kong, 1841–1880* (Hong Kong: Hong Kong University Press, 2001), 29.
11. Davis to Keying, 4 January 1845, CO 129/11, fo. 53–54.
12. Pottinger to Aberdeen, 5 May 1843, FO 17/63, fo. 145.
13. Davis to Stanley, 21 October 1844, CO 129/7, fo. 108.
14. Ordinance No. 16 of 1844, CO 129/7, fo. 208.
15. Merchants' Address to the Governor and Legislative Council, 19 October 1844, CO 129/7, fo. 209.
16. Merchants' Address to the Governor and Legislative Council, 19 October 1844, CO 129/7, fo. 209.
17. Stanley to Pottinger, 6 April 1843, CO 403/1, pp. 2–6. On the politics of colonial self-government in the mid nineteenth century, see J. M. Ward, *Colonial Self-Government: The British Experience, 1759–1856* (London: Macmillan, 1976).

18. Labouchere to Bowring, 29 July 1856, CO 403/6, 482–490, cited in Frederick Madden and David Fieldhouse, *The Dependent Empire and Ireland, 1840–1900: Advance and Retreat in Representative Government (Select Documents on the Constitutional History of the British Empire and Commonwealth, Volume V)* (Westport, CT: Greenwood Press, 1991), 483–4.
19. Minute by Merivale, CO 129/62, cited in Madden and Fieldhouse, *Dependent Empire and Ireland*, 486.
20. Davis to Stanley, 6 November 1844, CO 129/7, fo. 198–200.
21. Munn, *Anglo-China*, 128–9.
22. Davis to Stanley, 6 November 1844, CO 129/7, fo. 198–201.
23. Ordinance No. 18 of 1844, s. 2, and Davis to Stanley, 4 December 1844, CO 129/7, fo. 245–247.
24. Bowring to Lytton, 18 September 1858, CO 129/69, fo. 246–249; Munn, *Anglo-China*, 67.
25. Ordinance No. 18 of 1844, CO 129/7, fo. 245.
26. Ordinance No. 16 of 1844, CO 129/7, fo. 208.
27. Ordinance No. 18 of 1844, ss. 3, 6.
28. Davis to Stanley, 28 December 1844, CO 129/7, fo. 322; Davis to Stanley, 3 February 1845, CO 129/11, fo. 79–81.
29. Minutes of the Executive Council of Hong Kong, 24 June 1845, CO 131/1, fo. 142.
30. Minutes of the Executive Council of Hong Kong, 24 June 1845, CO 131/1, fo. 305–308.
31. Minutes of the Executive Council of Hong Kong, 24 June 1845, CO 131/1, fo. 307.
32. Ordinance No. 7 of 1846, s. 2, CO 130/2, fo. 111. This Ordinance was partly a response to another report by Fearon of 1 October 1846, CO 129/19, fo. 60–65.
33. Ordinance No. 7 of 1846, ss. 2, 13, 17.
34. Ordinance No. 7 of 1846, ss. 5, 13.
35. Davis to Stanley, 15 October 1845, CO 129/13, fo. 239.
36. Lau to Caine, 30 August 1843, CO 129/2, fo. 424–426. See Chapter 1.
37. Bruce to Caine, 13 September 1844, HKRS 100-3, fo. 107.
38. Davis to Stanley, 15 October 1845, CO 129/13, fo. 239.
39. Caine to Hillier, 30 September 1845, HKRS 100-3, fo. 190.
40. Ordinance No. 1 of 1845, CO 129/11, fo. 43.
41. Robert J. Antony, *Unruly People: Crime, Community, and State in Late Imperial South China* (Hong Kong: Hong Kong University Press, 2016), 107–15, 194–6.
42. Antony, *Unruly People*, 201–12.
43. Davis to Acting Viceroy Ching, 15 May 1844, CO 129/8, fo. 274–275; Davis to Aberdeen, 20 December 1844, CO 129/7, fo. 302.
44. Davis to Aberdeen, 20 December 1844, CO 129/7, fo. 302.

45. Keying to Davis, 17 December 1844, CO 129/7, fo. 305.
46. Ordinance No. 1 of 1845, CO 129/11, fo. 43.
47. Davis to Keying, 22 December 1844, CO 129/11, fo. 46.
48. Charles Egan, *The Law of Extradition Comprising the Treaties Now in Force between England and France, and England and America* (London: W. W. Robinson, 1846), 1–12.
49. Keying to Davis, 30 December 1844, CO 129/11, fo. 48.
50. Keying to Davis, private letter received on 3 January 1845, CO 129/11, fo. 51.
51. Davis to Keying, 4 January 1845, CO 129/11, fo. 53–54.
52. Proceedings of the Executive Council of Hong Kong, 8 January 1845, CO 131/1, fo. 100.
53. Davis to Keying, 15 May 1844, CO 129/8, fo. 274–275.
54. Stanley to Davis, 28 June 1845, CO 129/11, fo. 41–42.
55. Stanley to Davis, 28 June 1845, CO 129/11, fo. 42.
56. Ordinance No. 12 of 1845, s. 1, CO 130/2, fo. 76.
57. Caine to Hillier, letters of 5 August and 8, 9, and 28 September 1846, HKRS 100-3, fo. 292, 312–314.
58. Shelley to Caine, 27 March 1846, HKRS 100–3, fo. 243.
59. Davis to Grey, 22 October 1846, and Extract from a Case of 54 Chinese Prisoners Tried before C. B. Hillier, Esq, Assistant Magistrate of Police, CO 129/17, fo. 282–287.
60. Ordinance No. 10 of 1844, CO 130/1, s. 25.
61. Question by John Bowring, 4 August 1846, UK House of Commons Debates, vol. 88, cc. 340–341.
62. *The Friend of China and Hong Kong Gazette*, 29 April 1846, p. 1176, Centre for Research Libraries Digital Resources, online: http://ddsnext.crl.edu/titles/18432#?c=0&m=175&s=0&cv=0&r=0&xywh=-195%2C-666%2C4854%2C3424 (accessed 20 February 2023).
63. Davis to Grey, 22 October 1846, CO 129/17, fo. 282. Not everyone agreed that rattan caning was less severe than flogging. See, for example, the testimony of William Scott, 'Report from the Select Committee on Commercial Relations with China', C. (1st series) 654, UK House of Commons Papers V.1 (1847), 278. On corporal punishment in colonial Hong Kong, see generally Frank Dikötter, '"A Paradise for Rascals": Colonialism, Punishment and the Prison in Hong Kong (1841–1898)', *Crime, History and Societies* 8, no. 1 (2004): 49–63.
64. Davis to Grey, 22 October 1846, CO 129/17, fo. 282–283.
65. Hawes, Minute of 29 December 1846, CO 129/17, fo. 284.
66. Grey, Minute of 30 December 1846, CO 129/17, fo. 284.
67. 'Report from the Select Committee on Commercial Relations with China' (1847), 167.
68. Ordinance No. 2 of 1850, CO 130/2, fo. 144, preamble and section 1.
69. Ordinance No. 2 of 1850, s. 3.

70. The Act of 8 & 9 Vict. c. 120 was cited in Bonham to Grey, 21 March 1850, CO 129/32, fo. 160–161. This Act added to the Acts 6 & 7 Vict. c. 75 (implementing the extradition agreement with France) and c. 76 (implementing the agreement with the United States).
71. Bonham to Grey, 21 March 1850, CO 129/32, fo. 161.
72. Ordinance No. 2 of 1850, s. 2.
73. 6 & 7 Vict. c. 75, s. 1, and c. 76, s. 1.
74. Ordinance No. 2 of 1850, s. 3.
75. 6 & 7 Vict. c. 75, s. 4, and c. 76, s. 4.
76. Bonham to Grey, 27 December 1848, CO 129/26, fo. 307; Bonham to Grey, 24 May 1849, CO 129/29, fo. 155–156; Inglis to Caine, 21 May 1849, CO 129/29, fo. 160–161.
77. Bonham to Grey, 24 May 1849, CO 129/29, fo. 155–156; Bonham to Grey, 7 September 1849, CO 129/30.
78. Bowring to Labouchere, 9 December 1856, CO 129/59, fo. 218–220. On Daniel Caldwell's chequered career, see Kaori Abe, 'Middlemen, Colonial Officials, and Corruption: The Rise and Fall of Government Compradors in Hong Kong, 1840s–1850s', *Modern Asian Studies* 52, no. 5 (2018): 1774–805; Christopher Munn, 'Colonialism "in a Chinese atmosphere": The Caldwell Affair and the Perils of Collaboration in Early Colonial Hong Kong', in Robert Bickers and Christian Henriot, eds., *New Frontiers: Imperialism's New Communities in East Asia, 1842–1953* (Manchester: Manchester University Press, 2000).
79. Ordinance No. 6 of 1857, CO 130/2, ss. 7, 35, 39.
80. Ordinance No. 2 of 1857, CO 130/2.
81. Munn, *Anglo-China*, 272.
82. Proclamation by Governor-General Ye of 28 October 1856, 'Papers Relating to the Proceedings of Her Majesty's Naval Forces at Canton', C. (1st series) 2206, UK House of Commons Command Papers XLIII.1 (1857), 40.
83. Ordinance No. 2 of 1857.
84. Ordinance No. 9 of 1857, CO 130/2; Labouchere to Bowring, 2 May 1857, CO 129/62, fo. 61–64.
85. Michael Lobban, *Imperial Incarceration: Detention without Trial in the Making of British Colonial Africa* (Cambridge: Cambridge University Press, 2021), 9–20; Lyndall Ryan, 'Martial Law in the British Empire', in Philip Dwyer and Amanda Nettelbeck, eds., *Violence, Colonialism and Empire in the Modern World* (Cambridge: Cambridge University Press, 2017), 93. Martial law was later declared in Jamaica following the notorious Morant Bay Rebellion of 1865: R. W. Kostal, *A Jurisprudence of Power: Victorian Empire and the Rule of Law* (Oxford: Oxford University Press, 2005).
86. Bowring to Labouchere, No. 19 of 29 January 1857, CO 129/62, fo. 154–157. More suspicious characters were detained in February: Proceedings of the Executive Council of Hong Kong, 26 February 1857, CO 131/4, fo. 62–63.

87. Bowring to Labouchere, No. 19 of 29 January 1857, CO 129/62, fo. 154–155.
88. Bowring to Labouchere, 20 January 1857, CO 129/62, fo. 108–109.
89. Norton-Kyshe, *History of the Laws and Courts of Hong Kong, Volume 1*, 414–18.
90. Kate Lowe and Eugene McLaughlin, '"Caution! The Bread Is Poisoned": The Hong Kong Mass Poisoning of January 1857', *Journal of Imperial and Commonwealth History* 43, no. 2 (2015): 189–209, 204. Compare with J. Y. Wong, *Deadly Dreams: Opium, Imperialism, and the Arrow War (1856–1860) in China* (Cambridge: Cambridge University Press, 1998), 26.
91. Labouchere to Bowring, 8 May 1857, CO 129/62, fo. 227–228; Bridges to Bowring, 12 August 1857, CO 129/64, fo. 114–119.
92. Choi Chi-cheung, 'Cheung Ah-Lum, A Biographical Note', *Journal of the Hong Kong Branch of the Royal Asiatic Society* 24 (1984): 282–7.
93. Merivale's and Ball's Minutes of 20 and 21 March 1857, CO 129/62, fo. 158.
94. Bowring to Labouchere, 28 February 1857, CO 129/62, fo. 338–339.
95. Ball's Minute of 4 May 1857, CO 129/62, fo. 340.
96. Ball's Minute of 7 May 1857, CO 129/62, fo. 341.
97. Merivale's Minutes of 6 and 7 May 1857, and Labouchere to Bowring, 9 June 1857, CO 129/62, fo. 341–344.
98. Jan Martin Lemnitzer, *Power, Law and the End of Privateering* (Basingstoke: Palgrave Macmillan, 2014).
99. Bruce A. Elleman, 'The Taiping Rebellion, Piracy, and the Arrow War', in Bruce A. Elleman, Andrew Forbes, and David Rosenberg, eds., *Piracy and Maritime Crime: Historical and Modern Case Studies* (Newport, RI: Naval War College Press, 2010), 51–63.
100. Lowe and McLaughlin, 'The Hong Kong Mass Poisoning of January 1857', 197.
101. Susanna Hoe and Derek Roebuck, *The Taking of Hong Kong: Charles and Clara Elliot in China Waters* (Richmond: Curzon Press, 1999), 261.
102. Stanley to Pottinger, 3 June 1843, CO 403/1, fo. 8–10.
103. 6 & 7 Vict. c. 80 (1843), s. 1.
104. 'Return of Names of Governors and Lieutenant Governors of Colonies', C. (1st series) 391, UK House of Commons Papers XXXI.403 (1852).
105. Benton and Ford, *Rage for Order*, 102–12.
106. Newcastle to Atherton and Palmer, 29 November 1862, CO 48/414/10592, cited in W. Ross Johnston, *Sovereignty and Protection: A Study of British Jurisdictional Imperialism in the Late Nineteenth Century* (Durham, NC: Duke University Press, 1973), 48.
107. Interestingly, the first High Commissioner for Southern Africa was none other than Henry Pottinger. Pottinger requested the creation of

this office in 1846 as a condition for taking up the governorship of the Cape Colony. He was offered the governorship because the Colonial Office needed an experienced administrator to keep the peace between white settlers and the native Xhosa people on the Cape frontier. See Johnston, *Sovereignty and Protection*, 46.

108. Inge van Hulle, *Britain and International Law in West Africa: The Practice of Empire* (New York, NY: Oxford University Press, 2020), 161.
109. W. David McIntyre, *The Imperial Frontier in the Tropics, 1865–75* (London: Palgrave Macmillan, 1967), 364–8; Peter Burroughs, 'Imperial Institutions and the Government of Empire', in Andrew Porter and Wm. Roger Louis, eds., *The Oxford History of the British Empire, Volume III: The Nineteenth Century* (Oxford: Oxford University Press, 1999), 170–97.
110. John K. Fairbank, *Trade and Diplomacy on the China Coast: The Opening of the Treaty Ports, Volume 1: 1842–1854* (Cambridge, MA: Harvard University Press, 1953), 24–8.
111. Paul A. van Dyke, *The Canton Trade: Life and Enterprise on the China Coast, 1700–1845* (Hong Kong: Hong Kong University Press, 2005).
112. 'Treaties between H.M. and Emperor of China, with Rules for Trade and Tariff of Duties', C. (1st Series) 2755, UK House of Commons Command Papers LXI.285 (1858–1860).
113. Richard S. Horowitz, 'The Opium Wars of 1839–1860', in Stephan Haggard and David C. Kang, eds., *East Asia in the World: Twelve Events that Shaped the Modern International Order* (Cambridge: Cambridge University Press, 2020), 164–87.
114. Order of Council of 17 April 1844, reproduced in Lewis Hertslet, ed., *Hertslet's Commercial Treaties: A Complete Collection of the Treaties and Conventions, and Reciprocal Regulations, at Present Subsisting between Great Britain and Foreign Powers, Volume 6* (London: Butterworth, 1845), 276. In the view of the Foreign Office, 'the chief superintendent of trade in China is what a consul-general was in former times. The consuls correspond directly with him, and he either decides points himself, or sends them home for decision'. For this quotation, see the 'Report of the Select Committee on the Consular Service and Appointments', C. (1st series) 482, UK House of Commons Papers VIII.1 (1857–8), 77.
115. Wong, *Deadly Dreams*, 262–3.
116. Philip Bowring, *Free Trade's First Missionary: Sir John Bowring in Europe and Asia* (Hong Kong: Hong Kong University Press, 2014), 66–7, 115–34.
117. Merivale, Minute of 11 April 1855, CO 129/49, fo. 125–128.
118. Peel to Bowring, 15 February 1854, CO 403/5, fo. 141–143.
119. Bowring to Grey, 28 February 1855, CO 129/49, fo. 181–182.

120. Palmerston, Minute of 15 April 1855, CO 129/49, fo. 128. On Bowring's acquaintance with Palmerston, see Bowring, *Free Trade's First Missionary*, 115–16.
121. Merivale, Minute of 11 April 1855, and Palmerston to Bowring, 28 April 1855, CO 129/49, fo. 118, 127–130.
122. Wong, *Deadly Dreams*, 70–4, 174–215.
123. On the imperial implications of the general election of 1857, see Alan Lester, Kate Boehme, and Peter Mitchell, *Ruling the World: Freedom, Civilisation and Liberalism in the Nineteenth-Century British Empire* (Cambridge: Cambridge University Press, 2021), 215–18.
124. Gregson to Clarendon, 6 January 1858, FO 17/279, cited in Wong, *Deadly Dreams*, 304.
125. Clarendon to Bowring, 10 March, 25 March, and 21 April 1857, FO 17/261, fo. 177–179, 221–223, 254.
126. 22 & 23 Vict. c. 9, s. 2 (1859).
127. Bulwer-Lytton to Bowring, 9 December 1858 and 26 March 1859, CO 403/8, fo. 203, 223.
128. Murray to Rogers, 29 July 1865, CO 129/109, fo. 164.
129. Alexander to Robertson, 15 June 1865, FO 17/613, fo. 35–36; Mercer, Memorandum of 22 June 1865, CO 129/105, fo. 466.
130. Robertson to Wade, 19 June 1865, FO 17/613, fo. 9, 15.
131. Wade to Russell, 8 July 1865, FO 17/613, fo. 4.
132. Cardwell to Mercer, 26 December 1865, CO 129/109, fo. 323.
133. Statement of Sun-He, 4 July 1867, CO 129/123, fo. 355–356.
134. Statement of Sun-He, 4 July 1867, CO 129/123, fo. 355–356.
135. Robertson to Smith, 18 July 1867, CO 129/123, fo. 360, 362.
136. MacDonnell to Buckingham, 29 July 1867, and Smith to Robertson, 22 July 1867, CO 129/123, fo. 350, 363–365.
137. Rogers, Minute of 19 September 1867, CO 129/123, fo. 351; Buckingham to MacDonnell, 25 October 1867, CO 129/127, fo. 457.
138. Twiss to Adderley, 9 October 1867, CO 129/127, fo. 458. On the extradition of fugitive slaves, see Chapter 5 of this book.
139. Smith, Memorandum of 16 December 1869, CO 129/147, fo. 429–430.
140. Smith, Memorandum of 16 December 1869, CO 129/147, fo. 430–433.
141. MacDonnell to Buckingham, 11 January 1869, CO 129/136, fo. 51–56.
142. Amanda Nettelbeck, 'Creating the Aboriginal Vagrant: Protective Governance and Indigenous Mobility in Colonial Australia', *Pacific Historical Review* 87, no. 1 (2018): 79–100.
143. Victoria Registration Ordinance, No. 7 of 1866, and Ordinance for the Maintenance of Order and Cleanliness, No. 8 of 1866, CO 130/3, fo. 129; Blue Book of Statistics for the Colony of Hong Kong, 1869, CO 133/26, fo. 105.

144. MacDonnell to Buckingham, 11 January 1869, CO 129/136, fo. 51, 54.
145. MacDonnell to Buckingham, 27 August 1867, CO 129/124, fo. 202–205.
146. MacDonnell to Buckingham, 11 January 1869, CO 129/136, fo. 55.
147. Minute by Granville, 4 March 1869, and Rogers to Hammond, 13 March 1869, CO 129/141, fo. 56, 67–70.
148. Hammond to Rogers, 3 May 1869, and Granville to MacDonnell, 10 May 1869, CO 129/141, fo. 128.
149. Robertson to Wade, 19 June 1865, FO 17/613, fo. 9–12; Mercer to Cardwell, 13 November 1865, CO 129/107, fo. 311–312.
150. Christopher M. Roberts and Hazel W. H. Leung, 'Governance through Vagrancy Law in Hong Kong, 1841–1939', in Cerian Griffiths and Łukasz Jan Korporowicz, eds., *English Law and Colonial Connections: Histories, Parallels, and Influences* (Oxford: Routledge, 2024), 194–5.
151. Christopher Munn, '"Our Best Trump Card": A Brief History of Deportation in Hong Kong, 1857–1955', in Michael Ng and John D. Wong, eds., *Civil Unrest and Governance in Hong Kong: Law and Order from Historical and Cultural Perspectives* (London: Routledge, 2017), 30–5; Christopher Munn, 'Margins of Justice in Colonial Hong Kong: Extrajudicial Power, Solicitors' Clerks, and the Case of Li Hong Mi, 1917–1920', *Law and Humanities* 11, no. 1 (2017): 102–20. On politically motivated deportations after the Second World War, see Michael Ng, *Political Censorship in British Hong Kong: Freedom of Expression and the Law (1842–1997)* (Cambridge: Cambridge University Press, 2022), 55–86.
152. The Registrar General and Protector of Chinese Inhabitants became the Secretary for Chinese Affairs in 1913, then the Secretary for Home Affairs in 1969: Ho Pui-yin, *The Administrative History of the Hong Kong Government Agencies, 1841–2002* (Hong Kong: Hong Kong University Press, 2002), 25–7. On the historical links between the rise of the registrar generalship and the professionalisation of the civil service in colonial Hong Kong – links that involved the appointment of 'cadet officers', one of the first of whom was Cecil Clementi Smith – see H. J. Lethbridge, 'Hong Kong Cadets, 1862–1941', *Journal of the Royal Asiatic Society (Hong Kong Branch)* 10 (1970): 36–56; Shiona Airlie, *Thistle and Bamboo: The Life and Times of Sir James Stewart Lockhart* (Hong Kong: Hong Kong University Press, 2010). On cadet officers in Hong Kong, Ceylon, and the Straits Settlements, see also Anthony Kirk-Greene, *Britain's Imperial Administrators, 1858–1966* (London: Macmillan, 2000), 127.
153. For modern accounts of disguised extradition, see, for example, Ivor Stanbrook and Clive Stanbrook, *Extradition Law and Practice*, 2nd ed. (Oxford: Oxford University Press, 2000), 345; M. Cherif Bassiouni,

International Extradition: United States Law and Practice, 6th ed. (New York, NY: Oxford University Press, 2014), 213–73.

154. Namely, the Deportation Ordinance 1917, cited in Geoffrey C. Gunn, *Ho Chi Minh in Hong Kong: Anticolonial Networks, Extradition and the Rule of Law* (Cambridge: Cambridge University Press, 2021), 162.
155. Munn, 'A Brief History of Deportation in Hong Kong', 37.
156. *The Times*, 7 September 1882, cited in Paul O'Higgins, 'Disguised Extradition: The Soblen Case', *Modern Law Review* 27 (1964): 521–39 at 521–2.
157. Speech of J. R. Clynes, 19 February 1931, UK House of Commons Debates, vol. 248, c. 1430, cited in Emily Whewell, 'Seeking Refuge in Hostility: The Caribbean "British Isle of Freedom" and the Right to Remove Fugitive Convicts', *Journal of Imperial and Commonwealth History* 48, no. 1 (2020): 149–67, at 156.
158. Whewell, 'Seeking Refuge in Hostility', 151.
159. Notably 33 Geo. III c. 4 (1793), 43 Geo. III c. 155 (1803), and 11 & 12 Vict. c. 20 (1848). There is reportedly no record of the Aliens Act 1848 being enforced against anyone before lapsing in 1850. See Bernard Porter, *The Refugee Question in Mid-Victorian Politics* (New York, NY: Cambridge University Press, 1979), 3. It was subsequently only in 1905 that the Crown acquired further powers to deport people from the British Isles, as Parliament took steps to control immigration from Eastern Europe: Alison Bashford and Catie Gilchrist, 'The Colonial History of the 1905 Aliens Act', *Journal of Imperial and Commonwealth History* 40, no. 3 (2012): 409–37.

3 Navigating Disorder

1. Robert J. Anthony, ed., *Elusive Pirates, Pervasive Smugglers: Violence and Clandestine Trade in the Greater China Seas* (Hong Kong: Hong Kong University Press, 2010).
2. Arnold J. Meagher, *The Coolie Trade: The Traffic in Chinese Laborers to Latin America 1847–1874* (Philadelphia, PA: Xlibris, 2008).
3. 'Return of Cases of Extradition of Prisoners under Treaty between Great Britain and United States', C. (2nd series) 1557/1621, UK Command Papers LXXXII.199, 207; Bernard Porter, *The Refugee Question in Mid-Victorian Politics* (New York, NY: Cambridge University Press, 1979), 144 n.
4. Davis to Keying, 13 November 1846, CO 129/17, fo. 323; Bowring to Labouchere, 22 July 1857, CO 129/63, fo. 472–480; MacDonnell to Alcock, 16 May 1866, CO 129/113, fo. 181.
5. Bradley Miller, *Borderline Crime: Fugitive Criminals and the Challenge of the Border, 1819–1914* (Toronto: University of Toronto Press, 2016), 155–61.

6. On the history of the idea of the universal jurisdiction over piracy, see Mark Chadwick, *Piracy and the Origins of Universal Jurisdiction: On Stranger Tides?* (Leiden: Brill-Nijhoff, 2019); Michael Kempe, '"Publique Enemies to Mankind": International Pirates as a Product of International Politics', in Stefan Eklöf Amirell, Bruce Buchan, and Hans Hägerdal, eds., *Piracy in World History* (Amsterdam: Amsterdam University Press, 2021), 35–59.
7. Lauren Benton, 'Toward a New Legal History of Piracy: Maritime Legalities and the Myth of Universal Jurisdiction', *International Journal of Maritime History* 23, no. 1 (2011): 225–40, at 225.
8. Alfred P. Rubin, *The Law of Piracy*, 2nd ed. (Honolulu, HI: University Press of the Pacific, 2006), 272.
9. Davis to Stanley, 8 March 1845, CO 129/11, fo. 157; Davis to Grey, 26 February 1848, CO 129/23, fo. 188.
10. Christopher Munn, *Anglo-China: Chinese People and British Rule in Hong Kong, 1841–1880* (Hong Kong: Hong Kong University Press, 2001), 152–6.
11. Blue Books of Statistics for the Colony of Hong Kong, 1856, CO 133/13, fo. 119–121.
12. Christopher Munn, 'The Hong Kong Opium Revenue, 1845–1885', in Timothy Brook and Bob Tadashi Wakabayashi, eds., *Opium Regimes: China, Britain, and Japan, 1839–1952* (Berkeley, CA: University of California Press, 2000).
13. Stephen's Memorandum of January 1840, CO 323/226, cited in John W. Cell, *British Colonial Administration in the Mid-Nineteenth Century: The Policy-Making Process* (New Haven, CT: Yale University Press, 1970), 12.
14. Bowring to Labouchere, 25 March 1858, CO 129/67, fo. 321–323.
15. Blue Books of Statistics for the Colony of Hong Kong, 1863, CO 133/20, fo. 178; Block Plan of Victoria Gaol, 1865, MPG 1/1113. As a devoted Benthamite, Bowring modelled the new Victoria Gaol after Jeremy Bentham's 'panopticon' penitentiary: May Holdsworth and Christopher Munn, *Crime, Justice and Punishment in Hong Kong: Central Police Station, Central Magistracy and Victoria Gaol* (Hong Kong: Hong Kong University Press, 2020), 193–6.
16. Blue Books of Statistics for the Colony of Hong Kong, 1856, CO 133/13, fo. 202; 1857, CO 133/14, fo. 110–111; 1859, CO 133/16, fo. 132.
17. Blue Books of Statistics for the Colony of Hong Kong, 1866, CO 133/23, fo. 126.
18. Proceedings of *R* v. *Chun Ah-tsup and others*, 17 August 1850, CO 129/33, fo. 188–191.
19. Bonham to Grey, 6 August 1850, CO 129/33, fo. 169–171.
20. Bonham to Grey, 6 August 1850, CO 129/33, fo. 169–171.
21. Bowring to Labouchere, 28 February 1857, CO 129/62, fo. 339.

22. Hulme to Grey, 8 July 1852, CO 129/41, fo. 206, cited in Munn, *Anglo-China*, 217. On the decline of capital punishment in England during the early nineteenth century, see Simon Devereux, *Execution, State and Society in England, 1660–1900* (Cambridge: Cambridge University Press, 2023), 284–320.
23. Blue Books of Statistics for the Colony of Hong Kong, 1852–58, CO 133/9, fo. 179; CO 133/10, fo. 158; CO 133/11, fo. 162; CO 133/12, fo. 184; CO 133/13, fo. 246; CO 133/14, fo. 116; CO 133/15, fo. 133. On the cost of transporting convicts from Hong Kong, see Christopher Munn, 'The Transportation of Chinese Convicts from Hong Kong, 1844–1858', *Journal of the Canadian Historical Association* 8, no. 1 (1997): 113–45, at 122.
24. Munn, 'The Transportation of Chinese Convicts from Hong Kong', 121.
25. Ceded to Britain by the Sultanate of Brunei under the Treaty of Labuan (1846), the island of Labuan became a Crown colony in 1848, a territory of the British North Borneo Company in 1890, and, finally, part of the Straits Settlements in 1907.
26. Labouchere to Bowring, 22 December 1858, CO 129/58, fo. 342–344.
27. Hilary M. Carey, *Empire of Hell: Religion and the Campaign to End Convict Transportation in the British Empire, 1788–1875* (Cambridge: Cambridge University Press, 2019).
28. Yue-shan Chan, 'A Study of the Adoption and Enforcement of Transportation in Hong Kong 1844–1858', PhD dissertation, University of Hong Kong (2009), 201–2; Ravindra K. Jain, 'South Indian Labour in Malaya, 1840–1920', in Kay Saunders, ed., *Indentured Labour in the British Empire, 1834–1920* (London: Croom Helm, 1984), 158–82.
29. Other colonial efforts to substitute Chinese migrant labour for the labour of slaves and convicts are discussed in Stan Neal, *Singapore, Chinese Migration and the Making of the British Empire, 1819–67* (Woodbridge: Boydell Press, 2019).
30. Bowring to Labouchere, 28 February 1857, CO 129/62, fo. 339.
31. Robinson to Cardwell, 9 August 1864, CO 129/99, fo. 332–333.
32. Blue Books of Statistics for the Colony of Hong Kong, 1849–66, CO 133/6, fo. 102; CO 133/16, fo. 189; CO 133/17, fo. 148; CO 133/18, fo. 166; CO 133/20, fo. 181; CO 133/21, fo. 177; CO 133/22, fo. 181; CO 133/23, fo. 191.
33. Robinson to Cardwell, 9 August 1864, CO 129/99, fo. 332–333.
34. The Hong Kong Court of Justice was the same court that the Crown had legislated for but not actually established in Canton during 1833–42 (see Chapter 1 of this book). An Order in Council of 4 January 1843 relocated the Court of Justice to Hong Kong, where it sat until it was replaced in October 1844 by the Supreme Court of Hong Kong, a creation of the colony's Legislative Council. The ordinance that established the Supreme Court granted it admiralty jurisdiction, but imperial officials

noted in 1845 that only the Queen could create such a jurisdiction. As a result, letters patent were issued in January 1846 to establish the Hong Kong Court of Vice-Admiralty. In 1849, however, an Act of Parliament abolished all colonial Courts of Vice-Admiralty, vesting the municipal courts of each colony with the jurisdiction to try all crimes committed within admiralty jurisdiction. As a result, the jurisdiction to try pirates was vested once again in the Supreme Court of Hong Kong. See Hong Kong Ordinances No. 15 of 1844 and No. 6 of 1845, CO 130/1–2; Stephen's Minute of 13 March 1845, and Stanley to Davis, 24 March 1845, CO 129/7, fo. 113–123; Admiralty Offences (Colonial) Act, 12 & 13 Vict. c. 96 (1849). On the Hong Kong Court of Vice-Admiralty, see J. W. Norton-Kyshe, *History of the Laws and Courts of Hong Kong, Volume 1* (London: T. F. Unwin, 1898), 95, 282. On colonial Courts of Vice-Admiralty more generally, see Bevan Marten, 'Constitutional Irregularities in the British Imperial Courts of Vice Admiralty during the Mid-Nineteenth Century', *Journal of Legal History* 37, no. 2 (2016): 215–43.

35. Grace Fox, *British Admirals and Chinese Pirates, 1832–1869* (New York, NY: Routledge, 2019), 107–12; C. Nathan Kwan, '"Putting Down a Common Enemy": Piracy and Occasional Interstate Power in South China during the Mid-Nineteenth Century', *International Journal of Maritime History* 32, no. 3 (2020): 697–712, at 707.
36. Bowring to Labouchere, 13 October 1856, CO 129/58, fo. 341, 364–365.
37. Order in Council of 9 March 1865, ss. 119–126, reproduced in Lewis Hertslet, *Hertslet's Commercial Treaties: A Complete Collection of the Treaties and Conventions, and Reciprocal Regulations, at Present Subsisting between Great Britain and Foreign Powers, Volume 12* (London: Butterworth, 1871), 308–310. See generally Christopher Roberts, *The British Courts and Extra-territoriality in Japan, 1859–1899* (Leiden: Global Oriental, 2014), 15–19; Emily Whewell, 'British Extraterritoriality in China: The Legal System, Functions of Criminal Jurisdiction, and Its Challenges, 1833–1943', PhD dissertation, University of Leicester (2015), 48–61.
38. Pär Kristoffer Cassel, *Grounds of Judgment: Extraterritoriality and Imperial Power in Nineteenth-Century China and Japan* (Oxford: Oxford University Press, 2012), 68.
39. Order in Council of 9 March 1865, ss. 54 and 98. On the British perpetration of 'creek piracy' along Chinese rivers during the 1850s and 1860s, see Alexander Thompson, *British Law and Governance in Treaty Port China 1842–1927: Consuls, Courts and Colonial Subjects* (Amsterdam: Amsterdam University Press, 2024), 93–111.
40. The British consular courts' lack of jurisdiction over non-British criminals was confirmed in an opinion of the Law Officers of the Crown, reproduced in Clive Parry, ed., *Law Officers' Opinions to the Foreign*

Office, 1793–1860, Volume 20 (Farnborough: Gregg International Publishers, 1970), 179.

41. Robinson to Cardwell, 9 August 1864, CO 129/99, fo. 332.
42. Bonham to Grey, 6 August 1850, CO 129/33, fo. 170–173.
43. Robinson to Cardwell, 9 August 1864, CO 129/99, fo. 334.
44. Robinson to Cardwell, 9 August 1864, CO 129/99, fo. 335–336.
45. Grey to Bonham, 12 November 1850, CO 129/33, fo. 183–186.
46. Bonham to Grey, 29 January 1851, CO 129/36, fo. 56.
47. Robinson to Cardwell, 9 August 1864, CO 129/99, fo. 334–335.
48. *China Mail*, 24 March 1853, quoted in Fox, *British Admirals and Chinese Pirates*, 118.
49. Bowring to Russell, 4 September 1855, CO 129/51, fo. 209–210.
50. Ordinance No. 4 of 1855, CO 130/2, fo. 206.
51. Ordinance No. 4 of 1855, CO 130/2, fo. 206.
52. J. Y. Wong, *Deadly Dreams: Opium, Imperialism, and the Arrow War (1856–1860) in China* (Cambridge: Cambridge University Press, 1998), 58.
53. Wong, *Deadly Dreams*, 43–68.
54. Robert Bickers, *The Scramble for China: Foreign Devils in the Qing Empire, 1832–1914* (London: Allen Lane, 2011), 145.
55. Mercer's Memorandum on the Kowloon Peninsula Question, 6 June 1859, CO 129/74, fo. 97–107, at 102.
56. Mercer's Memorandum on the Kowloon Peninsula Question, 6 June 1859, CO 129/74, fo. 101–102.
57. Article 6 of the Convention signed at Peking, 24 October 1860, reproduced in 'Treaties between H.M. and Emperor of China, with Rules for Trade and Tariff of Duties', C. (1st Series) 2755, UK House of Commons Command Papers LXI.285 (1858–1860).
58. MacDonnell to Carnarvon, 25 September 1866, CO 129/115, fo. 139.
59. MacDonnell to Carnarvon, 25 September and 12 October 1866, CO 129/115, fo. 139, 229.
60. John Rolt, J. B. Karslake, and Robert Phillimore to Stanley, 15 January 1867, CO 129/127, fo. 235–246 at 244.
61. Pauncefote's Legal Opinion of 11 October 1866, CO 129/115, fo. 229.
62. John Rolt, J. B. Karslake, and Robert Phillimore to Stanley, 15 January and 16 July 1867, CO 129/127, fo. 235–246, 354–355.
63. Alcock to Stanley, 28 September 1867, CO 129/127, fo. 541–543; Alcock to MacDonnell, 28 September 1867, CO 129/125, fo. 196–201.
64. Rogers' Minute of 7 January 1868, CO 129/125, fo. 191–193.
65. 'Convention between United Kingdom and China respecting the Extension of Hong Kong Territory', C. (2nd series) 9087, UK Parliamentary Command Papers CIX.639 (1898).
66. Proceedings of the Executive Council of Hong Kong, 26 March 1845, CO 131/1, fo. 131.

67. John K. Fairbank, *Trade and Diplomacy on the China Coast: The Opening of the Treaty Ports, Volume 1: 1842–1854* (Cambridge, MA: Harvard University Press, 1953), 243.
68. *China Mail*, 26 August and 28 October 1847, CO 132/1.
69. Proceedings of the Executive Council of Hong Kong, 20 July 1848, CO 131/2, fo. 28–43.
70. Bonham to Grey, 21 October 1850, CO 129/34, fo. 78. On Chinese indentured labourers in Peru, see Watt Stewart, *Chinese Bondage in Peru: A History of the Chinese Coolie in Peru, 1849–1874* (Durham, NC: Duke University Press, 1951).
71. David Northrup, *Indentured Labor in the Age of Imperialism, 1834–1922* (New York, NY: Cambridge University Press, 1995).
72. Meagher, *The Coolie Trade*, 190.
73. Hillier to Caine, 7 October 1850, CO 129/34, fo. 85–88.
74. Bonham to Grey, 21 October 1850, CO 129/34, fo. 80.
75. Bonham to Grey, 21 October 1850, CO 129/34, fo. 81; 'Convention between Her Majesty and the King of French, for the Mutual Surrender, in Certain Cases, of Persons Fugitive from Justice, signed at London, February 13, 1843', C. (1st series) 444, UK House of Commons Command Papers LX.487 (1843).
76. Grey to Bonham, 1 February 1852, CO 129/34, fo. 84.
77. Merivale's Minute of 26 December 1850, CO 129/34, fo. 81; French Extradition Act, 6 & 7 Vict. c. 75 (1843).
78. Robert L. Irick, *Ch'ing Policy toward the Coolie Trade, 1847–1878* (Taipei: Chinese Materials Center, 1982), 33 n.
79. Bridges to Caine, 14 June 1852, CO 129/40, fo. 146–147; Irick, *Ch'ing Policy toward the Coolie Trade*, 36.
80. Eileen P. Scully, *Bargaining with the State from Afar: American Citizenship in Treaty Port China, 1844–1942* (New York, NY: Columbia University Press, 2001), 67.
81. Bridges to Caine, 14 June 1852, CO 129/40, fo. 146–148.
82. Merivale's Minute of 25 August 1852, and Merivale to the Law Officers of the Crown, 14 September 1852, CO 129/40, fo. 141–142.
83. Opinion of the Law Officers of the Crown, 21 September 1852, CO 129/41, fo. 103–105.
84. Pakington to Jervois, 30 September 1852, CO 129/40, fo. 144.
85. Irick, *Ch'ing Policy toward the Coolie Trade*, 43.
86. Ball's and Merivale's Minutes of 6–7 May 1857, CO 129/62, fo. 341.
87. Hong Kong Ordinance No. 2 of 1850, s. 1, CO 130/2, fo. 144. See Chapter 2 of this book.
88. Labouchere to Bowring, 9 June 1857, CO 129/62, fo. 343–344.
89. Bowring to Labouchere, 22 July 1857, and Labouchere to Bowring, 14 October 1857, CO 129/63, fo. 472–479.
90. Labouchere to Bowring, 14 October 1857, CO 129/63, fo. 472–479.

91. Robinson to Cardwell, 9 August 1864, CO 129/99, fo. 332.
92. Cardwell to Mercer, 10 April 1865, CO 129/109, fo. 58–59.
93. Hong Kong Ordinance No. 13 of 1865, CO 130/3, fo. 115.
94. Cardwell to Mercer, 26 January 1866, CO 129/117, fo. 235.
95. Robinson to Newcastle, 23 March 1860, CO 129/77, fo. 158–159.
96. Statement of Ing A-soong, 19 January 1860, CO 129/77, fo. 172–178.
97. Extract from the February Sessions of the Criminal Calendar of Hong Kong, 1860, CO 129/77, 196.
98. Robinson to Newcastle, 23 October 1861, CO 129/82, fo. 232–236.
99. Testimonies of Chun Ahyoong, Ng Ahng, Low Ahtoo, and Yong Ahng, 3 December 1861, CO 129/82, fo. 421–439.
100. Robinson to Newcastle, 23 October 1861, CO 129/82, fo. 238–240.
101. Chinese Passengers Act, 18 & 19 Vict. c. 104 (1855).
102. 'Minute of Information Obtained in Investigation on board the *Ville D'Agen*, September 23rd–26th 1861', CO 129/82, fo. 283–289.
103. Thomsett to Mercer, 19 September 1861, CO 129/82, fo. 159–161.
104. Robinson to Newcastle, 23 October 1861, CO 129/82, fo. 241–244.
105. Harding, Atherton, and Palmer to Hammond, 22 February 1862, FO 83/2251, fo. 141–147.
106. Newcastle to Robinson, 26 February 1862, CO 129/89, fo. 194–196.
107. Slave Trade Act, 5 Geo. IV c. 113 (1824); Adams to Robinson, 10 December 1861, CO 129/82, fo. 447.
108. Robinson to Newcastle, 23 October 1861, CO 129/82, fo. 248.
109. Lao to the Allied Commissioners in Canton, 22 September 1861, CO 129/82, fo. 303–306.
110. Robinson to Newcastle, 23 October 1861, and Mercer to the Allied Commissioners in Canton, 26 September 1861, CO 129/82, fo. 245–247, 307–308.
111. Adams to Robinson, 10 December 1861, CO 129/82, fo. 448.
112. Warrant for the arrest of Juan Pastor, 29 November 1861, CO 129/82, fo. 416.
113. Extract from the Minutes of the Executive Council, CO 129/82, fo. 408–410.
114. Smale's Report of 14 December 1861, CO 129/82, fo. 411–412.
115. Article 10, Treaty between H.M. and United States of America, Washington, C. (1st series) 424, UK Command Papers LXI.1 (1842); Article 1, Convention between H.M. and King of the French, for Mutual Surrender of Persons Fugitive from Justice, C. (1st series) 444, UK Command Papers LX.487 (1843).
116. 6 & 7 Vict. c. 75 and c. 76 (1843).
117. Smale, Report of 14 December 1861 and Robinson to Newcastle, 13 December 1861, CO 129/82, fo. 402–406, 413–414.
118. Adams to Robinson, 10 December 1861, CO 129/82, fo. 447–454 (emphasis added).

119. Robert Phillimore, *Commentaries Upon International Law, Volume 1* (Philadelphia, PA: T. & J.W. Johnson, 1854), 247–53.
120. *Le Louis* (1817) 165 E.R. 1464. See Rubin, *The Law of Piracy*, 192 n.; Chadwick, *Piracy and the Origins of Universal Jurisdiction*, 161–2.
121. 'First Report from the Select Committee on the Slave Trade', C. (1st series) 308, UK House of Commons Papers XIX.1 (1849).
122. Jenny S. Martinez, *The Slave Trade and the Origins of International Human Rights Law* (Oxford: Oxford University Press, 2012), 114–39.
123. 5 Geo. IV c. 113, s. 9.
124. Harding, Atherton and Palmer to Newcastle, 21 February 1862, and to Russell, 22 February 1862, CO 129/89, fo. 74–78, 190–191.
125. Hammond to Rogers, 25 February 1862, and Newcastle to Robinson, 26 February 1862, CO 129/89, fo. 65, 194–196.
126. The Peruvian Minister in London to Russell, 7 February 1862, CO 129/89, fo. 82–88.
127. Russell to The Peruvian Minister in London, 3 and 5 March 1862, CO 129/89, fo. 89–92.
128. Robinson to Newcastle, 26 February 1862, CO 129/85, fo. 169–176, 180.
129. Newcastle to Robinson, 15 May 1862, CO 129/85, fo. 195–200.

4 Rationalising Reciprocity

1. Palmerston to Bonham, 24 January 1850, FO 17/164, fo. 41–42.
2. Treaty of Tianjin, Article 16 (emphasis added), reproduced in 'Treaties between Her Majesty and the Emperor of China, with Rules for Trade and Tariff of Duties', C. (1st Series) 2755, UK Parliament Command Papers LXI.285.
3. Treaty of Tianjin, Article 21.
4. Rogers, Minute of 8 August 1866, CO 129/117, fo. 390, 392.
5. Evidence of Hammond and Holland, in 'Report from the Select Committee on Extradition (1868); Together with the Proceedings of the Committee, Minutes of Evidence, and Appendix', UK House of Commons Papers VII.129, No. 393 (1868), 2, 10–14, 49–51.
6. I. A. Shearer, *Extradition in International Law* (Manchester: Manchester University Press, 1971), 31–2.
7. 6 & 7 Vict. c. 75, 76 (1843); 8 & 9 Vict. c. 120 (1845); 25 & 26 Vict. c. 70 (1862); 29 & 30 Vict. 121 (1866).
8. Charles Egan, *The Law of Extradition Comprising the Treaties Now in Force between England and France, and England and America* (London: W. W. Robinson, 1846); Edward Clarke, *A Treatise upon the Law of Extradition* (London: Steven and Haynes, 1867); Frederick Waymouth Gibbs, *Extradition Treaties* (London: William Ridgway, 1868).

9. Muriel E. Chamberlain, *Lord Aberdeen: A Political Biography* (London: Longman, 1983); Samuel John Butcher, 'Lord Aberdeen and Conservative Foreign Policy, 1841–1846', PhD dissertation, University of East Anglia (2015). On the historical connection between extradition arrangements and peace settlements, see Joanna Harrington, 'The Making of Modern International Extradition Law', in Neil Boister, Sabine Gless, and Florian Jessberger, eds., *Histories of Transnational Criminal Law* (New York, NY: Oxford University Press, 2021), 276–86.
10. On the origins of the Webster–Ashburton Treaty of Washington, see Howard Jones and Donald A. Rakestraw, *Prologue to Manifest Destiny: Anglo-American Relations in the 1840s* (Wilmington, DE: S. R. Books, 1997).
11. Chamberlain, *Lord Aberdeen*, 344.
12. Nicholas Adams, 'British Extradition Policy and the Problem of the Political Offender (1842–1914)', PhD dissertation, University of Hull (1989), 24–43.
13. Adams, 'British Extradition Policy', 50.
14. Christine van den Wijngaert, *The Political Offence Exception to Extradition: The Delicate Problem of Balancing the Rights of the Individual and the International Public Order* (Deventer: Kluwer, 1980), 13.
15. Adams, 'British Extradition Policy', 80–90.
16. Colonial Office Circulars No. 8 of 13 May 1837, No. 96 of 14 January 1839, and No. 113 of 16 July 1839, CO 854/2.
17. Edward D. Jervey and C. Harold Huber, 'The *Creole* Affair', *Journal of Negro History* 65, no. 3 (1980): 196–211.
18. Chamberlain, *Lord Aberdeen*, 310–14; Lawrence C. Jennings, 'France, Great Britain, and the Repression of the Slave Trade, 1841–1845', *French Historical Studies* 10, no. 1 (1977), 101.
19. Jervey and Huber, 'The *Creole* Affair', 207.
20. Canning to Stephen, 21 August 1845, CO 295/148, fo. 60.
21. Wilson to Macleod, 18 July 1845, CO 295/148, fo. 72–73.
22. Canning to Hope, 4 December 1845, CO 295/148, fo. 75–76.
23. MacLeod to Wilson, 19 February 1846, and Wilson to Palmerston, 18 August 1846, CO 295/154, fo. 126–131.
24. Manrique to Wilson, 17 August 1846, CO 295/154, fo. 137–139.
25. Addington to Stephen, 2 October 1846, CO 295/154, fo. 120–121.
26. Trinidad Ordinance No. 6 of 1847, CO 854/4, fo. 36.
27. 'Report from the Select Committee on Extradition' (1868), 99. In 1849, the Crown colony of Antigua comprised the island territories of Antigua, Barbuda, Anguilla, Dominica, Nevis, Montserrat, St Christopher, and the Virgin Islands. The combined government of Anguilla and St Christopher was empowered more generally to surrender fugitives to 'any foreign territory or dominion' that was willing to reciprocate.

28. Colonial Office Circulars No. 165 of 3 April 1848 and No. 184 of 3 March 1849, CO 854/4, fo. 35, 65.
29. 16 Vict. c. 3 (1852) (Act of the Superintendent of British Honduras).
30. Legislative Council of Malta Ordinance No. 1 of 1863, s. 11. The Crown colony of Labuan also enacted an ordinance in 1857 for the surrender of fugitives to the 'Sultanate of Borneo', better known as Brunei. The Labuan ordinance was enacted pursuant to an informal understanding of reciprocity, but it did not contain any special commencement mechanism. See the 'Report from the Select Committee on Extradition' (1868), 48, 103–4.
31. There was one partial exception: the Parliament of Upper Canada enacted a statute in 1833 (Fugitive Offenders Act, 3 Will. IV c. 7) to authorise the surrender of fugitives to foreign countries in the absence of any international arrangements. On the contested legality of this statute, see G. V. La Forest, *Extradition to and from Canada*, 2nd ed. (Toronto: Canada Law Book Ltd, 1977), 3–4.
32. Francis Piggott, *Extradition: A Treatise on the Law Relating to Fugitive Offenders* (London: Butterworth & Co., 1910), 5.
33. See Chapter 3 of this book for a discussion on the idea that ships flying a state's flag were an extension of the state's physical territory.
34. Adams, 'British Extradition Policy', 55–6.
35. Bradley Miller, *Borderline Crime: Fugitive Criminals and the Challenge of the Border, 1819–1914* (Toronto: University of Toronto Press, 2016).
36. Chapter 1 of this book.
37. Keying to Davis, 21 June 1844, CO 129/8, fo. 284–285; Pottinger to Aberdeen, 23 September 1843, FO 17/69, fo. 205, 207.
38. Keying to Davis, 21 June 1844, CO 129/8, fo. 285.
39. Davis to Keying, 24 June 1844, CO 129/8, fo. 286.
40. Davis to Keying, 15 May 1844, CO 129/8, fo. 274–275.
41. Davis to Aberdeen, 20 December 1844, CO 129/7, fo. 302.
42. See Chapter 2 of this book.
43. Bruce to Caine, 25 March 1845, HKRS 100–3, fo. 135.
44. Bruce to Caine, 25 March 1845, HKRS 100–3, fo. 135.
45. Davis to Keying, 27 September 1847, CO 129/21, fo. 154.
46. Davis to Keying, 27 September 1847, CO 129/21, fo. 154–155 (emphasis added).
47. The Elders of Tunggan Village to Davis, 3 November 1847, CO 129/21, fo. 157.
48. Keying to Davis, 10 November 1847, CO 129/21, fo. 159–160.
49. Davis to Palmerston, 13 November 1847, CO 129/21, fo. 151. On the colonial control of Chinese domestic and commercial servants in mid nineteenth-century Hong Kong, see Christopher Munn, 'Hong Kong, 1841–1870: All the Servants in Prison and Nobody to Take Care of the House', in Douglas Hay and Paul Craven, eds., *Masters, Servants, and*

Magistrates in Britain and the Empire, 1562–1955 (Chapel Hill, NC: University of North Carolina Press, 2004), 365–401.

50. British witnesses testified that the two officers were 'not excited by wine' when they left the barracks, but Chinese witnesses testified that they were drunk when they arrived in the village.
51. Testimony of Lo Yaong-shing, *The China Mail*, 8 March 1849, CO 132/2, fo. 19–20; *The China Mail*, 13 March 1851, CO 132/2, fo. 177–178. Lo Chun-she's name was printed as 'Lo Chow-she' in some reports, but the latter seems to be her mother-in-law.
52. In fact, Chui A-po served in the grand fleet of Shap-ng-tsai, the pirate chief that the Royal Navy defeated in 1849. See Grace Fox, *British Admirals and Chinese Pirates, 1832–1869* (New York, NY: Routledge, 2019), 107–9; J. W. Norton-Kyshe, *History of the Laws and Courts of Hong Kong, Volume 1* (London: T. F. Unwin, 1898), 260.
53. *The China Mail*, 8 March 1849, CO 132/2, fo. 19–20.
54. Bonham to Grey, 21 March 1849, CO 129/28, fo. 360–361.
55. *The China Mail*, 8 March 1849, CO 132/2, fo. 19–20.
56. Bonham to Grey, 21 November 1849, CO 129/30, fo. 324–326.
57. Bonham to Grey, 21 November 1849, CO 129/30, fo. 325.
58. See Chapters 2 and 3 of this book.
59. Bonham to Grey, 21 November 1849, CO 129/30, fo. 326.
60. Bonham to Grey, 21 November 1849, CO 129/30, fo. 327.
61. Blackwood's Minute of 30 January 1850, CO 129/30, fo. 329 (emphasis in original).
62. Blackwood's Minute of 30 January 1850, CO 129/30, fo. 329.
63. Merivale's Minute of 31 January 1850, CO 129/30, fo. 329.
64. Palmerston to Bonham, 24 January 1850, FO 17/164, fo. 41–42.
65. Speech of Lord Brougham, 14 February 1842, UK House of Lords Debates vol. 60 cc. 317–327, cited in Robert Phillimore, *Commentaries Upon International Law, Volume 1* (Philadelphia, PA: T. & J. W. Johnson, 1854), 310.
66. Egan, *The Law of Extradition*, 1–12; Travers Twiss, *The Law of Nations Considered as Independent Political Communities* (Oxford: Oxford University Press, 1861), 344–6. See also Phillimore, *Commentaries upon International Law, Volume 1*, 298–302.
67. Bonham to Grey, 21 March 1851, CO 129/36, fo. 72–74.
68. Grey to Bonham, 9 June 1849, CO 403/4, fo. 364; Hong Kong Government Notification of 1 March 1849, CO 129/28, fo. 368.
69. *The China Mail*, 13 March 1851, CO 132/2, fo. 177–178.
70. *The China Mail*, 13 March 1851, CO 132/2, fo. 178.
71. *The China Mail*, 3 April and 10 April 1851, CO 132/2, fo. 183–186; Bonham to Grey, 29 March 1851, CO 129/36, fo. 105.
72. Christopher Munn, *Anglo-China: Chinese People and British Rule in Hong Kong, 1841–1880* (Hong Kong: Hong Kong University Press,

2001), 204–7; Eric Marcks, 'English Law in Early Hong Kong: Colonial Law as a Means for Control and Liberation', *Texas International Law Journal* 35, no. 2 (2000): 265.

73. Harry Gelber, *Battle for Beijing, 1858–1860: Franco-British Conflict in China* (London: Palgrave MacMillan, 2016).
74. Clarendon to Elgin, 20 April 1857, reproduced in, 'Correspondence Relative to the Earl of Elgin's Special Missions to China and Japan, 1857–1859', C. (1st series) 2571, UK House of Commons Command Papers XXXIII.1, 4–6.
75. 'Correspondence Relative to the Earl of Elgin's Special Missions to China and Japan', 4–6.
76. Hope's Minute of 12 February 1843, CO 129/3, fo. 94.
77. Law Officers to Aberdeen, 18 March 1843, CO 129/3, fo. 169–170; Law Officers to Stanley, 29 January 1842, in Clive Parry, ed., *Law Officers' Opinions to the Foreign Office, 1793–1860, Volume* 72 (Farnborough: Gregg International Publishers, 1970–73), 172–94; Stanley to Pottinger, 6 April 1843, CO 403/1, p. 2.
78. Mercer to Cardwell, 11 July 1865 and Mercer's Memorandum of 22 June 1865, CO 129/105, fo. 458, 466–471; Robertson to Alexander, 26 June 1865, FO 17/613, fo. 82.
79. Jui-Lin to Robertson, 22 June 1865, FO 17/613, fo. 75–76.
80. Mercer's Memorandum of 22 June 1865, FO 17/613, fo. 65.
81. Alexander to Robertson, 26 June 1865, FO 17/613, fo. 78–79.
82. Wade to Mercer, 19 September 1865, CO 129/107, fo. 113.
83. Mercer to Cardwell, 25 October 1865, CO 129/107, fo. 107, 108.
84. Pauncefote's Legal Opinion of 3 July 1865, FO 17/613, fo. 255–257.
85. Pauncefote's Legal Opinion of 3 July 1865, FO 17/613, fo. 255–257 (emphasis added).
86. Undated Minute by Rogers, likely 5 January 1866, CO 129/105, fo. 462.
87. Rogers' Minute of 8 August 1866, CO 129/117, fo. 390; Clarendon to Alcock, 11 December 1865, FO 17/613, fo. 441–443; Cardwell to Mercer, 10 January 1866, CO 129/107, fo. 117.
88. Rogers' Minute of 8 August 1866, CO 129/117, fo. 390, 392.
89. Robinson's Memorandum of 2 August 1866, CO 129/117, fo. 382–384.
90. J. W. Norton-Kyshe, *History of the Laws and Courts of Hong Kong, Volume* 2 (London: T. F. Unwin, 1898), 46. Many thanks to Christopher Munn for drawing this case to my attention.
91. The subjects of non-treaty powers were normally represented by the consular officers of treaty powers acting in official or unofficial capacities. For example, British officers often acted for other European states and subjects because Britain had the largest consular network in China. See John K. Fairbank, *Trade and Diplomacy on the China Coast: The Opening of the Treaty Ports, Volume 1: 1842–1854* (Cambridge, MA: Harvard University Press, 1953), 212–15.

92. Hong Kong Ordinance No. 1 of 1844, s. 3 (in force from 1844 to 1865), and Order in Council of 9 March 1865 for the Government of British Subjects in China and Japan, s. 44 (in force from 1865) reproduced in Lewis Hertslet, ed., *Hertslet's Commercial Treaties: A Complete Collection of the Treaties and Conventions, and Reciprocal Regulations, at Present Subsisting between Great Britain and Foreign Powers, Volumes 6 and 12* (London: Butterworth, 1845/1871).
93. 6 & 7 Vict. c. 34 (1843). This statute was later repealed and replaced by the Fugitive Offenders Act, 44 & 45 Vict. c. 69 (1881), which also authorised the rendition of fugitives charged with misdemeanours, in addition to felonies. For a contemporary discussion of intra-imperial rendition, see Piggott, *Extradition*, 274–302.
94. Alexander Thompson, 'The British State at the Margins of Empire: Extraterritoriality and Governance in Treaty Port China, 1842–1927', PhD dissertation, University of Bristol (2018), 134–8; Robert Bickers, *The Scramble for China: Foreign Devils in the Qing Empire, 1832–1914* (London: Allen Lane, 2011), 103; Fairbank, *Trade and Diplomacy on the China Coast*, 215–17. On the legal status of Straits-born people of Chinese descent in the nineteenth and early twentieth centuries, see Siew-Min Sai, 'Dressing Up Subjecthood: Straits Chinese, the Queue, and Contested Citizenship in Colonial Singapore', *Journal of Imperial and Commonwealth History* 47, no. 3 (2019): 446–73; Eddie Tang, 'British Policy towards the Chinese in the Straits Settlements: Protection and Control, 1877–1900 (With Special Reference to Singapore)', PhD dissertation, Australian National University (1970).
95. Clarendon to Alcock, 9 November 1865 (private), FO 17/613, fo. 361, 363–364.
96. In the mid nineteenth century, British subject status was only transmitted by patrilineal descent, and only for two generations. In other words, the foreign-born *great* grandchildren of natural-born subjects were regarded as aliens at birth. But the law was later amended in 1914 to let unlimited generations of foreign-born children inherit subject status. See 4 Geo. II c. 21 (1731); 13 Geo. III c. 21 (1773); 4 & 5 Geo. 5 c. 17 (1914); Rieko Karatani, *Defining British Citizenship: Empire, Commonwealth, and Modern Britain* (London: Frank Cass, 2003), 41; Ann Dummett and Andrew Nicol, *Subjects, Citizens, Aliens and Others: Nationality and Immigration Law* (London: Weidenfeld and Nicolson, 1990), 36.
97. Fairbank, *Trade and Diplomacy on the China Coast*, 215.
98. *Report of the Royal Commissioners for Inquiring into the Laws of Naturalization and Allegiance* (London: H.M. Stationery Office, 1869), Appendix, 47.
99. *Report of the Royal Commissioners for Inquiring into the Laws of Naturalization and Allegiance*, Appendix, 65–8.

100. Marginal Notes by Hammond and Clarendon against Clarendon's despatch to Alcock of 11 December 1865, FO 17/613, fo. 443; Law Officers to the Foreign Office, 29 May 1867, reproduced in Clive Parry, ed., *A British Digest of International Law, Volume 5* (London: Stevens and Sons, 1965), part VI, chapter 15, 394.
101. All natural-born British subjects of Chinese descent were considered eligible for British protection in China from 1904 until the end of the treaty port era. See Thompson, 'The British State at the Margins of Empire', 158–61.
102. Cardwell to Mercer, 10 January 1866, CO 129/107, fo. 117.
103. Robinson, Minute of 2 August 1866, CO 129/117, fo. 379, 384.
104. 'Correspondence Respecting the Revision of the Treaty of Tien-Tsin', C. (2nd Series) 389, UK House of Commons Command Papers LXX.125.
105. Evidence of Edmund Hammond, 'Report from the Select Committee on Extradition' (1868), 10–14.
106. Evidence of Edmund Hammond, 'Report from the Select Committee on Extradition' (1868), 2.
107. Evidence of H. T. Holland, 'Report from the Select Committee on Extradition' (1868), 49–51.
108. Extradition Act, 33 & 34 Vict. c. 52, s. 4 (1870).
109. The Anglo-Swiss Treaty of 1880 was implemented by an Order in Council issued under the Extradition Act 1870. It was a rare exception that proved the rule, or the trend, that British treaties signed between 1870 and 1989 generally exempted signatories' own nationals from extradition to foreign countries: Piggott, *Extradition*, 64, 237–8; Ivor Stanbrook and Clive Stanbrook, *Extradition Law and Practice*, 2nd ed. (Oxford: Oxford University Press, 2000), 312–13.
110. Piggott, *Extradition*, Appendix p. 260; 'Convention between Great Britain and China, giving effect to Article III of the Convention of July 24, 1886, relative to Burmah and Thibet, Signed at London, March 1, 1894', C. (2nd series) 7547, UK Command Papers XCVI.89. Although the Anglo-Siamese agreement covered fugitives escaping between Siam and any 'British territory', it was made specifically with Burma in mind. On the Sino-British Conventions of 1886–97 and British consular activity in Western China, see Emily Whewell, *Law Across Imperial Borders: British Consuls and Colonial Connections on China's Western Frontiers, 1880–1943* (Manchester: Manchester University Press, 2019).

5 Founding Alsatia

1. 'Report from the Select Committee on Extradition; Together with the Proceedings of the Committee, Minutes of Evidence, and Appendix', UK House of Commons Papers VII.129, No. 393 (1868).

2. Bowen to Derby, 31 December 1883, CO 129/213, fo. 289–290. On the legally dubious sanctuary that debtors and other wanted people enjoyed at Whitefriars, see James R. Hertzler, 'The Abuse and Outlawing of Sanctuary for Debt in Seventeenth-Century England', *Historical Journal* 14, no. 3 (1971): 467–77.
3. Mercer to Newcastle, 30 October and 25 November 1862, CO 129/88, fo. 114–116, 181.
4. Stephen R. Platt, *Autumn in the Heavenly Kingdom: China, the West, and the Epic Story of the Taiping Civil War* (New York, NY: Vintage Books, 2012), xxiii.
5. Philip A. Kuhn, 'The Taiping Rebellion', in John K. Fairbank, ed., *The Cambridge History of China, Volume 10: Late Ch'ing 1800–1911, Part 1* (Cambridge: Cambridge University Press, 1978), 264–317.
6. Stephen R. Platt, 'British Intervention in the Taiping Rebellion', in Robert Bickers and Jonathan J. Howlett, eds., *Britain and China, 1840–1970: Empire, Finance and War* (Oxford: Routledge, 2016), 41–57.
7. Hong Kong Ordinance No. 1 of 1855, 'to enforce neutrality during the contest now existing in China'.
8. Mercer to Newcastle, 30 October 1862, CO 129/88, fo. 114–116.
9. Atherton, Palmer, and Phillimore to Russell, 24 February 1863, FO 83/2251, fo. 219–222.
10. Rogers' Minute of 8 January 1863, CO 129/88, fo. 117.
11. Hammond to Rogers, 7 April 1863, and Newcastle to Mercer, 11 April 1863, CO 129/95, fo. 80–82, 92.
12. Christine van den Wijngaert, *The Political Offence Exception to Extradition: The Delicate Problem of Balancing the Rights of the Individual and the International Public Order* (Deventer: Kluwer, 1980), 9–12.
13. Christopher H. Pyle, *Extradition, Politics, and Human Rights* (Philadelphia, PA: Temple University Press, 2001), 11.
14. See the discussion on Solomon Moseby's case (1837) in David Murray, *Colonial Justice: Justice, Morality, and Crime in the Niagara District, 1791–1849* (Toronto: University of Toronto Press), 196–216.
15. Hackett was surrendered under a legally contested colonial statute, the Fugitive Offenders Act, 3 Will. IV c. 7 (1833), which the Parliament of Upper Canada enacted, controversially, in the absence of treaty arrangements: Alexander L. Murray, 'The Extradition of Fugitive Slaves from Canada: A Re-evaluation', *Canadian Historical Review* 43, no. 4 (1962): 298–314.
16. 'Treaty between Her Majesty and the United States of America, signed at Washington, August 9, 1842', C. (1st series) 424, UK House of Commons Command Papers LXI.1 (1843).
17. On colonial regimes of extradition, see Chapter 4 of this book.
18. 'Correspondence Respecting the Case of the Fugitive Slave, Anderson', C. (1st series) 2813, UK House of Commons Command Papers LXIV.293;

Paul Finkelman, 'International Extradition and Fugitive Slaves: The John Anderson Case', *Brooklyn Journal of International Law* 18 (1992): 765–810. On the political implications of Anderson's case, see Patrick Brode, *The Odyssey of John Anderson* (Toronto: University of Toronto Press, 1989).

19. *In re Ternan* [1864] 33 QB 201 (emphasis added).
20. *In re Ternan* [1864] 33 QB 201. Justices Crompton and Blackburn also considered the argument that the mutiny might not be a crime at all, if it was a legitimate act of belligerents engaged in war. However, it was not clear if Ternan and his men were acting under orders of the Confederate government. The facts were clearer, by contrast, in another case in which Confederate soldiers fled to Canada after raiding the town of St Albans, Vermont, in October 1864. A police court in Montreal decided that, as lawful belligerents, the raiders were not extraditable. See L. N. Benjamin, *The St. Albans Raid* (Montreal: John Lovell, 1865).
21. Bradley Miller, *Borderline Crime: Fugitive Criminals and the Challenge of the Border, 1819–1914* (Toronto: University of Toronto Press, 2016), 144–7.
22. Keate to Lytton, 23 May 1859, CO 295/204, fo. 262, cited in Nicholas Adams, 'British Extradition Policy and the Problem of the Political Offender (1842–1914)', PhD dissertation, University of Hull (1989), 66.
23. See Chapter 3 of this book.
24. Robert J. Anthony, ed., *Elusive Pirates, Pervasive Smugglers: Violence and Clandestine Trade in the Greater China Seas* (Hong Kong: Hong Kong University Press, 2010), 7–8. See also Robert J. Antony, *Like Froth Floating on the Sea: The World of Pirates and Seafarers in Late Imperial South China* (Berkeley, CA: University of California Institute of East Asian Studies, 2003).
25. Wensheng Wang, *White Lotus Rebels and South China Pirates* (Cambridge, MA: Harvard University Press, 2014); Joseph MacKay, 'Pirate Nations: Maritime Pirates as Escape Societies in Late Imperial China', *Social Science History* 37, no. 4 (2013): 551–73; Paolo Calanca, 'Piracy and Coastal Security in Southeastern China, 1600–1780', in Antony, ed., *Elusive Pirates, Pervasive Smugglers*.
26. Dian H. Murray, 'Living and Working Conditions in Chinese Pirate Communities, 1750–1850', in David J. Starkey, E. S. van Eyck van Heslinga, and J. A. de Moor, eds., *Pirates and Privateers: New Perspectives on the War on Trade in the 18th and 19th Centuries* (Exeter: University of Exeter Press, 1997), 49.
27. Officially, the 'East Indies and China Station' until 1865.
28. Sablé to Swinhoe, 10 August 1866, FO 17/614, fo. 207.
29. Timothy Brook, Jérôme Bourgon, and Gregory Blue, *Death by a Thousand Cuts* (Cambridge, MA: Harvard University Press, 2008); Robert J. Antony, *Unruly People: Crime, Community, and State in Late Imperial South China* (Hong Kong: Hong Kong University Press, 2016), 8, 248.

30. Hammond to Alcock, private letter of 9 November 1865, FO 17/613, fo. 363.
31. *The Canton Observer*, 5 June 1865, CO 129/106, fo. 287.
32. 'Execution of a Taeping Chief in Canton', *The Standard*, 22 July 1865; Extract from the *Overland Trade Report*, 30 May 1865, copied in 'Correspondence respecting Rendition by Acting Governor of Hong Kong, to Chinese Authorities at Canton, of Person described as Mo-Wong and his Execution', UK House of Commons Papers L.1, No. 120, p. 4.
33. Platt, *Autumn in the Heavenly Kingdom*, 179–81.
34. Sykes to Russell, 25 July 1865, FO 17/613, fo. 101–102.
35. Cardwell to Mercer, 10 August 1865, CO 129/109, fo. 170–171.
36. Cardwell to Mercer, 11 September 1865, CO 129/109, fo. 199–201.
37. Cardwell to Mercer, 10 April 1865, CO 129/109, fo. 58–60.
38. Cardwell's undated minute of late August 1865, CO 129/109, fo. 198.
39. Cardwell to Mercer, 10 April 1865, CO 129/109, fo. 58–60.
40. Mercer to Cardwell, 20 September 1865, CO 129/106, fo. 237–238.
41. Requisition for How Yook-Tin, CO 129/106, fo. 247–248.
42. Mercer to Cardwell, 20 September 1865, CO 129/106, fo. 238.
43. Proceedings before the Police Magistrate, 24 April and 1 May 1865, CO 129/106, fo. 263–271.
44. 'Correspondence respecting Rendition by Acting Governor of Hong Kong, to Chinese Authorities at Canton, of Person described as Mo-Wong and his Execution', UK House of Commons Papers L.1, No. 120.
45. Rogers' Minute, undated (November 1865), CO 129/106, fo. 246.
46. Jenny Huangfu Day, 'The Enigma of a Taiping Fugitive: The Illusion of Justice and the "Political Offence Exception" in Extradition from Hong Kong', *Law and History Review* (2021): 1–36. See also a revised version of this narrative in Jenny Huangfu Day, *Transborder Fugitives, Extradition, and Political Crimes in Modern China* (Cambridge: Cambridge University Press, in press).
47. Robertson to Hammond, 6 October 1865, FO 405/12, fo. 11, cited in Day, 'The Enigma of a Taiping Fugitive', at 16–17.
48. Mercer to Cardwell, 20 September 1865, CO 129/106, fo. 237.
49. See Chapter 3 of this book.
50. Cardwell to MacDonnell, 26 December 1865, CO 129/109, fo. 323–326.
51. Cardwell's Minute of 3 December 1865, CO 129/109, fo. 322.
52. Cardwell to MacDonnell, 26 December 1865, CO 129/109, fo. 323–326.
53. Cardwell to MacDonnell, 26 December 1865, CO 129/109, fo. 323–326.
54. Cardwell to MacDonnell, 26 December 1865, CO 129/109, fo. 323–326.
55. Cardwell to Mercer, 26 January 1866, CO 129/117, fo. 235.
56. Hammond to Alcock, private letter of 9 November 1865, FO 17/613, fo. 361.
57. Hammond to Alcock, private letter of 9 November 1865, FO 17/613, fo. 361.

58. Palmer, Collier, and Phillimore to Clarendon, 25 November 1865, CO 129/109, fo. 329, 332; Clarendon to Alcock, 11 December 1865, FO 17/613, fo. 447–449. On the non-reciprocity of Article 21 of the Treaty of Tianjin, see Chapter 4 of this book.
59. Robertson to Layard, 25 September 1865, FO 17/613, fo. 145, 149.
60. Hammond to Alcock, 9 November 1865 (conveying Clarendon's instructions), FO 17/613, fo. 365 (emphasis added).
61. Hammond to Alcock, 9 November 1865, FO 17/613, fo. 365.
62. Wade's Memorandum on Prince Kung's Despatch, 6 May 1866, FO 17/614, fo. 127–128.
63. Alcock to Kung, 11 April 1866, FO 17/614, fo. 135–136.
64. Alcock to Clarendon, 11 May 1866, FO 17/614, fo. 118.
65. See Chapter 1 of this book for an account of judicial torture in China, articulated by Governor Henry Pottinger in *The Queen* v. *Lo A-tow* (1843). Pottinger's successors surrendered criminals to China without requesting guarantees against torture or *lingchi*. See, for example, Robinson to Cardwell, 9 August 1864, CO 129/99, fo. 337.
66. Alcock to Clarendon, 11 May 1866, FO 17/614, fo. 119–120.
67. Commandant of Kowloong City to MacDonnell, 24 April 1866, CO 129/113, fo. 342–343.
68. Proceedings at the Police Court, Victoria, 1 May 1866 and Opinion of Julian Pauncefote, 15 May 1866, CO 129/113, 346–355, 367. Kwok Leong-hee's barrister may have been W. H. Mitchell, a former assistant magistrate in Hong Kong who retired from the colonial service 1862 and took the bar in 1865. See G. B. Endacott, *A Biographical Sketch-Book of Early Hong Kong* (Singapore: Eastern Universities Press Limited, 1962), 118.
69. Proceedings at the Police Court, Victoria, 30 May 1866, and Report by Pauncefote, 4 June 1866, CO 129/113, fo. 379–421.
70. Jui-Lin to Robertson, 24 May 1866, CO 129/113, fo. 377.
71. Mercer to Robertson, 17 May 1866, Robertson to Rennie, 5 June 1866, and MacDonnell to Cardwell, 11 June 1866, CO 129/113, fo. 332–337, 369–371, 428.
72. Cox's Minute of 6 August 1866, and Carnarvon to MacDonnell, 4 September 1866, CO 129/113, fo. 338–339, 433.
73. MacDonnell to Alcock, 8 February 1867, CO 129/120, fo. 452–454.
74. Proceedings at the Police Court, Victoria, 30 May 1866, CO 129/113, fo. 379–420.
75. Alcock to Stanley, 18 May 1868, FO 17/615, fo. 129–130.
76. Alcock to Stanley, 18 May 1868, FO 17/615, fo. 133–136.
77. Hammond's Memorandum of 29 August 1868, FO 17/615, fo. 185–186.
78. 'Report from the Select Committee on Extradition' (1868). A similar proposal, also rejected, was later made by the Royal Commission on Extradition of 1878.

79. 33 & 34 Vict. c. 52 (1870), s. 2.
80. 'Report from the Select Committee on Extradition' (1868), 14.
81. 'Report from the Select Committee on Extradition' (1868), 49–50.
82. Minutes of Proceedings at the Police Court, Victoria, 19 January to 4 February 1871, CO 129/149, fo. 418–423; Dabry to Robertson, 15 November 1870, and Robertson to Wade, 17 November 1870, reproduced in 'Correspondence Respecting the Emigration of Chinese Coolies from Macao', UK House of Commons Papers LXX.183, No. 504.
83. 33 & 34 Vict. c. 52 (1870), s. 27 and Third Schedule.
84. Smale to Austin, 14 January 1871, CO 129/153, fo. 167.
85. Peter Wesley-Smith, 'Kwok-A-Sing, John Smale, and the Macao Coolie Trade', *Law Lectures for Practitioners (Hong Kong)* (1993): 124–34.
86. Smale to Austin and Pauncefote, 14 January 1871, CO 129/153, fo. 167–173 (emphasis in original).
87. Pauncefote to Smale, 14 January 1871, CO 129/153, fo. 167–173.
88. Ordinance No. 9 of 1857, CO 130/2, fo. 237.
89. Whitfield to Kimberley, 21 February 1871, CO 129/149, fo. 184–185.
90. Minutes of the Executive Council of Hong Kong, 24 February 1871, CO 129/153, fo. 164.
91. Opinion of the Law Officers of the Crown, 21 September 1852, CO 129/41, fo. 103–105.
92. Whitfield to Kimberley, 21 February 1871, CO 129/149, fo. 184–185.
93. Extradition Act 1866, 29 & 30 Vict. c. 121. Under this statute, authenticated depositions taken in the United States were also accepted in relation to fugitives requested by the United States.
94. Extradition Act, 33 & 34 Vict. c. 52 (1870), s. 14. See Adams, 'British Extradition Policy', 101–36.
95. Whitfield to Kimberley, telegram of 21 February 1871, copied in CO 129/149, fo. 184.
96. Whitfield to Kimberley, 31 March 1871, CO 129/149, 391. On the connection of Singapore to the British imperial telegraph network, see Roland Wenzlhuemer, *Connecting the Nineteenth-Century World: The Telegraph and Globalization* (Cambridge: Cambridge University Press, 2013), 241.
97. Wenzlhuemer, *Connecting the Nineteenth-Century World*, 241.
98. Whitfield to Kimberley, telegram of 21 February 1871, copied in CO 129/149, fo. 184.
99. Extradition Act 1870, s. 6 and First Schedule.
100. Kimberley to Whitfield, telegram of 8 March 1871, CO 129/154, fo. 168.
101. '*In the Matter of Kwok-a-Sing on Habeas Corpus: Judgment* (29 March 1871)', *Hong Kong Daily Press*, 5 April 1871, CO 129/149, fo. 427–428.
102. *Kwok-a-Sing* (29 March 1871), CO 129/149, fo. 427–428.

103. Kennedy to Kimberley, 20 November 1872, reproduced in *Papers Relative to the Measures Taken to Prevent the Fitting Out of Ships at Hong Kong for the Macao Coolie Trade* (London: H.M. Stationery Office, 1873), 192.
104. Chinese Passengers Act, 18 & 19 Vict. c. 104 (1855).
105. Pauncefote's Report of 25 May 1871, CO 129/150, fo. 228–231.
106. Robertson to Wade, 17 November 1870, reproduced in 'Correspondence Respecting the Emigration of Chinese Coolies from Macao', UK House of Commons Command Papers LXX.183, No. 504 (1871).
107. Grace Fox, *British Admirals and Chinese Pirates, 1832–1869* (Oxford: Routledge, 2019), 181–3; Treaty of Tianjin, Article 53.
108. Jonathan Chappell, 'Maritime Raiding, International Law and the Suppression of Piracy on the South China Coast, 1842–1869', *International History Review* 40, no. 3 (2018): 473–92.
109. Robert J. Antony, 'Piracy on the South China Coast through Modern Times' in Bruce A. Elleman, Andrew Forbes, and David Rosenberg, eds., *Piracy and Maritime Crime: Historical and Modern Case Studies* (Newport, RI: Naval War College Press, 2010), 44.
110. Extradition Act 1870, s. 2.
111. *Kwok-a-Sing* (29 March 1871), CO 129/149, fo. 428.
112. Pauncefote to Austin, 18 April 1871, CO 129/149, fo. 415. The discharge was delayed because Smale offered to keep Kwok-a-Sing remanded pending the colonial government's appeal to the Privy Council, but only on the condition that Kwok-a-Sing was compensated if the appeal was dismissed. The colonial government declined this constitutionally dubious offer.
113. '*In re Kwok-A-Sing: Judgment* (22 May 1871)', *Hong Kong Daily Press*, 23 May 1871, CO 129/150, fo. 235.
114. Extradition Act 1870, s. 17.
115. Draft ordinance enclosed in Whitfield to Kimberley, 18 April 1871, CO 129/149, fo. 405.
116. Ordinance No. 2 of 1871, CO 130/3, fo. 228.
117. C.L. de la Forest to Whitfield, 25 April 1871, CO 129/150, fo. 229.
118. Pauncefote's Report of 25 May 1871, CO 129/150, fo. 228–229.
119. A. S. de Souza to Whitfield, 5 May 1871, CO 129/150, fo. 230.
120. 31 Cha. II, c. 2, s. 6.
121. *Kwok-A-Sing* (22 May 1871), CO 129/150, fo. 235.
122. Arnold J. Meagher, *The Coolie Trade: The Traffic in Chinese Laborers to Latin America 1847–1874* (Bloomington, IN: Xlibris, 2008), 188.
123. *Kwok-A-Sing* (22 May 1871), CO 129/150, fo. 235.
124. Pauncefote's Memorandum of 5 July 1871, CO 129/151, fo. 39.
125. Whitfield to Kimberley, telegram of 10 June 1871, CO 129/150, fo. 353: 'Great scandal. No appeal [for Pauncefote]. May Chief Justice be ordered home on leave & the Pirates be brought to trial?'

126. Pauncefote to Austin, 18 July 1871, CO 129/151, fo. 136.
127. Whitfield to Kimberley, 6 July and 20 July 1871, CO 129/151, fo. 34, 140. Francis later applied for a new trial against Pauncefote, but (perhaps sensing its futility) Smale rejected this application in December 1871: MacDonnell to Kimberley, Telegram of 8 December 1871, CO 129/153, fo. 186). Pauncefote, on the other hand, never made another attempt to have Kwok-a-Sing tried for piracy. This is a point of confusion in Elliott Young, 'Chinese Coolies, Universal Rights and the Limits of Liberalism in an Age of Empire', *Past and Present* 227 (2015): 121–49, at 140.
128. The Colonial Office considered giving the chief justiceship of Hong Kong to Pauncefote, who briefly coveted it. However, officials decided that this would have been impolitic under the circumstances: Herbert's Minute of 6 September 1871, CO 129/151, fo. 143; Holland's and Kimberley's Minutes of 18 and 21 January 1872, CO 129/153, fo. 155.
129. Herbert to the Law Officers of the Crown, 22 July 1871, CO 129/150, fo. 240.
130. Hugessen's Minute of 21 July 1871, CO 129/150, fo. 227.
131. Hugessen's Minute of 10 August 1871, CO 129/150, fo. 418.
132. Herbert's Minute of 10 August 1871, CO 129/150, fo. 418. Kwok-a-Sing was never convicted of any crime in Hong Kong, contrary to the account in Jennifer Wells, 'Clashing Kingdoms, Hidden Agendas: The Battle to Extradite Kwok-A-Sing and British Legal Imperialism in Nineteenth-Century China', *East Asia Law Review* 7 (2011): 161–93, at 172.
133. Collier, Coleridge, and Twiss to Kimberley, 29 July and 17 August 1871, CO129/154, fo. 95–97, 105.
134. Kimberley's Minute of 11 August 1871, CO 129/150, fo. 418.
135. Records of the Judicial Committee of the Privy Council, 1845–1874, PCAP 9/3–7.
136. The Queen's Proctor to Holland, 1 February 1872, CO 129/160, fo. 212.
137. *Attorney General of Hong Kong* v. *Kwok-A-Sing* (1873) LR 5 PC 179 at 197.
138. *Kwok-A-Sing* (1873) at 197–8.
139. *Kwok-A-Sing* (1873) at 201.
140. *Kwok-A-Sing* (1873) at 190.
141. *Kwok-A-Sing* (1873) at 201–2.
142. *Kwok-A-Sing* (1873) at 200.
143. *Papers Relative to the Measures Taken to Prevent the Fitting Out of Ships at Hong Kong for the Macao Coolie Trade* (London: H.M. Stationery Office, 1873).
144. Hong Kong Ordinances No. 3 of 1873 ('to make better provision for the regulation, inspection, and approval of the fittings of ships intended for the conveyance of Chinese emigrants, to be embarked at ports or places out of the Colony') and No. 6 of 1873 ('for the better protection of Chinese women and female children').

145. Hong Kong Ordinance No. 5 of 1873 ('to make further provision for the repression of abuses in relation to Chinese emigration').
146. Meagher, *The Coolie Trade*, 293.
147. Robert L. Irick, *Ch'ing Policy toward the Coolie Trade, 1847–1878* (Taipei: Chinese Materials Center, 1982), 257–73; Yen Ching-Hwang, *Coolies and Mandarins: China's Protection of Overseas Chinese During the Late Ch'ing Period (1851–1911)* (Singapore: Singapore University Press, 1985), 72–122.
148. Pauncefote's Report of 25 May 1871, CO 129/150, fo. 231.
149. Pauncefote to Herbert, 25 February 1874, CO 129/169, fo. 705.
150. Holland's Minute of 17 March 1874, CO 129/169, fo. 703.
151. Kennedy to Carnarvon, 8 February 1875, CO 129/170, fo. 90.
152. Bramston to Austin, 31 January 1875, CO 129/170, 98.
153. Brian L. Blakeley, *The Colonial Office, 1868–1892* (Durham, NC: Duke University Press, 1972), 80.
154. Leigh R. Wright, *Julian Pauncefote and British Imperial Policy, 1855–1889* (Lanham, MD: University Press of America, 2002).
155. Pauncefote's Memorandum of 25 March 1875, and Carnarvon to Kennedy, 15 May 1875, CO 129/170, fo. 84–85, 138–141.
156. Draft Ordinance for the Extradition of Chinese Criminals (1875), CO 129/171, fo. 262.
157. Tenterden to Herbert, 29 February 1876, CO 129/176, fo. 171.
158. G. W. Johnson's minute of 24 September 1888, Knutsford to Des Voeux, 8 October 1888, and Russell's memorandum of 25 May 1888, CO 129/238, fo. 462, 504, 511.
159. Des Voeux to Knutsford, 8 August 1888, CO 129/238, fo. 466–498. See Day, *Transborder Fugitives* for an account of a notable dispute in 1887, in which the Hong Kong government, citing *Kwok-a-Sing*, refused to extradite a Chinese fugitive upon a charge that pertained to the Chinese civil service examinations – a 'peculiar' crime, in the words of the Privy Council.
160. Des Voeux to Knutsford, 8 August 1888, CO 129/238, fo. 466–498.
161. Webster and Clarke to Knutsford, 15 December 1888, CO 129/240, fo. 85.
162. Johnson and Wingfield's minutes of 24 and 25 September 1888, CO 129/238, fo. 464–465.
163. Wingfield's and Knutsford's minutes of 25 and 30 September 1888, CO 129/238, fo. 465.
164. Hong Kong Chinese Extradition Ordinance, No. 7 of 1889. Section 13(1) states that:

> whenever the Governor shall from the Magistrate's Report or otherwise have reason to suppose, that any fugitive criminal, who has been committed to the Victoria Gaol to await the further order of the Governor, has been resident in the Colony for one year or upwards, the depositions and evidence taken before the Magistrate on the investigation of the case

shall together with the Magistrate's Report thereon be considered by the Governor in Council, who shall be assisted in such consideration by the Chief Justice of the Colony and the Governor in Council shall decide whether such fugitive criminal shall be surrendered or not.

165. Report by the Acting Attorney General on Ordinance No. 26 of 1889, CO 129/241, fo. 835; Proceedings of the Legislative Council of Hong Kong, 1889, CO 131/18, fo. 33–44. The Chinese Extradition Ordinance of 1889 was later amended in 1897. Authenticated depositions taken in China were made admissible as evidence to support requests for fugitives, not being permanent residents of Hong Kong, who were charged with murder, piracy, and other serious crimes.
166. Des Voeux to Knutsford, 29 July 1889, CO 129/241, fo. 829–834.
167. Wingfield to Currie, 13 September 1889, CO 129/241, fo. 836–837.
168. John McLaren, *Dewigged, Bothered, and Bewildered: British Colonial Judges on Trial, 1800–1900* (Toronto: University of Toronto Press, 2011), 262.

Conclusion

1. Stephen's Minute of 8 July 1843, CO 129/3, fo. 219.
2. In the representative words of Antony Anghie, 'unequal treaties' were 'unequal not only because they were the product of unequal power, but because they embodied unequal obligations'. See Anthony Anghie, *Imperialism, Sovereignty and the Making of International Law* (Cambridge: Cambridge University Press, 2004), 72. On the origins of the term 'unequal treaties' in early twentieth-century Chinese nationalist and communist politics, see Dong Wang, *China's Unequal Treaties: Narrating National History* (Oxford: Lexington, 2005).
3. Thom's Memorandum of 10 July 1843, FO 17/68, fo. 110–111.
4. Li Chen, *Chinese Law in Imperial Eyes: Sovereignty, Justice, and Transcultural Politics* (New York, NY: Columbia University Press, 2016). On American perceptions of Chinese law since the nineteenth century, see also Teemu Ruskola, *Legal Orientalism: China, the United States, and Modern Law* (Cambridge, MA: Harvard University Press, 2013).
5. Fugitive Offenders and Mutual Legal Assistance in Criminal Matters Legislation (Amendment) Bill (Hong Kong SAR).
6. C. L. Lim, *Treaty for a Lost City: The Sino-British Joint Declaration* (Cambridge: Cambridge University Press, 2022), 200–15.
7. Press Release of the Hong Kong Bar Association (HKBA), 6 June 2019, online: www.hkba.org/events-publication/press-releases-coverage/2019 (19 May 2024), cited in Sonny Shiu-Hing Lo, Steven Chung-Fun Hung, and Jeff Hai-Chi Loo, *The Dynamics of Peaceful and Violent Protests in Hong Kong: The Anti-extradition Movement* (Singapore: Palgrave Macmillan, 2021), 68.

8. Albert H. Y. Chen, 'A Perfect Storm: Hong Kong–Mainland Rendition of Fugitive Offenders', *Hong Kong Law Journal* 49, no. 2 (2019): 419–30, at 426.
9. C. L. Lim, 'The Hong Kong Extradition Bill', *Law Quarterly Review* 136 (January 2020): 19–23, at 23.
10. Janice M. Brabyn, 'Extradition and the Hong Kong Special Administrative Region', *Case Western Reserve Journal of International Law* 20 (1988): 169–94, at 185 n.
11. Fugitive Offenders Ordinance 1997, c. 503, s. 2(1)(a).
12. Lo, Hung, and Loo, *The Anti-extradition Movement*, 2.
13. Articles 20–35 of the Law of the People's Republic of China on Safeguarding National Security in the Hong Kong Special Administrative Region, online: www.gld.gov.hk/egazette/pdf/20202448e/egn2020244872.pdf (accessed 5 May 2024).
14. Articles 44 and 55–60 of the Law of the People's Republic of China on Safeguarding National Security in the Hong Kong Special Administrative Region.
15. Sonny Lo, 'Hong Kong in 2020: National Security Law and Truncated Autonomy', *Asian Survey* 61, no. 1 (2021): 34–42.

Index

Studies in Legal History

(continued from page ii)

Kristin A. Olbertson, *The Dreadful Word: Speech Crime and Polite Gentlemen in Massachusetts, 1690–1776*

Edgardo Pérez Morales, *Unraveling Abolition: Legal Culture and Slave Emancipation in Colombia*

Lyndsay Campbell, *Truth and Privilege: Libel Law in Massachusetts and Nova Scotia, 1820–1840*

Sara M. Butler, *Pain, Penance, and Protest: Peine Forte et Dure in Medieval England*

Michael Lobban, *Imperial Incarceration: Detention without Trial in the Making of British Colonial Africa*

Stefan Jurasinski and Lisi Oliver, *The Laws of Alfred: The Domboc and the Making of Anglo-Saxon Law*

Sascha Auerbach, *Armed with Sword and Scales: Law, Culture, and Local Courtrooms in London, 1860–1913*

Alejandro de La Fuente and Ariela J. Gross, *Becoming Free, Becoming Black: Race, Freedom, and the Law in Cuba, Virginia, and Louisiana*

Elizabeth Papp Kamali, *Felony and the Guilty Mind in Medieval England*

Jessica K. Lowe, *Murder in the Shenandoah: Making Law Sovereign in Revolutionary Virginia*

Michael A. Schoeppner, *Moral Contagion: Black Atlantic Sailors, Citizenship, and Diplomacy in Antebellum America*

Sam Erman, *Almost Citizens: Puerto Rico, the U.S. Constitution, and Empire*

Martha S. Jones, *Birthright Citizens: A History of Race and Rights in Antebellum America*

Julia Moses, *The First Modern Risk: Workplace Accidents and the Origins of European Social States*

Cynthia Nicoletti, *Secession on Trial: The Treason Prosecution of Jefferson Davis*

Edward James Kolla, *Sovereignty, International Law, and the French Revolution*

Assaf Likhovski, *Tax Law and Social Norms in Mandatory Palestine and Israel*

Robert W. Gordon, *Taming the Past: Essays on Law and History and History in Law*

Paul Garfinkel, *Criminal Law in Liberal and Fascist Italy*

Michelle A. McKinley, *Fractional Freedoms: Slavery, Intimacy, and Legal Mobilization in Colonial Lima, 1600–1700*
Karen M. Tani, *States of Dependency: Welfare, Rights, and American Governance, 1935–1972*
Stefan Jurasinski, *The Old English Penitentials and Anglo- Saxon Law*
Felice Batlan, *Women and Justice for the Poor: A History of Legal Aid, 1863–1945*
Sophia Z. Lee, *The Workplace Constitution from the New Deal to the New Right*
Mitra Sharafi, *Law and Identity in Colonial South Asia: Parsi Legal Culture, 1772–1947*
Michael A. Livingston, *The Fascists and the Jews of Italy: Mussolini's Race Laws, 1938–1943*

Printed by Integrated Books International,
United States of America